ESSAYS IN
MUSICAL ANALYSIS

By

DONALD FRANCIS TOVEY

IN SIX VOLUMES

CONTENTS

ESSAYS IN
MUSICAL ANALYSIS

By

DONALD FRANCIS TOVEY

REID PROFESSOR OF MUSIC IN THE
UNIVERSITY OF EDINBURGH

Volume II

SYMPHONIES (II), VARIATIONS AND ORCHESTRAL
POLYPHONY

LONDON
OXFORD UNIVERSITY PRESS
HUMPHREY MILFORD

OXFORD
UNIVERSITY PRESS
AMEN HOUSE, E.C. 4
London Edinburgh Glasgow New York
Toronto Melbourne Capetown Bombay
Calcutta Madras
HUMPHREY MILFORD
PUBLISHER TO THE
UNIVERSITY

FIRST PRINTED   1935
SECOND IMPRESSION 1936
THIRD IMPRESSION   1939
FOURTH IMPRESSION 1942

FOREWORD TO THE SECOND IMPRESSION

I HAVE already disclaimed for these essays any research except the verifying of quotations where they are not best unverified. On page 46 there is a glaring instance where the verifying of a quotation has been indiscreet. The whole point of my diatribe against the honoured name of Rubinstein was my assumption that the 'great artist' in memory of whom Tchaikovsky wrote his Trio was the author of scandalous attacks upon the larger works of Schumann, as well as being a brother of the great Anton. It is, I think, a fact that the huge and splashy compositions of Rubinstein and Tchaikovsky have all the defects of Schumann's larger forms, with few traces of the wit which goes far to justify Schumann in his methods. In that sense the name of Rubinstein is by no means irrelevant, even though his playing of such lyrics as *Vogel als Prophet* was one of the most angelic performances that ever deserved to become immortal. The moral evidently is that it is better not to quote at all than to verify at the expense of the point.

D. F. T.

January 1936.

CONTENTS

SIBELIUS

VAUGHAN WILLIAMS

LX–LXIII
VARIATIONS
BEETHOVEN

BRAHMS

DVOŘÁK

C. HUBERT H. PARRY

MENDELSSOHN

DVOŘÁK

BRAHMS

LXVIII–LXXXIII
ORCHESTRAL POLYPHONY
BEETHOVEN

BACH

HANDEL

JULIUS RÖNTGEN

VAUGHAN WILLIAMS

GUSTAV HOLST

XLII. HERE AND ELSEWHERE

IN so far as this volume has a plan it falls into four parts. First, there is an account of Beethoven's Ninth Symphony, sufficiently full to include some discussion of its influence on later music. Secondly, there are essays dealing with works written during and after what is commonly called the 'Romantic Period', and including some quite recent works, but not including anything in which the purely musical issues are interfered with by literary or descriptive elements. Thirdly, there are a few essays on variations, beginning with Beethoven's Choral Fantasia which is nothing else; and orchestral pieces other than symphonies. Lastly, a completely new subject is introduced by a full discussion of Beethoven's Overture *Zur Weihe des Hauses*. This subject is the problem of orchestral polyphony, and it is illustrated by a series of works ranging from Bach to contemporary composers.

The choice of works here analysed is limited, not by my outlook on modern music, but by the encouragement given to local musicians by the musical public opinion of the capital of Scotland. Far be it from me to say that the contemporary music analysed in these volumes is not of my own choosing. No gentleman could make such a selection only to disavow it; and if critics blame me for liking works which they dislike, let us by all means stick to our various tastes. But I emphatically decline to be judged by the modern works that I have *not* yet produced and analysed. My choice, both of them and of the classics, has been limited by the following circumstances.

First, my orchestra has, for the greater part of its existence, been kept together as such by what wages it can earn and what ensemble it can learn by three hours' rehearsal in a week. In the last few years this has been expanded to a precarious six hours in the week. I hold to the heresy that modern music requires from its players not less practice and familiarity than the classics. My orchestra has been in existence at this date (1934) for eighteen years, in the course of which it has played the most hackneyed item on its programmes fourteen times. That is to say, fourteen performances in eighteen years are the nearest approach it has achieved towards making an item hackneyed from its own point of view.

My supporters are numerous, energetic, and loyal. But they have not as yet outvoted the traditional popular 'slogan' that Edinburgh ought to be musically a suburb of Glasgow. The slogan, if a slogan can exist in secret, is not thus expressed, but the doctrine is unmistakable and is believed to be infallible.

Glasgow is the happy possessor of a first-rate orchestra which is now in a position to rehearse for thirty hours a week, and which relies upon Edinburgh for a considerable part of its public support. I am the last person to grudge model conditions to any orchestra; my friend Casals has devoted his life's energies to establishing his orchestra in Barcelona on a twenty-five hour week, with triumphant success. But neither I nor my orchestral colleagues find six hours enough, nor do we see why we should be condemned for ever to snatch it from cinema-work and theatre floor-sweepings. Edinburgh is not the only place that suffers from the belief that all good music must come from elsewhere. There soon will be no elsewhere for it to come from. Whatever the term 'modern music' may be held to include, I can represent no comprehensive view of it, so long as I can produce no works containing Wagner tubas, no works with six horns, seldom any works with three instead of two of each wind instrument, and no work that my people cannot learn in twelve hours. Soon such works will be heard nowhere.

Robert Louis Stevenson, in his charming book on Edinburgh, said severe things about the climate of the Scottish capital. In the second edition of that book he added a footnote, saying that he understood that these strictures had given pleasure in a certain other city. Upon which he also remarked 'I have not written a book about Glasgow'.

It is always good news to me when, as happens fairly often, the musicians who have been expelled from Edinburgh by the severity of its musical climate succeed in doing better elsewhere. But I have not written about the musical climates of other towns. Like most towns, including those of nations reputedly more musical, Edinburgh owes its capacity to retain orchestral musicians and chamber-musicians almost wholly to those theatres and cinemas that provide steady daily employment at a living wage. The only thing more destructive to a player's technique than the daily practice of theatre trash is his sole alternative of death by starvation. From the serene heights of a University Chair whose occupant was appointed *ad vitam aut culpam* (that is to say before an age-limit was fixed, and on condition that his indictable offences, if committed, shall remain undiscovered), it is easy to play the part of an apostle of culture. I receive many compliments from the press and public for my efforts in that line and for the educational aspect of my concerts. But I make no such claim; on the contrary, I do not care two hoots for an apostleship of culture that allows the local musicians to be systematically driven out of the town and thrown on to the scrap-heap; and I have no interest in promoting a musical education that can lead to nothing better than the life of a theatre-musician in the capital of Scotland in 1934.

As a relief from such a life, six hours' decent music a week is not enough. But though the Scottish Orchestra of Glasgow is endowed for six times the wage-earning work of the Reid Orchestra, we must not conclude that the musical climate of Glasgow is six times as favourable as that of Edinburgh. On the contrary, public opinion is openly boastful, in both Edinburgh and Glasgow, that without its Edinburgh season the Scottish Orchestra could not survive. The suggestion has even been strongly urged that it would be a patriotic musical policy for me to confine my activities and my orchestra to the precincts of the University. To which the fit reply is Example 2 from my analysis of Elgar's *Cockaigne*,

if my interpretation of that admirable theme is correct.

The Reid Orchestra has produced fully twice as many contemporary works as appear in these volumes; not that that amounts to much. In several cases I have been able to obtain the composer's own analysis which, however modestly expressed, has an authority to which I obviously cannot claim, though I have sometimes intervened in footnotes when the composer's modesty has been actually misleading.

The experience of the awful consequences of my writing the analyses of my own works elsewhere suffices to warn me against mentioning the cases where composers have thus helped me in the Reid Concerts.

Other hands have come to my help when I was abroad or ill: notably Dr. Mary Grierson, who has analysed several works by Delius and other composers; and Mr. Henry Havergal, who wrote an admirable little essay on Vaughan Williams's incidental music to *The Wasps*, I having dealt only with the Overture. I have always had the ambition to write an essay on Bantock's Hebridean Symphony, a work which is on its way to becoming hackneyed for the Reid Orchestra, inasmuch as we have played it no less than three times, including performances at two successive concerts in 1920. Our later performance was in 1929; and the occasion was for us more solemn than the general public realized. The performance was broadcast, and we had the privilege of knowing that the great collector of the Hebridean songs, Mrs. Kennedy Fraser, then far advanced in a fatal illness, was listening to us. My ambition to write a new analysis of the Hebridean Symphony was checked by the realization that I could do no better than once more avail myself of the permission to use the analysis by Bantock's friend and biographer, H. Orsmond Anderton, in whose recent death we have lost an accomplished poet, composer, and, among other things, the inventor of an immense improvement in musical notation, perfectly practical in manuscript, thoroughly satisfactory to musical scholars, and difficult to achieve in print only because our age of mass-production is inevitably an age of stagnation when such mass-products as printed music come into question.

No; I am not going to give a list of the other more or less modern works that have been performed at my concerts without my writing their analysis. A series of Sunday concerts, ranging from pianoforte recitals to such orchestral concerts as we can afford, serves as a contribution to the funds of the Reid Orchestra; and at these concerts we cannot afford analytical programmes. But modern works have been represented at them. Still, I rely upon the Judge's Rules and decline to say anything further that can be used as evidence against me, about my choice of modern music, whether as restricted by the musical climate of Edinburgh or as I would have it if fair play were given to Edinburgh musicians.

BEETHOVEN

XLIII. NINTH SYMPHONY IN D MINOR, OP. 125
—ITS PLACE IN MUSICAL ART

It is well known that Beethoven had in his earliest period the ambition to set Schiller's 'Ode to Joy'. This project had in itself nothing to do with the idea of a choral symphony. At the time he was sketching his Seventh and Eighth Symphonies, he had already made up his mind that the next symphony should be in D minor, though he did not jot down any themes for it. This project again had nothing to do with Schiller's 'Ode'. Years later, after the Choral Symphony had been produced, Beethoven, no doubt in a moment of depression, said to some friends that the choral finale was a mistake, and that perhaps he might some day write an instrumental finale. This, in fact, had been his first intention, and the early sketches of the Ninth Symphony give the theme of the finale of the great A minor Quartet in D minor as the finale of the symphony. Beethoven had not hitherto written much choral music; and the study of that stagnant backwater of musical history, the choral art as practised by composers for the church and the stage in Vienna at the beginning of the nineteenth century, does not reveal the existence of anything like a 'good school' in this branch of composition. Nobody cares for the choral works of Beethoven's contemporaries, and so the extravagant compass Beethoven assigns to his voices looks like some enormous violence of Beethoven's genius; whereas it is but little worse than the habits of contemporaries of his who were under no excitement whatever. Other difficulties more enormous and less effective in Beethoven's choral writing arise from the fact that his two great choral works, the Ninth Symphony and the Mass in D, are for him, morally speaking, early works in this art. The Mass in D is longer than the whole of the Ninth Symphony, and is choral from beginning to end; yet, enormously difficult as is the Mass, the finale of the Choral Symphony is more exhausting in twenty minutes than the whole Mass in an hour and a quarter.

Beethoven was only fifty-seven when he died of a complication of disorders aggravated by a neglected chill. Constitutionally, in spite of his deafness and the moodiness it naturally engendered, he was on the whole a healthier and stronger man than, say, Samuel Johnson; and there is nothing but accident that deprived the art of music of a fourth period in Beethoven's development, which should have been distinguished by a body of choral work fully equal in power and perfection to the symphonies and string quartets.[1]

The arguments which would persuade us that the chorale finale of the Ninth Symphony is the outcome of a discontent with instrumental music are by this time discredited. Wagner committed some indiscretions on these lines, but they were too obviously grist to the official Wagnerian mill to survive in a musical civilization which recognizes Wagner as one among the greatest composers instead of putting him into a category which excludes all the rest of music. On the other hand, those arguments are equally futile which would persuade us that the choral finale was a 'mistake', because of some fundamental fallacy in the introduction of voices and words into a symphony. Contemporary performances, and contemporary judgements of the work, gave Beethoven abundant cause for moments of depression. At Aachen not only did the choral parts not arrive in time for performance, but the conductor, Beethoven's favourite pupil Ries, had to make large cuts in the slow movement simply because the orchestra could not master its difficulties. The only way to understand, not only the choral finale, but the other three movements of the symphony, is to attend strictly to the music from its own point of view as Beethoven wrote it; and not to be distracted by what he may have said about it when he was thinking of writing something else. We have no right to dismiss it as a mistake until we have thoroughly followed its meaning, whether we like it or not. The more we study it, from whatever point of view, the more obvious do its real mistakes become; and the more obvious they become, the more readily, and even impatiently, will the music-lover with a sense of proportion dismiss them from his mind as trivial accidents. The question as to the 'legitimacy' of bringing voices and words into a symphony is an exploded unreality. Professor Andrew Bradley, without saying a word about music, exploded it for all time when, in his inaugural lecture in the Chair of Poetry at Oxford in 1901, he discussed 'Poetry for Poetry's sake', and showed the fundamental fallacy in theories of artistic 'absoluteness', viz. the fallacy of separating form from matter at all. In the case of a choral symphony the essential facts are these; first, that all instruments and all harmonic and contrapuntal arts imitate, on the one hand, voices,

[1] This view has been hotly challenged by critics who urge, as a fatal objection to it, that Beethoven shows no appreciation of the beauty of the unaccompanied chorus. Such critics must extend their objection to the whole of classical choral music between the death of Palestrina and the maturity of Brahms. Bach, Handel, Mozart, and Haydn wrote not a line of unaccompanied choral music, unless you count canons scribbled on menu cards. Bach's so-called 'unaccompanied' motets all require instrumental support.

and on the other hand, dance rhythms or pulse rhythms: secondly, and consequently, the voice is the most natural as well as the most perfect of instruments as far as it goes; so that its introduction into instrumental music arrests the attention as nothing else will ever do, and hence must not be admitted without the intention of putting it permanently in the foreground: thirdly, that the introduction of the voice normally means the introduction of words, since that is how the human race uses its voice: and lastly, that it follows from this that the music must concern itself (conventionally or realistically or how you please) with the fit expression of the sense of the words. The correct application of Professor Andrew Bradley's philosophy (a classical statement of the case which, though not addressed to musicians, every musician should know) will show that there is no inherent impossibility in thus reconciling the claims of absolute music with those of the intelligent and intelligible setting of words. There is no part of Beethoven's Choral Symphony which does not become clearer to us when we assume that the choral finale is right; and there is hardly a point that does not become difficult and obscure as soon as we fall into the habit which assumes that the choral finale is wrong. I am not arguing that it is necessary to prove that it or any other work of art is perfect. That is never necessary, and most people would rashly say that it is never possible. All that is required is a point of view which assumes that Beethoven is not an inattentive artist who cannot keep his own plan in mind, until we have clear evidence to the contrary. If Beethoven were a Berlioz, a Bruckner, or a Mahler, we should find him out all the sooner by assuming that he is nothing of the kind. Hot-headed enthusiasts for these three composers fail to realize the gravity of their inconsistencies, because they assume that Beethoven was no better. The criticism which discovers the inconsistencies starts by assuming that these composers are as consistent as Beethoven. They break down under the test; but the critic who has applied it admires them more than the blind enthusiasts, because he sees more in the art of music whereever he finds it.

If a great work of art could be made responsible for all subsequent failures to imitate it, then Beethoven might have had cause for doubting whether the opening of his Ninth Symphony was worth the risk. It is a privilege of the greatest works of art that they can, if they will, reveal something gigantic in their scale, their range, and their proportions at the very first glimpse or moment. This power is quite independent of the possibility that other works may be larger; it is primarily a matter of proportion, and the actual size enters into the question only when the work of art is brought by some unavoidable accident into relation with the actual size of the spectator. Thus Macaulay once shrewdly observed that the size of the Great Pyramid was essential to its sublimity, 'for what could be more vile than a pyramid thirty feet high?' And thus the faithful reproduction of the noblest proportions will not give sublimity to an architectural model that you can put under a glass case. The truth is that in architecture the size of the human frame is one of the terms, perhaps the principal term, of the art. In pictures this is not so, or rather it is so with a more elastic relativity: you can give any proportions you like to your pictures by introducing human figures or other known objects on whatever scale you please. Music has, like architecture, a fixed element to deal with, the subtlest and most implacable of all. It is no use comparing the dimensions of music for a few instruments with those of music for vast masses: the string quartets of Beethoven are in the most important of all their dimensions fully as large as the symphonies. It is no use saying that the string quartet is a pencil drawing, and the symphony an oil painting or a fresco: pencil drawings are not executed on the scale of frescoes. It is no use saying that the string quartet is monochrome, while the symphony has all the tone colours of the orchestra: people who seriously talk of string-quartet style as monochromatic are probably tone-deaf, and certainly incapable of recognizing anything short of the grossest contrasts in orchestral music. Yet there is what you may call a dimensional difference between a string quartet and an orchestra; and the difference is hardly greater in volume of tone than in range of tone colour. These differences, again, cannot fail to have some effect on the architecture of the works designed for few or for many instruments, but such effects on the designs are not less subtle than profound; and the composer himself is so far from recognizing them until his plans are matured that, as we have already seen, Beethoven for a long time thought that what eventually became the finale of his A minor Quartet was to be the finale of the Ninth Symphony.

The all-pervading, constant element in musical designs is time. Beethoven's chamber music (extending the term so as to include everything from one to eight instruments) is for the most part on the same time-scale as his symphonies. That scale was from the outset so large that his First Symphony, a masterly little comedy, shows him taking the precaution to design his first independent orchestral work on a smaller scale than much that he had already written for solo instruments. But while it was obvious from the outset that his compositions were on the largest known scale, it only gradually became evident that that scale was growing beyond all precedent. Beethoven himself did not avow this fact until he recommended that the Eroica Symphony, being longer than usual, should be placed nearer the beginning than the end of the concert.[1] And the Eroica does not from the outset promise to be larger than the Second Symphony, nor indeed in its first sketches did it show any signs of being so large. Contemporary critics throughout Beethoven's career were continually deceived about the scale of his designs, or they would not so constantly have considered Beethoven inferior to Mozart in power of construction. With the rarest exceptions they always listened to a work of Beethoven in the expectation that its proportions would be those of a work of Mozart; and the mere measurement of the actual length of the work as a whole would not suffice to correct that assumption, for several very perfect works of Mozart may be found which are considerably longer than some characteristic great works of Beethoven. The enlargement of the time-scale is not a matter of total length; it is a matter of contrasts in movement. Mozart's aesthetic system does not admit of such broad expanses side by side with such abrupt and explosive actions as are perfectly natural in Beethoven's art. The first signs of intelligence in this matter came from those contemporary critics of Beethoven who had the sense to be bewildered by many things which are now accepted inattentively. Two of Weber's notorious gibes will clear up the matter once for all. He regarded the introduction to the Fourth Symphony as a monstrous and empty attempt to spread some four or five notes over a quarter of an hour. This shows that he had a sense of something new in Beethoven's time-scale. The other case was that of the sustained note five octaves deep towards the end of the first movement of the Seventh Symphony; a feature which he declared showed that Beethoven was now ripe for the madhouse. This shows that he perceived something unprecedented in Beethoven's scale of tone. Now the scale of tone is a very much more difficult matter to discuss than the scale of time, and I must be content, for the present, to leave all statements about it in the form of dogmatic assertion. It naturally is more easily measured in orchestral works than in works where there is less volume of tone to deal with; but again, as with the time elements, it is not a question of the actual volume, but of the range of contrast. In Beethoven's string quartets it is not less manifest than in his orchestra. In short, just as it is possible in the very first notes of a work to convey to the listener the conviction that this is going to be something on a large scale of time, so is it possible, however small the instrumental means employed, to arouse in the listener a confident expectation of an extraordinary depth and range of tone.

[1] His notion of 'nearer the beginning than the end' was 'after, perhaps, an overture, an aria, and a concerto'. When he produced his next symphony, the Fourth, he preceded it with the First, the Second, and the Eroica. Four hours was short for a concert in those days.

The opening of the Ninth Symphony is an immediate revelation of Beethoven's full power in both of these ways. Of all passages in a work of art, the first subject of the first movement of Beethoven's Ninth Symphony has had the deepest and widest influence on later music. Even with an ordinary instrumental finale, the Ninth Symphony would have remained the most gigantic instrumental work extant; its gigantic proportions are only the more wonderful from the fact that the forms are still the purest outcome of the sonata style. The choral finale itself is perfect in form. We must insist on this, because vast masses of idle criticism are still nowadays directed against the Ninth Symphony and others of Beethoven's later works in point of form; and these criticisms rest upon uncultured and unclassical text-book criteria as to musical form; mere statements of the average procedure warranted to produce tolerable effect if carefully carried out. We shall never make head or tail of the Ninth Symphony until we treat it as a law unto itself. That is the very treatment under which Berlioz and Bruckner break down; and it is also the treatment under which a Mozart symphony proves itself to be a living individual, though he wrote so many other symphonies externally similar in form.

The opening of the Ninth Symphony is, then, obviously gigantic. It is gigantic in relation to the sonata style of which it is still a perfect specimen. But its gigantic quality is so obvious in itself that it has been the actual and individual inspiring source of almost all the vast stream of modern music that has departed from the sonata style altogether. The normal opening for a sonata movement is a good, clear, pregnant theme. Whatever happens before the statement of such a theme is evidently introductory, and the introduction is generally so separable that it is in an obviously different tempo, whether or not it does itself consist largely of something broadly melodious. But it would hardly do to call the opening of the Ninth Symphony an introduction: it is impossible to imagine anything that more definitely plunges us into the midst of things. No later composer has escaped its influence. Nearly all modern music not on sonata lines, and a great deal that is on sonata lines, assumes that the best way to indicate a large scale of design is to begin with some mysteriously attractive humming sounds, from which rhythmic fragments gradually detach themselves and combine to build up a climax. When the climax is a mighty theme in unison for the whole orchestra, and the key is D minor, the resemblance to Beethoven's Ninth Symphony becomes almost absurd. And this is actually the case in Bruckner's third and ninth symphonies; while he hardly knows how to begin a first movement or finale without a long tremolo. It is no exaggeration to say that the typical opening of a modern orchestral work has become as thoroughly conventionalized on these lines as any tonic-and-dominant sonata formula of the eighteenth century. There is no objection to this, so long as the composer can draw the rest of his work to scale. Only through lifelong mastery of the sonata style could such an opening be continued in anything resembling sonata form; and the crushing objection to the forms of Berlioz and Bruckner is not their departure from sonata principles, but their desperate recourse to them in just the most irrelevant particulars. Another set of difficulties arises when the composer continues such an opening without relying upon sonata forms. The orthodox reproach that is levelled against 'symphonic poems' is that of form-lessness: it is generally a foolish reproach because it is based on some foolish text-book notion of form as the average classical procedure. The real trouble with an unsuccessful symphonic poem is generally that it either fails to maintain the scale set up by its ninth-symphony type of opening, or makes an even more radical failure to come to a definite beginning on any scale at all; as, for instance, in the extreme case of Liszt's *Ce qu'on entend sur la montagne*. This work consists of an introduction to an intro-duction to a connecting link to another introduction to a rhapsodic interlude, leading to a free development of the third introduction, leading to a series of still more introductory developments of the previous introduction, leading to a solemn slow theme (which, after these twenty minutes, no mortal power will persuade any listener to regard as a real beginning), and so eventually leading backwards to the original mysterious opening by way of conclusion.

The whole difference between Wagner and such interesting but unconvincing pioneers is that Wagner, when he abandoned the sonata time-scale, thoroughly mastered his own new proportions. He talked partisan nonsense about Beethoven's attitude to 'abso-lute' musical forms, but he made no mistakes in maturing his own musical style; and the fact that his medium was music-drama must not mislead us into denying the validity of his mature sense of musical form as a factor in the purely instrumental music of later times.

This opening of the Ninth Symphony has, then, been a radiating point for all subsequent experiments for enlarging the time-scale of music; and the simplest way to learn its lessons is to set our mind free to expect to find in the Ninth Symphony the broadest and most spacious processes side by side with the tersest and most sharply contrasted statements and actions. There are listeners (indeed their complaint is one of the intellectual fashions of the day) to whom it is a cause of nervous irritability that the Ninth Symphony is recognized by orthodoxy as the most sublime musical composi-tion known. Orthodoxy happens to be perfectly right here, and for the same reason that it is right about Handel's *Messiah*, and Bach's *Matthew Passion* and Mass in B minor. These things do not rest upon fashion: they rest upon the solid fact that these works deal truthfully with sublime subjects. As a modern poet has remarked, 'All is not false that's taught at public schools'; and if there are large numbers of contemporary music lovers who are in heated revolt against the aesthetics of Beethoven's music, that is a nervous condition which concerns nobody but themselves.[1] There will always be still larger numbers of music lovers who have not yet heard anything like as much classical music as they wish to hear. It is just as well that they should realize that there is nothing more than an irritated condition of nerves behind the talk that still goes on about the need of a revolt against Beethoven. No artist of such a range as Beethoven has ever set up a tyranny from which revolt is possible. We hear a great deal about the way in which English Music was 'crushed by the ponderous genius of Handel'. It was crushed by nothing of the sort; it was crushed simply by the fact that the rank and fashion of English music patrons would for centuries listen only to Italian singers and Italian composers. Handel's methods were Italian, and he benefited accordingly. The real objection that is felt against Beethoven's aesthetics is the eternal dread felt by the artist of *genre* in the presence of the sublime. Modern British music has derived much stimulus from highly specialized *genres* of French music, and these *genres* do not aim at the sublime. They thus do not blend well with the Ninth Symphony, though they are conspicuously free from the false sublime that would blend infinitely worse.

We have seen that there are two factors which cause the impression of the enormous size in the opening of the Ninth Symphony. The one factor, that of proportion in time, we have already dealt with, and on that head all that remains is to explain how the actual length of the opening is not exceptional. Indeed, the whole first movement, as Sir George Grove has pointed out, is, though the greatest of Beethoven's compositions in this form, by no means the longest. And this does not mean that it is more terse than longer movements such as the first movement of the Eroica Symphony. Those longer movements are not diffuse; but the compression of Beethoven's later style is balanced by a still wider power of expansion. What happens is that, as we have already

---

[1] The quaintest manifestations of the revolt were those of the writers who at the centenary of Beethoven's death told us that the 'humanism' of Beethoven's slow movements was antiquated. From time to time the Superman *may* seem to be as fashionable as all that: but nevertheless he does not exist as yet.

pointed out, the range of contrasts in phrase-length is greater; and the result is that more space is gained by compression than will ever be filled up by expansion. Sir George Grove pointed out how, already as soon as the first mysterious sounds begin to make their crescendo, the rhythmic fragments are compressed and hurried. So much, then, for the rhythmic side of this opening.

The rest of its enormous effect is the result of the scale of tone. And here again the Ninth Symphony, like the Fifth and the *Leonora* Overtures, teaches us that there is for the massive treatment of the orchestra a criterion which many modern orchestral composers have entirely forgotten. Orchestral music since Beethoven has undergone its greatest developments chiefly at the hands of composers who contemplated music from the standpoint of the theatre. It is true that Liszt wrote nothing for the theatre, and that Berlioz's operas were brilliant failures; but the fact remains that nearly everything that marks an advance in nineteenth-century orchestral technique since Beethoven is an advance in essentially dramatic orchestration; and this in the narrow sense, that the characteristic orchestral discoveries would be even more useful in an opera than in a purely symphonic work. Finally, it is universally admitted, even by partisans, that Liszt and Berlioz did not often achieve complete mastery of their art problems, and that if we are to find a style for the post-Beethoven orchestra which we can always confidently expect to say what it means and mean what it says, we must turn to the later music-dramas of Wagner. It is no more necessary to prove that these are perfect works of art than to prove the perfection of ethics, theology, science, and sentiment throughout *Paradise Lost*. But you can, on the whole, find mastery wherever you look in the later works of Wagner, just as you can in Milton, without taking any precaution to select specially inspired passages; whereas with Liszt and Berlioz you will find mastery about as sporadically as you will find it in Walt Whitman. Wagner is, in short, the most authoritative classic of the orchestral technique of the age after Beethoven; and Wagner's life's work is for the stage.

Now there are two far-reaching consequences of this that we must take into account before we adopt Wagner as a criterion for the symphonic orchestra. The composer for the stage (like the composer of symphonic poems on the basis of Liszt and Berlioz) is constantly occupied by illustrating something outside the music. This *may* tend to limit his capacity for inventing sounds which do not obviously illustrate something external; and it *must* limit his opportunities for developing such sounds. The purely symphonic composer has no use for illustrative sounds unless they are also useful to a purely musical design; and as soon as they are so useful, their imitative aspect ceases to attract notice. There is a very large

class of orchestral procedure which is thus common to the symphonic orchestra and the stage; and so long as music confined itself
to Mozart's range of expression the distinction between symphonic
and dramatic orchestration remained a subtlety. In music of his
period you might perhaps be able to distinguish between first-rate
and second-rate mastery of the orchestra in this way, that with
second-rate composers the dramatic orchestral devices lacked
musical point, while the musical devices lacked dramatic point.
But the divergence of interests did not as yet amount to this, that
a composer could write symphonic orchestration which would be
impossible in stage music. All that had happened was that much
which was tolerable or even effective on the stage, would be too thin
and commonplace for the symphonic orchestra. The mature works
of Wagner are far too highly organized in all respects for this to be
crudely manifest; but it is self-evident that the orchestration of
Wagnerian opera contains much that is not only out of place but
inadequate for symphonic writing. And practically this is a more
important truth to the modern composer than the converse truth,
that the mastery of a symphonic style for full modern orchestra is
in itself no qualification for the handling of operatic orchestration.
There are far more composers who can write a good modern
opera than there are composers of good modern symphonies.

But the subtle aesthetic distinction between the dramatic and
symphonic in orchestration is not more important than the very
much simpler practical fact which determines the opera-writer's
orchestral outlook. Nine-tenths of the opera-writer's orchestration
is designed for the accompanying of voices. It does not matter
whether, like Wagner, he puts all his invention into the orchestra
and gets the voice to declaim through the orchestral design as it
best can, or whether, like Mozart, he puts his primary invention
into the voice. Whatever he does, he knows that the voice must be
heard somehow; and his orchestral climaxes are severely restricted
to situations in which there is either no solo singing, or the voices
are able actually to interrupt the full orchestra, and so to convey an
ingenious illusion of dominating the storm when all the time the
orchestra gives way to the singer with the readiest tact. The
imagination of the public and of students is impressed by the
extent to which Wagner enlarged the orchestra; and Wagner is
one of the greatest composers in the handling of massive orchestration; but massive orchestration seems such a simple thing, and the
immense majority of Wagner's interesting orchestral devices are
so closely associated with the singer on the stage (even where they
are not actually accompanying the voice) that very few critics and
students pay much attention to Wagner's handling of an orchestral
tutti. Hence there arises a conception of the modern orchestra as

an organization which on the one hand can make an alarmingly loud noise, and on the other hand can indulge in astounding complexities of musical spider-lines. The attempts of ordinary go-ahead composers to handle the tutti of a modern orchestra with no technique at all, or perhaps with a humdrum military bandmaster's technique, can hardly fail to produce a noisy impression; 'noisiness' being a popular term for bad balance of tone. The position, then, with commonplace exploitations of the modern orchestra is that the tuttis are apt to be scored with no technique to speak of, and that the rest of the writing, though often very interesting and clever, is unwittingly based upon a conception which reduces itself to the art of accompanying a voice. Again and again the inner history of an ambitious piece of contemporary orchestration has been that it was scored in some complicated and interesting way; and that, after the usual disheartening experiences of inadequate rehearsals, the composer has found that the full passages had better be expressed in the old scrubbing-brush of tremolo, with the theme entrusted to the trumpet as the only person capable of carrying it through.

The real method for scoring a tutti will be found in Wagner, in Richard Strauss, and Elgar, and a very few other composers since Beethoven; and it will be found to be in all essentials surprisingly like Beethoven's method. Now the clue to the whole orchestration of the Ninth Symphony is to be found in the statement of I forget what French authority that the whole work, or at all events a great part of it, is one grand tutti. This must not be taken to mean that it is full of useless doublings, or that it does not contain numberless passages in which single instruments weave delicate threads. What it does mean is that the composition is for a whole orchestra employed for its own sake, and that no part of its aesthetic system is concerned with the accompaniment of anything else—until, of course, the voices enter in the finale. And there we find proof of how curiously irrelevant that present-day style of criticism is which patronizes Beethoven for having 'attempted' in the Ninth Symphony an orchestration which only the resources of Wagner could have enabled him to carry out successfully. No such criticism can tackle the choral part of the symphony at all; for, whatever may be said against Beethoven's choral writing (and choral technique is no strong feature in modern musical progress), Beethoven is completely at his ease in *accompanying* the voice. There is, in fact, very little trouble with the orchestration of the choral finale; nor is there much difficulty in getting the slow movement to sound clear, although there is a prevalent and very gross misunderstanding of a certain horn passage therein, which we will discuss in its place. The whole set of difficulties of the orchestration of the Ninth

Symphony is confined to the first movement and to one famous theme in the scherzo. Wagner adjusted these matters easily; Weingartner adjusts them more accurately: with a large orchestra such as that of Dresden, with 150 players and triple wind (six flutes, six oboes, and so on), the adjustment becomes purely the business of the conductor, and of some one's marking the extra wind parts according to his directions.[1] The first movement of the Ninth Symphony is no doubt the most troublesome of all Beethoven's scores; but no virtuoso has ever written a work for the pianoforte which does not, in proportion to its size, throw far more responsibility upon the player for adjusting its balance of tone.

The first thing, then, to realize about the Ninth Symphony is that it is a work for the orchestral tutti; and that nine-tenths of the patronizing criticism that is nowadays directed against it is based on a judgement that is frankly incapable of following any genuine orchestral tutti whatever. If your ear is accustomed entirely to the pianoforte, the clearest organ-playing in the world will be a chaos of echoes to you. If you know nothing but music for the full orchestra, your first impressions of the finest string quartet will consist mainly of squeak and scrape. And if your only conception of the orchestra is fundamentally operatic, it is no use to argue that Beethoven's symphonies are so often performed that you have nothing to learn from them; a cathedral choir-boy may have sung in the church services every day, and yet have escaped understanding the English of the Bible and Prayer Book. I have noticed that any truly symphonic orchestration sounds to me, for the moment, impenetrably thick after I have got my ears into focus for operatic or otherwise illustrative modern orchestration. Of course the impression is only momentary, because I know by experience that such impressions are mere physiological effects of contrast; the mind learns its accommodations just as the eye or the ear. But it will not learn its accommodations if it is told that there is no moon because the first step out of a brilliantly lighted room seems to be a step into pitch darkness.

ANALYSIS

1 *Allegro ma non troppo, un poco maestoso.*
2 SCHERZO: *Molto vivace* alternating with *Presto.*
3 *Adagio molto e cantabile* alternating with *Andante moderato.*

---

[1] It has been objected that all bad scoring can be defended and rectified on these lines. This is not so. Errors of calculation are not defects of imagination. Beethoven's imagination never fails; and there is no master of modern instrumentation who could trust himself to publish fewer miscalculated passages than Beethoven, if he were, like Beethoven, deprived of the opportunity for correcting his scoring at rehearsals.

4 FINALE: *Presto* alternating with quotations from previous movements, and leading to *Allegro assai*; leading to recapitulation
of *Presto* with a Baritone solo followed by the Choral Finale,
which consists of variations and developments of the theme of
the *Allegro assai* as follows:

Allegro assai: theme and two variations (quartet and chorus),
Allegro assai vivace alla marcia: variation with tenor solo and
male chorus; fugal episode; variation with full chorus.

Andante maestoso: new theme with full chorus.

Allegro energico, sempre ben marcato: double fugue on the two
themes.

Allegro ma non tanto (with changes of tempo) leading to *Prestissimo*: coda with quartet and chorus.

FIRST MOVEMENT

When we compare the opening of the Ninth Symphony with
many of those imitations of it that have almost become a normal
procedure in later music, two characteristic features reveal themselves. First that, as has already been indicated, Beethoven
achieves his evidences of gigantic size in a passage which is, as a
matter of fact, not very long; and secondly that this moderate
length is filled with clearly marked gradations, which succeed one
another more rapidly as the intensity increases. It is interesting to
see how few composers have ever by any refinement of technique
and apparatus mastered the natural aesthetics of climax as shown
in any of Beethoven's crescendos and most simply of all in this
opening. External details have been echoed by later composers
with excellent though sometimes obviously borrowed effect.
Bruckner's Ninth Symphony even gets in Beethoven's characteristic anticipation of the tonic chord on an outlying bassoon under
the dominant chord before the full orchestra bursts in with the
mighty unison theme.

Ex. 1.

But such resemblances are fatal; there is only one ninth-symphony
opening, and that is Beethoven's. If anybody else could get
those proportions right, he would arrive at Beethoven's Ninth
Symphony and not his own. If his own is going to be different
enough to justify its existence, it will not adopt, long after its
harmonies have moved into all manner of foreign keys and emotional tones, a characteristic external detail the whole point of
which was that the harmony had not yet begun to move at all.
And the real sublimity of Beethoven's conception has not yet fully
appeared with the entry of the mighty unison theme in the tonic

after this mysterious crescendo on the dominant (mysterious, by the way, because, as the harmony was nothing but bare fifths and octaves, that characteristic anticipation by the bassoon was the first indication that it was not the tonic chord of either A major or A minor). This opening is indeed gigantic, but its full power begins to manifest itself in the fact that it is not unwieldy. The mighty unison theme leads to a variety of short melodic and harmonic sequences, no two phrases being of easily predictable length; and it comes to a kind of full close very characteristic of Beethoven's latest work, a close in which the tonic chord has been arrived at without the intervention of the dominant as a penultimate. And so the theme, as Weingartner says, disappears into the ground like some Afrit vanishing in a column of smoke. And now we find ourselves on the tonic, with the same mysterious bare fifth quivering and growing until it pervades the whole orchestra. Immediately before the climax the bass changes the harmony, this time in the unexpected direction of B flat; and in this key the unison theme bursts out again, soon to make its way back to the dominant chord, where another new and terse theme appears.

Ex. 2.

This new theme leads, by a movement of its last three notes downward in a very few further steps, to the famous pathetic introduction to the second subject; a passage which attracted the eager attention of the musical symbolists who surrounded Liszt, on account of its superficial and entirely accidental resemblance to the theme of the *Ode to Joy*.

Ex. 3.

It cannot be too often or too strongly urged that no such thematic resemblances are of the slightest importance unless the composer himself establishes the connexion on the spot by the most unmistakable formal methods.[1] We shall find plenty of such methods in the Ninth Symphony and in any late work of Beethoven; which will conclusively prove that what is said about Beethoven's revolutionary tendencies in musical form is, for the most part, nonsense which it would be a mistaken courtesy to treat as anything but

[1] Strange to say, no English musician has been more strongly bitten by the Lisztian view than Stanford, who always upheld Liszt as the awful example of lack of musical logic; in spite of the fact that Liszt was a fanatic pioneer of music on a single leitmotif.

ignorance. Here it will suffice to say that Beethoven's forms become more and more precise in his later works; and that if thereby they become less and less like each other, this is what anybody who understands the nature of artistic forms as compared to living forms ought to expect. I am obliged to leave these general statements dogmatic where I am dealing with only one work; if proof is required I am ready for it with any work and any part of a work in Beethoven's third period; no very large field of survey, comprising, as it does, only thirteen works in sonata form, and not half a dozen other important compositions.

The second subject, at which we have now arrived, consists of a large number of different themes grouped into paragraphs of every imaginable size and shape. Of these I quote five: the consolatory opening cantabile divided between wind instruments of contrasted tone—

the stormy figure of scales in contrary motion—

the energetic theme with its contrast between sharp rhythm and cantabile, leading to the famous modulation into a distant key (flat supertonic)—

which in its turn leads to the most flowing and elaborate paragraph in this exposition where all is so flowing and rich; and so to the complicated and expressive dialogue between wind and strings (a difficult passage where Wagner's and Weingartner's suggestions are valuable in the interests of clearness)—

and the final triumphant tutti on the tonic chord of B flat—

which ends the exposition and collapses dramatically onto the dominant of D and back to the cloudy opening.

In discussing the first subject we saw the advantage of terseness in the very act of establishing an impression of immense size, for we noted that Beethoven was enabled thereby to give two great waves rising from mystery to their sublime crash. It might be argued that these two great waves are perhaps not so enormous as the longer passages often achieved by later composers, where it is inconceivable that the passage should be given twice over in its entirety. Very well then; Beethoven can do this greater type of passage also. The mysterious opening is now going to develop; it remains intensely quiet without crescendo, its periods marked by a distant boom of drums and flashes of red light from the trumpets, an extraordinarily solemn resource in the primitive classical treatment of these instruments already well known to Mozart and often used by him with sublime effect. The novelty in the present instance consists in the very low pitch of the trumpets. The harmonies drift through a major chord to the subdominant. The passage still remains intensely quiet, but in the subdominant the articulate main theme gathers shape in dialogue between the wind instruments. Suddenly on a fierce discord the energetic rhythmic figure of Ex. 8 bursts out on the full orchestra. The following plaintive treatment of figure (b) then makes, with the addition of four closing chords, a six-bar phrase.

This closes into G minor, and the dialogue on figure (a) is resumed. Now it leads to C minor, and again Ex. 8 intervenes on the full orchestra and yields to the six-bar phrase. This time the last two bars are repeated with a crescendo, and the orchestra plunges into a vigorous triple fugue with figure (*b*) (Ex. 1) for its main subject and a pair of admirably clear and contrasted counterpoints. This drifts with the grandest and simplest breadth straight through from C minor to G minor, D minor, and so to A minor. On reaching this key its energy abates until it subsides into a famous and exquisitely plaintive passage, which Sir George Grove was fond of quoting as an example of Beethoven's peculiar use of the word *cantabile*. Grove indicates that Beethoven applies the term rather specially to passages of a simplicity which makes them liable to be overlooked. To this we may add that as long as Beethoven refrains from using the German language he can hardly find any word that will give the player the chance of putting what the Germans call *Innigkeit* into his rendering. Beethoven does not want to prescribe what he calls *intissimo sentimento* here: his best chance of getting what he wants is to tell the player to sing, and as the passage is too quiet to lend itself to obvious swellings of tone, the mere action of getting a singing quality into its calm will go far to express its inwardness.[1]

This A minor cantabile develops itself almost happily in its own touching way (notice, for example, the place where the whole mass of wood-wind gathers itself together in a staccato crescendo). Suddenly, with childlike pathos the main theme of the second subject (Ex. 4) appears. The basses take it up in F major, and in that consolatory key the dialogue on figure (*b*) is resumed. Nothing indicates that the situation is going to change in any near future. The development has in fact been on fully as large a scale as the rest of the movement, but the present passage has every appearance of being in the middle of its flow. If Beethoven had left the movement unfinished here, no mortal could have made a better guess at the sequel than that somehow or other Beethoven would climb to another climax, and from it build a passage of anticipation of return which should surpass in length and excitement any of the famous returns he had achieved before; such as the return to the tonic in the Eroica Symphony, or the return three times anticipated in the first movement of the First Rasoumovsky Quartet. It would,

---

[1] I know of no more crushing evidence of racial incompatibility of temper than is furnished by Debussy's beautiful arrangement of Schumann's pedal pianoforte studies. The French composer shows all his exquisite sensibility for pianoforte tone and his scrupulous scholarship in every note of these arrangements, yet where Schumann writes *innig* Debussy translates it *très expressif*, which is as flatly the opposite term as any two languages could supply between them. This leaves open the question whether Debussy has not after all correctly interpreted Schumann's sentiments, which hardly reach Beethoven's *Innigkeit*.

however, be difficult to know exactly what a long and exciting preparation of a return is to prepare for in this case; for the opening of the Ninth Symphony is itself a long and exciting passage of preparation. There are people who talk *a priori* nonsense about the sonata forms, as if these forms were stereotyped moulds into which you shovel your music in the hope that it may set there like a jelly. The real facts of sonata form seem complicated only because we have to describe them in purely musical terms, just as the facts of pictorial forms would seem enormously complicated if we had to describe them in geometrical terms. In reality such a fact of sonata form as this matter of 'return to the tonic for the first subject', is the barest definition of the capacity of the music to make us expect to return to anything whatever.

Beethoven's conduct of this great development has so far contrived the course of events as to make us feel thoroughly in the swing of an almost happy conversational episode, when suddenly, with a change of harmony, four abrupt bars carry us roughly into the tonic major, and the whole development is at once a thing of the past, a tale that is told.

This return to the recapitulation is utterly unlike any other in Beethoven's works; and we shall always find that in these cardinal features of form, no two works of Beethoven are really alike. In this matter of return to the first subject Beethoven achieved every conceivable gradation, from famous record-breaking lengths of anticipation to not less record-breaking abruptness; nor did he neglect the possibilities of bringing about the return with all Mozart's quiet formal beauty and symmetry. The present catastrophic return now reveals fresh evidence of the gigantic size of the opening. Hitherto we have known the opening as a pianissimo, and only the subtlety of Beethoven's feeling for tone has enabled us to feel that it was vast in sound as well as in spaciousness. Now we are brought into the midst of it, and instead of a distant nebula we see the heavens on fire. There is something very terrible about this triumphant major tonic, and it is almost a relief when it turns into the minor as the orchestra crashes into the main theme, no longer in unison, but with a bass rising in answer to the fall of the melody. Each phrase given out by the strings is now echoed by the wood-wind (it is ridiculous to complain of Beethoven's orchestration here, when the whole difficulty of such passages might easily be remedied by simply doubling and trebling certain of the wind parts—a purely financial question). The whole first subject is thus on the one hand amplified by this dialogue treatment, while on the other it is mightily compressed by being gathered up in one single storm from the outset of its introduction down to its abrupt subsidence into the consolatory preparation for the second subject.

From this point the recapitulation follows bar for bar the course of the exposition, but there are new details of far-reaching significance. There is an interesting historic process in the expression of pathos in sonata form. The first great master in whose hands sonata forms became definitely dramatic is Haydn. When Haydn writes a sonata movement in the minor mode, his second subject will certainly be in the relative major key. What will happen to it in the recapitulation? If the work is of Haydn's maturity and the character of the movement is blustering and impetuous, Haydn's sunny temperament is almost certain to impel him to recapitulate his second subject in the major, and so to end with childlike happiness. Not so Mozart, who rises to his highest pathos by translating the second subject from the relative major to the tonic minor, and translating it by no means literally, but in every way heightening the pathos in both harmony and melody. Beethoven has further resources at his command, and his practice in such a case depends upon his power to design a coda equal in importance to the whole development of a movement. Accordingly, if Beethoven chooses to recapitulate the whole of his second subject in the tonic major, this does not commit him to a happy ending; on the contrary it is, for him, a powerful expression of tragic irony. Nowhere since Greek tragedy do we so forcibly feel the pathos of the messenger who comes with what has the appearance of good news but which really brings about the catastrophe, as when we have in a tragic work of Beethoven the comfort of the recapitulation of the second subject in the tonic major. In the Ninth Symphony, however, Beethoven has achieved a yet more powerful pathos; he can get both major and minor wherever he pleases. For six bars the second subject proceeds happily in the major, and then, sorrowfully repeating the fifth and sixth bars in the minor, continues in minor, with the exception of the pleading second phrase of Ex. 6. The wonderful modulation to the flat supertonic in this passage looks much simpler as a modulation from D minor to E flat than it did when it was written as a modulation from B flat, not to C flat, but to B natural. Gevaert and other eminent writers on music have argued from this that it actually sounds less remarkable here; but with all respect I submit that they are misled by appearances. The modulation was, in the first instance as in the second, a simple modulation to the flat supertonic; and if Beethoven chose in the first instance to spell it in an extraordinary fashion, that is no reason for playing it out of tune. Classical and modern music from the time of Mozart onwards is constantly offering us passages in which the notation is enharmonic while the sense is diatonic. On the other hand, many real enharmonic changes are not visible in the notation at all. The real difficulty here between the first and the

second passages is that in the first instance the whole context is in
a major key, whereas now in the recapitulation we are in the minor
tonic, and so to this extent it is true that the modulation to the flat
supertonic is less remote. On the other hand it is more pathetic,
and Beethoven contrives to heighten the pathos by a subtle change
in the position of the loud figure. From the following crescendo
onwards, all the rest of the recapitulation is in the minor, including
the once triumphant energetic close (Ex. 8).

What is going to happen next? Put this into technical language,
and ask how Beethoven is going to begin his coda. The superior
person who assumes that everything is silly as soon as it can be
designated by a technical term will hereupon quote the gentleman
who asked the painter where he was going to put his brown tree.
But this is not a true parallel to our question. A fair parallel would
be, what are you going to put in the middle distance on the left-
hand side of your picture? or what form of dome, tower, or spire
are you going to have in the middle of your cathedral roof? These
technical terms for the sonata forms describe no more than the
points of the compass, and there is no more resemblance between
the standard examples of even the most particularized of these
forms than there is between them and works in totally different
forms. If we once more imagine that the movement be left
unfinished at this point, we should find it just as difficult to guess
the next event as we did at the end of the development. The coda
of the first movement of the Eroica Symphony began with an
astounding and mysterious modulation which carried it off into
distant keys. Other codas of Beethoven begin as if to lead into the
development again in the same way as the close of the exposition
did; others bring the main theme or some other theme out in a
great climax; others settle down at once to a comfortable tonic-and-
dominant swinging passage on some important figure. Nearly
every great coda will contain some such passage as its most natural
means of expressing finality in the action of the piece. I suppose
that if we did not know how Beethoven's coda was to begin here,
our first guess would be some dramatic stroke of genius. Bruckner's most enthusiastic admirers are the first to deplore the fatal
ease with which their master strikes his dramatic stroke whenever
his huge creations try to lift their acreage of limbs without muscles
to work them. One of the reasons why the first movement of the
Ninth Symphony dwarfs every other first movement, long or short,
that has been written before or since, is that, more evidently than
in other compositions, it shows that no member of its organization
is so large as to lose freedom in its function as part of a larger whole.
The whole, when it has been heard, proves greater than the sum
of its parts. In works of art which take time instead of space, it is

inevitable that the highest organization should be concentrated towards the beginning; thus the first movement of a great classical work is normally the most highly organized. What has just been said of the first movement of the Ninth Symphony is true of every other mature work of Beethoven. It is only more easily seen here, and more profitably pointed out, because of the enormous influence this particular movement has had upon later music dealing with totally different forms. The technicalities or points of the compass of sonata form are merely relative; the principles of form are universal. As every part of the Ninth Symphony presents us with a constantly increasing impression of greatness in due proportion to a whole which is still greater than the sum of its parts, so does this movement stand towards the rest of the symphony. It matters not that the other movements are all simpler in organization; or rather, it is necessary that they should be. The simplicity means increase of breadth, and it is so organized that the mind is always fully occupied with the right actions and reactions.

And now for Beethoven's coda. We have just heard the end of the exposition, an emphatic close to one of the most flowing and elaborate paragraphs ever written in music or words. And instead of any abrupt modulation, Beethoven quietly and in a gentle vein of melancholy continues a flowing dialogue with the figures of the mighty first subject (Ex. 1), as if mysterious introductions and stormy outbursts were but old ancestral memories. The form of the dialogue is that which arose out of the mysterious introduction at the beginning of the development, but the tone-colour is not mysterious now; it is a grey noonday. Gradually and without change of key, the dialogue rises in an impassioned crescendo and bursts into a storm paragraph developing Ex. 5, which is followed up by a sequence based on Ex. 8. Suddenly the whole mass of strings stands hushed and overawed while the horns, softly in the full major tonic, are heard developing figure (b) of the main theme. This moment of distant happiness has never been surpassed for tragic irony. It is very characteristic of Beethoven, and many parallel passages can be found, besides what has been adduced above as to his habit of finding room for the major tonic in recapitulations where his main key was minor. Here it is evident that his translating most of his second subject into the minor was done as much for the sake of throwing this passage into relief as for its own pathos at the moment. Soon the whole mass of strings takes the theme up in four octaves, while isolated wood-wind instruments give out the semiquaver countersubject of the big fugue passage in the development. The strings carry on their quaver figure in a menacing crescendo. Neither in numbers nor in tone do the wood-wind make the slightest effort to be heard through this crescendo; but as Weingartner points out, there is something peculiarly fascinating in the very effect of their disappearance behind this rising granite mass of sound, and their quiet emergence again as the mass subsides. No sooner has it subsided than Ex. 5 bursts out again with the utmost passion. (In the score the entry of the first violin of this theme shows a capricious change of octave which looks exactly like an accidental omission of the *ottava* sign[1]; it is always corrected accordingly in performance, perhaps rightly. Other cases of the kind are frequent throughout the symphony, but are sometimes much more difficult to deal with, as Beethoven purposely made capricious changes of octave a feature of his later style.) This passage suddenly ends with the pathetic ritardando phrase (Ex. 9) which preceded the triple fugue passage in the development. It now leads to the final tragic passion. We have noted that a great symphonic coda is pretty sure to contain a passage that swings from tonic to dominant on some important figure. One such passage we had when those horns entered so suddenly in the tonic major. We now have the most famous of all tonic-and-dominant passages, in the minor; the famous dramatic muttering in semitones of the whole mass of strings, beginning with the basses and rising until it is five octaves deep in the violins. Next to the opening of the symphony this passage has been more imitated by ambitious later composers than any other in music, classical or modern. As Beethoven has it, the universal quality in it is its normal truth of emotional tone and musical form; its unique quality is that the melody that is sung above it is to all intents and purposes quite new.

EX. 10.

Of course the rhythm in dotted notes vaguely recalls the figure of the opening, which is more clearly alluded to by the trumpets and drums; but the fact remains that Beethoven here shows himself capable (as he has done elsewhere though never in a movement on so colossal a scale) of introducing at the very last moment a theme that has never been heard before. The procedure is perfectly logical. This melodic expression is external and emotional; the logic is no more to be looked for in melodic connexions of figure here than it is to be relied upon where such connexions are abundant. Like all musical logic, it lies in the proportions of

---

[1] The autograph, and the corrected MS. sent to the publishers, and every other authentic document, are in absolute agreement on this and almost every other disconcerting detail!

the rhythms and paragraphs. And so it is the most natural thing
in the world that the paragraph should finally burst into the mighty
unison of the main theme, and thus end the tragedy abruptly, yet
in the fullness of time, with its own most pregnant motto.

SCHERZO

After tragedy comes the satiric drama. The next movement is,
as Sir George Grove remarks, at once the greatest and the longest
of Beethoven's scherzos. The chord of D minor is thrown at us by
the strings in a rhythmic figure which pervades the whole; the
drums tuned in octaves supply the minor third of the chord, and
it is only as the work proceeds that we realize how this grotesque
introduction makes an eight-bar phrase.

Ex. 11.

Then the strings begin a very regular five-part fugue on the following subject, the wood-wind marking the first of every bar—

Ex. 12.

until almost the whole orchestra is mysteriously alive and busy.
Soon there is a short crescendo, and the theme bursts out in a tutti.
Suddenly the key swings round towards C major, the flat seventh
(a relationship, by the way, which Beethoven had only once before
brought into prominence, and that in one of his most mysterious
imaginations, the ghostly slow movement of the D major trio,
op. 70, no. 1). On the dominant of this key there is an exquisitely
harmonious passage of preparation, after which nothing less than a
broad second subject bursts out in the wood-wind which the
strings furiously accompany with the octave figure.

Ex. 13.

With Beethoven's scoring the theme cannot be heard with less than
double wind; and even triple wind would be better (as at Dresden,
for instance, where there are six flutes and six oboes, &c.), for they

can divide the parts among themselves according to their importance. For less well-endowed orchestras the measures indicated by
Wagner and Weingartner are absolutely necessary. They have this
disadvantage that the horns, to which Beethoven could not give
the melody because of their imperfect scale, now have the effect of
throwing the weight of tone into the lower octaves. The trouble
about all difficulties of balance with Beethoven is that his feeling
for tone-colour is invariably poetical and Beethovenish, while the
obvious ways of getting correct balance are apt to produce tone
which is neither.

So far the scherzo, including its grotesque opening, has pro-
ceeded in clear four-bar periods. Beethoven's scherzos, however,
will never permanently settle down to the spin of a sleeping top:
before the swing of the rhythm can cease to stimulate us it will be
enlivened by some momentary change of period. Here in the first
lull we have a six-bar period.

Ex. 14.

The wood-wind echo its last four bars, and then the exposition is
brought to a tonic-and-dominant end in an even number of two-bar
phrases with a new figure.

Ex. 15.

The initial figure now moves down a series of thirds in a harmonious pianissimo dialogue between strings and wind. Having
thus reached a D minor chord it stops abruptly, and the exposition
is repeated from the beginning of the fugue theme. After the
repeat the development begins by carrying on the dialogue in
descending steps of thirds which are so managed as to lead crescendo through an enormous range of key until the dialogue ends
angrily on the dominant of E minor, a key entirely alien to D minor.
And now comes the famous passage in three-bar rhythm, *ritmo di
tre battute*, which has drawn the attention of commentators to this
scherzo as containing an interesting rhythmic effect presumably
not to be found elsewhere. The truth is that this passage differs
from incidents such as that quoted (Ex. 14) only in being extended
over a wide region systematically enough for the special mention
of three-bar periods to save trouble in construing it. It is carried
out in great simplicity and breadth through E minor and A minor.

Suddenly the drums burst in with their figure on F, and the whole passage continues perfectly happily in F major. The entry of the drums has often been described as throwing the three-bar periods out again. It does nothing of the kind; it goes on making three-bar periods, giving figure (*a*), while the wind continue with figure (*b*). The key shifts in a leisurely way round to D minor. Now that we are in the tonic again, suddenly without the slightest break the rhythm relapses into four-bar periods, various instruments taking the theme up bar by bar.

Ex. 16.

The harmony drifts towards E flat (the flat supertonic), on the dominant of which the drums and horns mysteriously build up figure (*a*) into a chord. At last there is a crescendo, the chord suddenly changes to D minor, and the whole orchestra bursts out with the main theme in a tutti which stands for a recapitulation of the first subject. The key changes to B flat, where we have the harmonious transition passage. Again two odd bars are inserted bringing the passage on to the dominant of D; it is now expanded, with suggestions of the minor mode; and the second subject then bursts out, at first in D major; but from the ninth bar onwards it is translated into D minor. Otherwise this recapitulation is quite regular. The dialogue on figure (*a*) leads back to the development which is marked to be repeated, an injunction not often followed in these days of hustle. Afterwards this dialogue leads very simply to a short imitative coda. The tempo is hurried until the octave figure is compressed into duple time as follows—

Ex. 17.

And here a great confusion has arisen from the history of a certain change in Beethoven's way of writing the ensuing trio. The autograph shows that the bars of the trio were originally half their present length, and that the time was 2/4. With this notation it would have been impossible to conduct the trio too fast; and it is quite certain, from the very nature of the connecting passage, that Beethoven's intention is that two crotchets of the trio should correspond roughly to three (that is, one bar) of the scherzo. I say roughly, because a stringendo has intervened, and if the half-bar corresponds too exactly to the original tempo the effect will be heavy and stiff. Beethoven has given metronome marks throughout the symphony, and they have been much studied; with the general effect of confirming Beethoven's own recorded dissatisfaction with efforts so to fix the tempi. They do serve, however, to prove what tempo corresponds to what other tempo; and in general they prove *relative* tempi. Unfortunately, through the aid perhaps of a misprint, the trio, now that the notation is changed, still has a metronome mark indicating that its bars correspond to the bars of the scherzo; with the result that for the best part of a century violent efforts were made to take it twice as fast as it has any business to go. There is no possible doubt of Beethoven's real intentions; and the best tradition has no more been misled by the metronome mark than scholars would be misled by the reading *mumpsimus* instead of *sumpsimus*.[1]

The trio thus violently brought into being out of the stretto of the scherzo, proceeds with heavenly happiness on the following combination of themes.

Ex. 18.

The upper melody is as old as the art of music. Beethoven had already written something very like the whole combination, bass and all, long ago in the trio of the scherzo of his Second Symphony. Moreover, in some of the earlier sketches for the Ninth Symphony he reverts very nearly to the exact terms of this passage in the Second Symphony. The difference between the mature final idea and

---

[1] After this analysis was in the press, Sir Charles Stanford wrote to *The Times* (March 4th, 1922) conclusively proving, by a photograph of the page in question in the original edition, that the original metronome mark was for a minim and not a semibreve.

these earlier versions is that the final conception makes a point of its simplicity. The idea in the Second Symphony is childlike only in so far as it is without affectation and without introspection. A child-prodigy like Mozart or Mendelssohn might have invented it quite spontaneously as regards infant mental activity, but without any more understanding than is employed in the child's special faculty of mimicry. In the Ninth Symphony the meaning is very different: this naïve self-repetition with delicate differences (see the notes marked *) that carry more weight than they seem aware of; this swarm of fresh themes all ending in full closes; this piling up of the primitive little theme into a climax of mere tonic-and-dominant and merely square rhythms, but of grandiose proportions: all this is true of the child as seen by the poet who recognizes that the outward semblance belies the soul's immensity.

If Beethoven had read Wordsworth he would never have forgiven him for speaking of 'fading into the light of common day'. Nowhere is Beethoven's power more characteristically shown than when his ordinary daylight bursts in upon the trailing clouds of glory; as the mere formal da capo of the scherzo bursts in when the climax of the trio dies romantically away.

If this scherzo had been on a less gigantic scale, Beethoven would unquestionably have done as he did with his earlier great scherzos, and caused the alternating cycle of scherzo and trio to go at least twice round; that is to say, the scherzo would again lead to the trio, the trio would again be given in full, the scherzo would come round yet again and show every sign of again drifting into the trio, whereupon some drastic stroke would cut the process short. This double recurrence is possible only where the main body of the scherzo is worked out on a scale not greatly transcending what we may call the melodic forms, at least in its first strain. We have seen that the present scherzo, quite apart from the trio, is a fully differentiated and developed sonata movement; and the miracle therein is that it has never lost the whirling uniform dance-movement character essential to the classical scherzo. Amid all the variety of Beethoven's works you will always thus find each individual movement true to type. The minuet had already come to be regarded by Haydn and many of his contemporary critics as too slight an art-form longer to retain its place in the growing scheme of classical symphonies. Haydn's own minuets tend more and more to foreshadow the Beethoven scherzo, while Mozart's minuets never show what we may call the scherzo temperament; yet Mozart's are sometimes capable in their own calm way of being quite as big as the other movements of the work to which they belong. The most significant thing about the Beethoven scherzo is that it becomes worthy of its position in Beethoven's most gigantic works, not by abandoning the dance character, but by emphasizing it. There are people who apply to music certain eighteenth-century methods of criticising poetry; methods which simply measure the amount of information that would be conveyed if the art in question were reduced to prose. To such critics the double repetitions of Beethoven's scherzos are an idiotic mystery. Why should Beethoven say the same thing three times over in the same words? Why should dancers dance three times round the same ball-room? That depends upon the size of the ball-room, not upon the interest of its decorations. The size of the scherzo of the Ninth Symphony makes double repetitions out of the question; but an adequate expression of the characteristic perpetual circle is attained when for the second time the scherzo leads into the trio, and the first phrase (Ex. 18) starts on its course surrounded in a blaze from the whole orchestra, breaks off abruptly, and is closured by the two bars which have just led to it for the second time.

ADAGIO

In the slow movement Beethoven explores melody to its inmost depths. All musical form is melody 'writ large'; but there are forms in which the composition is felt not primarily as a single whole but as a series or colony of identical melodic schemes. The obvious case of this is the form of a theme with variations. The external form of the whole set of variations can tell us little about the composition except the number of variations, and the points, if any, at which they cease to confine themselves within the bounds of the theme. We are forced from the outset to attend to the emotional and other contrasts produced by their grouping; so that the analysis of a set of variations becomes instantly and automatically an analysis of style. The primitive simplicity of the external quasi-collective organism leaves us with nothing else to understand except the structure of the theme. Now when a great set of variations exists as a composition by itself, there is full scope for the variations to explore many aspects of the theme beyond the melody. Some of the greatest works in variation form have been based on themes of which melody was by far the least significant aspect. In these cases, at least the phrase rhythm of the theme will be found to be specially distinctive, so that its identity may be recognized in a totally different melody with totally different harmonies and totally different metric rhythm. In fact, this condition of things, which Sir Hubert Parry called rhythmic variation, is the highest type of independent variation form. If the phrase rhythm is not strong enough to support entirely new harmonies and melodies, then the harmonic scheme must be strong enough to support new melodies: the phrase rhythm, strong or weak, is prior to everything else, and cannot be altered without dissolving the sense of variation form. (Most modern sets of variations do thus dissolve the classical conception of the form, and compensate for the loss by retaining the melody far more constantly than Beethoven and Brahms think worth while.)

Now all this may seem a digression, inasmuch as the variations in the Ninth Symphony, both in the slow movement and the choral finale, are purely melodic. But it is worth while drawing attention to the fundamental importance of phrase rhythm in all classical variations; because until this is grasped the vaguest ideas are apt to prevail as to the value of purely melodic variations; and cases have been known where composers have introduced most interesting variations into works in sonata form, and wondered why procedures perfectly justifiable in an independent variation work somehow did not prove satisfactory in the sonata environment. We must not lose grasp of the principle that all sonata form works through external melody. It follows from this that variations must stick to the melody of their theme if they are to form part of a sonata scheme. It is also certain that a variation which is faithful to the melody is also faithful to the phrase rhythm. It is not good criticism to dismiss with contempt a merely ornamental variation as a poor thing; it is a simple thing, but it is also safe. If it is stupid, that is because the composer has a bad style. In the hands of the great composers the ornamental variation reaches the sublime just because of its utter simplicity and dependence upon the melody of the theme. In other words, the theme is pre-eminently sublime, and the variations are its glory. Some of the critics who have sneered at melodic variations should be more careful to make sure that they can recognize them.[1] I have seen more than one of the strictest of Beethoven's late slow movements in variation form described as 'a group of detached episodes with no discoverable connexion' by writers who are very full of 'the progress that has been made in the variation form since Beethoven's time'. And this is not a matter of speculative opinion; speaking generally I may say that no statement is made in any analysis of mine which the reader cannot verify for himself by following it in the score.

The slow movement of the Ninth Symphony is a set of variations on two alternating themes; at least, we could say so, if the second theme had more than one variation. On strict formal principles it does not matter whether the theme is actually varied at all so long as it is repeated: for instance, most of the slow movement of Beet-

---

[1] I have often been told that all good musicians deplore the disgraceful poverty of the first vocal variations in the choral finale. This does not represent a very advanced professional point of view. Good musicians do not estimate variations only as models for a student's exercises.

hoven's Seventh Symphony is aesthetically a set of variations, though the very essence of its variations is the cumulative effect of their repeating the same combination of melodies with no change except growing fullness of orchestration. In the Ninth Symphony Beethoven carries to its highest development a scheme for which he has given us only one exact counterpart, the Lydian Hymn of Thanks in the A minor Quartet; though he had written two earlier variation movements depending upon a pair of alternating themes, the slow movement of the Fifth Symphony, and the first allegretto which does duty for slow movement of the great E flat Trio, op. 70, no. 2. For all purposes except that of the antiquarian, it was Haydn who invented the idea of making variations on two alternating themes. Whichever theme was in the major, the other is in the minor; both themes are complete binary melodies with repeats, and the first impression on the listener is that the second theme is a contrasting episode like the trio of a minuet. Then the first theme returns, perhaps unvaried in its first strain, which however is repeated with ornamental variation, the rest of the theme continuing in the varied state. Then, just as Beethoven's most characteristic scherzos go twice through their cycle of repeating their trio, Haydn goes on to a variation of his second theme, and his scheme often goes far enough to include a third variation of the second theme, before the fourth variation of the first expands into a coda. Beethoven in his great E flat Trio adopts Haydn's form exactly, with the mock-tragic difference that, his first theme being in the major, he makes his coda end in pathetic childish wrath with a development of the minor theme. In the Fifth Symphony the two themes grow one out of the other in a more subtle way than Haydn's; and the second theme, though starting in the tonic, makes its point in the famous triumphant outburst in a bright foreign key. This is the only recorded sign of preparation for the bold and subtle art-form invented by Beethoven in his slow movements of the Ninth Symphony and the A minor Quartet. In these cases the two alternating themes are in brilliantly contrasted keys and tempi. In the Ninth Symphony the formal effect is enriched by the fact that the second theme is, on its second reappearance, in another contrasted key, so to speak twin, but not identical twin, with its first key. The scheme is as follows:

(1) First theme B flat major, 4/4.

(2) Second theme (*andante moderato*) D major, 3/4.

(3) Variation of first theme in tonic.

(4) Second theme in G major almost unvaried except for new scoring. As B major led back to B flat, so G major leads back to E flat as if to resume the first theme therein. This involves

(5) a modulating episode which will be described in due course. The episode leads suddenly back to the tonic where

(6) a complete second variation is given. At the point where the second theme should appear, the change of harmony which led back to it is replaced by a modulation to the sub-dominant, such as is typical of the last phase of a design that is to end quietly.

(7) The rest of the movement is coda, and the strong backbone of the most complicated parts of this coda consists of repetitions of melodic figures of the first theme, as will be shown in our musical illustrations.

Now let us look at the themes. I need not quote the two bars of introduction, famous as they are for their profound pathos. I write the melody on one stave, numbering its phrases; and on the upper stave I write the echoes of each phrase given out by the wood-wind

Ex. 19.

change of key

It will be seen that at first these echoes punctuate a melody that without them would be in symmetrical square phrases; but at last the wind instruments tend to develop something independently complete out of them, and end by taking over the climax of the main melody itself. They hesitate however at its close, and, while so hesitating, faint in the bright light of a change to a remote key.[1] The second theme is a single strain swinging along with glorious tenderness and warmth in its new key and rhythm.

Ex. 20.

The small notes in the musical illustration indicate the fragmentary counterpoint which enhances the effect of its immediate repetition. Its last bar is echoed with a change of harmony which plunges us back into the rich shadows of the main theme. Nowhere is the art of florid ornament more consummate than in the first violin part of the two complete variations in this slow movement. I say the first violin part, because the point of these variations is that, while the melody is given in Beethoven's finest florid ornament, the echoes of the wood-wind remain unvaried. If we had been given the theme, echoes and all, as the subject for a work in variation form, we might have felt at a loss to see what sort of variation could be made of it. To preserve the echoes as an unvaried background is a stroke of genius self-evident only because Beethoven has accomplished it. (He could not have accomplished it at once; for the first sketches of the theme show that at one time he seriously thought of making the wind instruments repeat regular whole sections instead of fragmentary echoes.) Now when the wood-wind take over the climax of the theme they still keep their part unvaried; and the

[1] I was not prepared, when I wrote this essay, to find that the slow movement of the Ninth Symphony was so out of fashion that an eminent critic could ask, apropos of this change, 'Where is the skill in abandoning your idea as soon as you have stated it?' To which the only fit answer is to ask, 'Where is the sense in supposing that the "idea" has been completely expressed before the first change of key or time that catches the eye by its appearance on paper?' People whose attention is not roused by that first modulation must be tone-deaf: people who don't see the point of its leading to an analogous but different key next time can have no memory. People who have noted it clearly both times will be wondering what will happen when the music approaches it for the third time; and when they hear the grand burst into the subdominant, they will have heard the complete statement of Beethoven's 'idea'. If critics are then going to argue that an idea cannot thus be spread over ten minutes, they must abandon any claim to understand Wagner, who spreads them over four whole evenings.

great change of harmony leads without effort to G major instead of D major. The melody of the second theme is not varied, but the scoring is now bright instead of deep, and the counterpoint added by the first violins is lighter. At the end, the change of harmony leads to E flat, and the clarinets give out the first two bars of the main theme unvaried. This is taken up by a horn, the clarinets giving a syncopated counterpoint. The slow figure of the theme descends into the depths and the key shifts to C flat major. The syncopated counterpoint is now given to the horn, the notes in this distant key being such as the player on the ordinary horn of Beethoven's time could produce only as closed notes by skilful use of his hand in the bell of the instrument. These notes are all very muffled and mysterious; they are not easy to produce in this way, and they therefore occurred so rarely in orchestral music that conductors used to need some experience and decision to protect themselves and Beethoven against the round assertion of the average player that the passage was impossible. It was, indeed, extremely difficult, but Berlioz (in the chapter which Strauss declares, in editing the *Grand Traité d'instrumentation*, to be of merely historic interest) quotes the very bar that culminates the difficulty, and demonstrates that it is skilfully written for the hand-horn. Now it has been discovered that Beethoven gave all these passages in this movement to the fourth horn, because he knew a fourth-horn player who possessed a pioneer two-valved specimen of the ventil-horn! The moral is not that we ought to play these passages with a boastful confidence to show that modern instruments make them child's-play, but that we ought to admire the sense of style and practical wisdom with which Beethoven uses the pioneer new instrument in the way best calculated to graft its resources on to the old stock.

The whole character of the passage is profoundly reflective, tender, and remote. Its dying fall seems about to be echoed; but instead of an echo the tone becomes rich and full, and the harmony brightens into a full daylight of the tonic. The second and last variation bursts in with the richest ornament achieved in music since Bach; and now we may appreciate fully the deep simplicity of Beethoven's most elaborate conceptions, inasmuch as throughout this variation the wood-wind have the theme without ornament except in so far as it is adapted to the prevailing triplet rhythm. The violins are silent while the wind instruments finish each phrase with its unadorned echo. In due course the point is reached where the wood-wind are dwelling upon the final cadence before breaking into one or other of the distant keys in which the second theme appeared. Instead of the exquisite soft foreign chord, there is now a sudden resolute modulation to the subdominant and an outburst of solemn triumph in which the trumpets enter for the first time. The drums also have their first forte; the drum-part being elsewhere throughout this movement remarkable for mysterious, soft rhythmic figures. The solemn outburst of triumph yields to a pleading development of the first two notes of the theme without ornament.

Ex. 21.

Mark well its four distinct entries within two bars, and note that the calm continuation in the tonic with what has the freshness of a new melody is simply an ornamental version of figure (a). As it proceeds, listen to the bass and you will find that the whole first phrase of the theme is moving upwards two bars at a time, each pair of bars being repeated.

Ex. 22.

Again the solemn triumph bursts out on the subdominant. Now see what becomes of the two bars of modulating sequence on figure (a). The magnificent plunge into the sombre key of D flat, with the four bars in which its consequences are worked out—these are the magnified version of those last two bars of Ex. 21, twice as slow and with richer harmonic detail.

Ex. 23.

They lead back to the new version of figure (*a*), which now continues happily, echoed bar by bar, with another new figure (note the dialogue between the drums and the basses).

Ex. 24.
Cantabile.

Drums.

Then the second phrase of the theme is taken up and treated in the same way; at first two bars at a time, then its last bar alone, until it expands into a final broad melodious climax. At last nothing is left but the solemn rhythmic figure of the drums and the basses, the dying sigh of the clarinets, and the throbbing of the strings, from which last arises one final majestic crescendo. And hereupon the movement, like most of Beethoven's late slow movements, closes with subtle allusions to figures of the principal melody, in such a way as to fill the last bar with articulate musical speech up to its last quarter.

FINALE

The great problem for Beethoven in the composition of the Ninth Symphony was obviously that of providing a motive for the appearance of the chorus. The general scheme of the whole symphony as a setting for Schiller's 'Ode to Joy' is simple and satisfactory enough. The first movement gives us the tragedy of life. The second movement gives us the reaction from tragedy to a humour that cannot be purely joyful, except in a childhood which is itself pathetic when contemplated from that distance of time at which alone it can be appreciated. The slow movement is beauty of an order too sublime for a world of action; it has no action, and its motion is that of the stars in their courses—concerning which, however, Beethoven has surprising things to tell us later on. But it is a fundamental principle in Beethoven's art that triumph is to be won in the light of common day. Only twice in all his works (Sonatas, opp. 109 and 111) has Beethoven allowed the conclusion of the whole matter to rest in a slow movement of this type—a paradise like that of Dante, in which the only action and the only movement are the ascent from Heaven to higher Heaven as measured by the enhanced glory in Beatrice's eyes.

Now we shall find that this account of the first three movements of the Ninth Symphony is Beethoven's own; and the Ninth Symphony is not the first work in which he had attempted something of the kind, a search for a theme on which the mind could rest as a final solution of typical human doubts and difficulties. The Fantasia, op. 77, adumbrates a search for happiness through a storm of conflicting emotions and humours: so bold is the sketch and so violent the contrasts during the conflict, that the work is hardly to be understood except in the light of the Ninth Symphony. Again in the Choral Fantasia a solo pianoforte executes a massive and cloudy introduction (which at the first performance Beethoven extemporized); the orchestra enters group by group, exchanging rhetorical questions with the pianoforte; and then the pianoforte settles down to a placid melody not unlike a childish foreshadowing of the great choral melody in the Ninth Symphony; a set of variations ensues which passes through various tempi and keys with developing episodes; until a dramatic crisis is reached, giving rise to further questions which are answered by the entry of voices, bringing the matter to a conclusion with a short ode in praise of music.

In the Ninth Symphony Beethoven's plan is to remind us of the first three movements just as they have been described above; and to reject them one by one as failing to attain the joy in which he believes. After all three have been rejected, a new theme is to appear, and that theme shall be hailed and sung as the Hymn of Joy. Beethoven's first idea was that a baritone should express all this process in words, from the outset, in an impassioned recitative. The orchestra was to start with a confused din expressing terror and violence; the singer was to rebuke it; whereupon the orchestra was to give out the opening of the first three movements, after each of which the singer was to point out why it was not to the purpose; until, on the appearance of the new theme, the singer was to accept it with triumph and set it to Schiller's Ode. Beethoven sketched all the recitatives with the necessary words, very sensibly making no effort to achieve a literary style in such a sketch, but writing the flattest prose to indicate what was going on. In any case it would have been a mistake to aim at poetic diction when *ex hypothesi* not only is the poem not yet begun, but the music of it has not been found. Plain prose is absolutely necessary to this scheme, if such a recitative is to be sung at all; that being so, Beethoven soon saw that he had better commit himself to the smallest amount of plain prose that could possibly suffice. Moreover, words without metre may be prose, but music without metre is recitative; and recitative, especially in a symphony, is by all historic association either the most lofty symbolism, or it is pretentious rubbish. Away, then, with these paragraphs of amateur prose attempting to describe emotions which only music can express. Let the basses of the orchestra seem on the point of articulate speech with their passionate recitative. Everything is there without words; nor could any words do justice to the pathos with which the recitative, after furiously rejecting the tragic solemnity of the first movement, seems to hope wistfully for something better, only to be stung into indignation by the playful theme of the scherzo. At the appearance of the slow movement the pathos touches perhaps the greatest height ever attained in recitative; fully as great as Bach and Handel achieved in accompanied recitative with voice and with Bible words. A few wind instruments give a halo of mysteriously luminous harmony above the basses so long as these remain softened. Then for a moment the passion breaks out again in despair; and now comes the new theme.

Ex. 25.

At once the situation is changed; the recitative of the orchestral basses greets the new theme with exultation. The wind-band closes the recitative with the old conventional final chords, and instantly the basses take up the theme and give it out in full. (It is customary to make an impressive pause before this definite entry of the theme; but Beethoven's notation of the final chords of the recitative is against this reading. There is no meaning in his putting the last chord at the end of a triple-time bar, unless it is to have the special rhythmic effect of leading straight into the next bar. It may be argued that this effect is not convincing; but whether it convinces us or not, it is thoroughly characteristic of Beethoven's later style and, like all such features, is the only possible alternative to an effect which, if convincing, is also the kind of commonplace Beethoven studiously avoids.)

Here now is the great theme which is to carry the stanzas Beethoven has collected from Schiller's 'Ode to Joy'. The melody is in two parts, of which the second is always repeated.

Ex. 26.

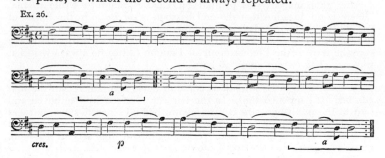

When the basses have given out the whole melody unharmonized, with its repeat, the violas in unison with the violoncellos go through it again in a higher octave also with the repeat. The double-basses have a melodious counterpoint, forming with the melody a very interesting two-part harmonic framework, to which the first bassoon adds an inner part melting occasionally into unison with the melody in a very subtle way.[1] The first violins enter in the soprano octave, and the theme is now in transparent widespread four-part harmony, to which the interior bassoon adds a more symphonic colour by doubling the melody at every odd pair of bars (see bars 3–4, 7–8, &c.). With the repeat there is now a crescendo: then the theme bursts out in the full wind-band, the trumpets blazing at high pitch with the melody, which is so simple that they can play every note of it in spite of the imperfect scale the trumpet had in Beethoven's time. (And yet such is Beethoven's delicate feeling that in one place in the eleventh bar he avoids a note which the trumpet has already played, because at this moment it is so harmonized as to suggest something beyond the natural character of the instrument.)

After the repeat the last four notes (*a*) of the theme are taken up and turned into a neat codetta, which henceforth becomes an integral part of the theme as treated in future variations.

Ex. 27.

I give it here as it occurs in the choral statements.

This codetta is developed in energetic sequences, rising to a climax in which fine detail is crowded together in short phrases such as we find in the most elaborate paragraphs in the first movement or in Beethoven's latest sonatas and quartets. A quite new phrase with a ritardando now appears, sounding a reflective note

[1] The second bassoon should play with the double-basses.

After this analysis was printed Sir Charles Stanford wrote to me, 'There is no question that the 2nd bassoon is *col Basso* in the Finale of the Ninth Symphony. It is in the autograph; it is written in *by himself* in the copy made for the King of Prussia in Berlin (I've seen it); and in the copy he sent to the Philharmonic of London (ditto) he always writes it thus / / / (I think) for about 30 bars'.

The autograph, now published in facsimile, is perfectly clear. How, then, did Beethoven's intentions come to be so contradicted in the first edition? It happened thus. In the fair copy revised by Beethoven and sent to the publishers, the contra-fagotto had no separate stave, but was indicated as playing *col. fag. 2do.* Beethoven suddenly saw a disastrous possibility at this point, and, forgetting about the second bassoon, scrawled 'contra-fagotto tacet', adding rests to make sure.

which becomes mysterious in a change to an extremely remote key (*poco adagio*).

Ex. 28.
poco ritenente.   *poco adagio.*

This is brushed cheerfully aside; but the doubt which it suggested receives tragic justification in the renewal of the panic of the introduction, which bursts out with greater violence than ever.

And now comes the revelation. The human voice is heard, summing up the beginning and the end of those instrumental recitatives. Beethoven's one piece of verbal prose is, after all, as fine as any master of style could make it. The situation demands a careful abstention from any diction that encroaches on poetry. Critics may cavil at the word *angenehm*, which the dictionary tells us means 'agreeable' or 'pleasant': but a German ear would be accustomed to it as a Biblical word without losing its familiar prosaic sense. Beethoven says 'Oh, friends, not these sounds; but let us attune our voices more acceptably and more joyfully'.[1]

The wood-wind give their first foreshadowing of the theme, the singer cries 'Freude' and is answered by the chorus basses; and then the singer gives out the great theme as a setting of the first stanza of Schiller's Ode. The repeat of the second half is given by the chorus in octaves without the sopranos, and then the orchestra concludes with the codetta.

> Praise to Joy, the god-descended[2]
> Daughter of Elysium,
> Ray of mirth and rapture blended,
> Goddess, to thy shrine we come.
> By thy magic is united
> What stern Custom parted wide:
> All mankind are brothers plighted
> Where thy gentle wings abide.

The next stanza is given by the vocal quartet, and the second part of it repeated by the full chorus in four-part harmony, the orchestra again concluding with the codetta.

> Ye to whom the boon is measured,
> Friend to be to faithful friend,
> Who a wife has won and treasured,
> To our strain your voices lend.

---

[1] Bülow wickedly used the phrase by way of prelude on the pianoforte when he had to play immediately after a dismally bad singer.

[2] Lady Macfarren's translation is reprinted here in revised version by permission of Novello & Co.

> Yea, if any hold in keeping
> Only one heart all his own,
> Let him join us, or else weeping,
> Steal from out our midst, unknown.

The third stanza is given in an ornamental variation by the quartet (probably the most difficult passage ever written for voices).

> Draughts of joy, from cup o'erflowing
> Bounteous Nature freely gives,
> Grace to just and unjust showing,
> Blessing ev'rything that lives.
> Wine she gave to us and kisses,
> Loyal friend on life's steep road:
> E'en the worm can feel life's blisses,
> And the Seraph dwells with God.

Again the full chorus repeats the second part with the utmost triumph, and this time the codetta is accompanied by massive vocal harmonies dwelling upon the last line—'und der Cherub steht vor Gott'. This is expanded with a modulation which suddenly plunges to the dominant of a darker key, B flat.

The blaze of glory vanishes. The solemn silence is broken by grotesque sounds in the depths of darkness. These sounds gather into rhythm, and take shape as the melody transformed into a military march, mysteriously distant, and filling a vast harmonic interval between deep bass and its shrill treble. Ruskin has finely described the Grotesque Ideal as a veil covering the terror of things too sublime for human understanding; and that is unquestionably one of Beethoven's reasons for this treatment of the stanza in which the poet exhorts mankind to run their course as joyfully as the stars in the heavens.

But there was another motive which impelled Beethoven towards the Grotesque Ideal here. He had dismissed all illusions about Napoleon as soon as Napoleon made himself Emperor, but he had not dismissed the poet's ideals of war and victory. No artist, certainly no musician, has more forcibly sounded the true note of military music than Beethoven. He did not often write or wish to write a military march, but whenever he did, he struck with unerring accuracy the formidable note which should underlie the strains which are to inspire those who march to them. Nowhere has the terror of war been so simply and so adequately presented as in the *Dona nobis pacem* of the Mass in D. Beethoven indulges in no silly realism (we may ignore his pot-boiler, the Battle Symphony): he tells us no details about war; but he unfailingly gives the note of terror wherever war is symbolized. In this light we must read the military character of his setting of Schiller's stanza about the stars in their courses. Thomas Hardy has said of the facts of astronomy that when we come to such dimensions the sublime ceases and ghastliness begins. Beethoven is not afraid of the depths of the starry spaces—not more afraid than he was of Napoleon's armies; and so it is his military note that he sounds when Schiller compares heroes with the stars in their courses.

> Glad as suns His will sent flying
> Through the vast abyss of space,
> Brothers, run your joyous race,
> Hero-like to conquest flying.

A solo tenor declaims the stanza triumphantly, but in broken phrases which seem to stagger dizzily across the rhythms of the variation. A male-voice chorus joins in on the repetition of the second part, which is concluded with the codetta. Then the orchestra breaks into a double fugue, of which the first subject is derived from the original melody, and the second subject from its transformation into march rhythm.

This double fugue is worked out with great energy, passing through various keys, and aiming at the dominant of B, on which there is a mighty unison climax. As this dies away, three notes of the main melody appear softly in B major, then again in B minor. The bass drops from B to A in an impressive way which we shall recognize again later—

and then the full chorus bursts out with the first stanza of the poem set to the unvaried original theme, while the whole string band accompanies with a running bass in the triplet rhythm. After the repeat the orchestra begins the codetta but breaks off abruptly at its second bar. A mighty new theme appears, sung by the tenors and basses and supported by the bass trombone, the first entry of the trombone since the scherzo. This is the song of the universal brotherhood of man, well-placed in harmonious reaction from that military note associated with the stars in their courses.

Ex. 31.

O   ye   mil - lions   I . . .   em - brace   ye !

Here 's   a   joy - ful   kiss   for   all !

The sopranos take up the new theme; and then the basses answer with another and yet more solemn note, 'Brothers above the starry vault there surely dwells a loving Father'. This, again, is repeated in full harmony by all the voices. To strike these solemn notes is only too easy for a small artist; but great artists, when they strike them, do as Beethoven does; they show by instinct, not by antiquarian knowledge, that these are the oldest harmonies in the world. Beethoven had opportunities for understanding the church modes as used by Palestrina; he was not as completely cut off from them by temperament and training as was, for instance, Mendelssohn. On the other hand, he had nothing like the scholarship in such matters shown in modern times by Sir Charles Stanford and Mr. Gustav Holst. Yet here, as in the 'Incarnatus' of the Mass in D and in the Lydian slow movement of the A minor Quartet, he shows exactly the Palestrina instinct for the expression of awe, mystery, and infinity, in terms of pure concord and subtle intermixture of key.

And now comes the stupendous claim that Joy is meant to raise us from our prostrate awe to the starry heights where the Godhead dwells. I give a literal translation, as here the printed English versions fail:[1]

> Ye millions, why fall prostrate?
> Dost thou, oh World, feel the presence of the Creator?
> Seek Him beyond the starry vault!
> Above the stars He surely dwells.

This is the central thought of the Ninth Symphony, and it also underlies Beethoven's whole treatment of the liturgical text of his Mass in D, where we have, throughout the Gloria, the Credo, and

---

[1] Lady Macfarren's translation, though skilfully designed for singing, here reverses Schiller's and Beethoven's conception, the point of which is *not* to fall prostrate, but to rise from prostration and look upwards to the Father above the starry vault.

the Sanctus, three conceptions continually emphasized; first the divine glory; secondly, and always in immediate contrast, the awe-struck prostration of mankind; and thirdly the human divinity of Christ ('Qui propter nos homines'; 'et homo factus est').

As in the Mass in D so here in the Ninth Symphony, the thought of divine glory overawes at first, only to inspire action. The chorus breaks into a torrential double fugue on the two main themes, the invocation to Joy, and the appeal to the brotherhood of mankind.

Ex. 32.

This fugue (the standard example of Beethoven's extreme demands on the voices, justified in this instance by convincing effect) rises to its notorious climax in which the sopranos hold a high A for twelve bars. After this terrific outburst there is an abrupt plunge into the deepest prostration, from which again mankind raises itself in contemplation of the Father above the starry vault. And now, before the final climax, comes that full revelation of Beethoven's range which is seldom absent from his greatest works; the note which only the greatest poets can master, and which lesser artists avoid because it offends their pride. The main theme has been given several complete variations for the orchestra and for the voices; it has been developed in episodes and interludes; the second theme has been stated; and the two themes have been combined in a double fugue. Now comes the coda. And the note of the coda is the purest happiness of childhood; nothing like it had been sounded in music since Mozart's *Magic Flute*; and if we are shocked at the notion of comparing Beethoven's endless round-canon (Ex. 33) with the happiness of Papageno and Papagena, why, then the poet and the composer may twit us with our slavery to fashion which sternly separates what the magic of joy reunites! Beethoven regards this childlike note as the very consummation of joy in *Gloria Dei Patris*. There is only one way to understand an artist of Beethoven's range, and that is to assume that he means what he says and that he has ample experience of the best way to say it.

Ex. 33.

&c.

It is not necessary to assume that he is infallible; but it is quite idle
to compare his range of style with something narrower, and to rule
out as in bad taste whatever exceeds those limits. It is strange but
true also of other artists besides Beethoven that the very points
which give most offence to superior persons are just those in which
the great artist most whole-heartedly echoes his predecessors. Not
only does the round just quoted recall Papageno and Papagena,
but when it suddenly drops into a slow tempo (*poco adagio*) as
Papageno and Papagena did, it rises to one of Mozart's most
characteristic forms of medial cadence.

Ex. 34.

Indeed we confidently expect the notes I have put in brackets; but
here the round intervenes again, gathering itself up as before into
the full chorus; and so leading again to the *poco adagio*. And then
a miracle happens. The solo voices enter in a bright new key, B
major, and turn the Mozartian medial cadence into a wonderful
florid cadenza that expands grandly and ends on the heights in this
distant region. It is the same region to which, after the military
variation of the stars in their courses, the energetic instrumental

fugue led; and now the same thing happens that happened then (Ex.
30), but in a much more subtle and simple form. The key of B
major becomes minor, and while its upper notes are still being held,
the bass drops down to A. It is as if the four solo voices had
ascended into the heavens, and had then expressed by their change
of harmony the link between heaven and earth. The orchestra at
first hesitating but with growing confidence, repeats the message
(that is to say, this mysterious step in the bass)—

Ex. 35.   *Poco allegro, stringendo.* . . . .

and in a moment the whole mass of singers and voices is ablaze
with the wildest outburst of joy. In all this final fury, with the
big drum, cymbals, and triangle marking time with frenzied
persistence, Beethoven maintains his Greek simplicity and subtlety
of proportion. It is only in externals that the music seems to break
all bounds; the substance and form are as exactly measured as the
most statuesque coda of any string quartet, and most of all in that
supreme stroke of genius, the sudden drop into a slow triple time
(*maestoso*) with a lyric turn of melody, on the words 'Daughter of
Elysium'.

Ex. 36.

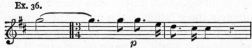

In this solemn tempo the chorus finishes, and then the orchestra
rushes headlong to the end. Even here there is no waste of energy,
no chaos nor anything perfunctory. The very last bars are a final
uprush of melody which happens to be quite new and might easily
have been an important theme.

SCHUMANN

XLIV. SYMPHONY IN B FLAT MAJOR, NO. I, OP. 38

1 *Andante un poco maestoso, leading to* 2 *Allegro molto vivace.*
3 LARGHETTO: *leading to* 4 SCHERZO: *Molto vivace.* 5 *Allegro
animato e grazioso.*

Schumann's first symphony is intended by him to express the
emotions of springtime, and does in fact express those of the
springtide of the happiest years of his life—his year of song,
1840, when he triumphed over all the obstacles which old Wieck

opposed to his marriage to his Clara, and poured out the first and greatest two volumes of his four volumes of songs; and 1841, when, with his powers as yet undiminished by illness, he devoted his attention to the larger forms of music. His adventures in these forms were to him a source of happiness akin to his marriage : and for at least five years the works that resulted were beautiful enough to justify his turning aside from the lyric forms in which his mastery was indisputable. But there are some things which you cannot have both ways. Schumann is a master of epigram. His ideas normally take the shape of gnomic sayings; and no writer is fuller of memorable *Einfälle*; of such 'good things' as, according to Mr. Puff, form the sole *raison d'être* of a plot. It has been observed by more than one eminent critic that the creators of such *Einfälle* seldom show high constructive genius on a larger scale. But what else can we expect? Large forms imply the expansion of initial ideas by development; and development is the very thing that an epigram will not bear. At the same time, it is a harsh judgement that forbids the epigrammatic artist to pile up his ideas into large edifices: his mind may be full of things that cannot be expressed except in works on a large scale. And if the artist cannot give such works an organic structure, why should he be forbidden to create artificial forms which enshrine his ideas as the coral-reef houses its millions of polypi? At all events, Schumann has abundantly proved that it is better for a symphony to be like a nobly rough mosaic with crude schematic forms than like a bad, sleek oil-painting. Indecently soon after Schumann's death, Joseph Rubinstein, no relation to the great Anton, wrote a famous article, in which Schumann's first symphony was thoroughly analysed with the systematic purpose of proving that Schumann could not compose at all. Every point that Rubinstein made is true; Schumann cannot develop an idea, he can only make sequences on it. He cannot even state an idea that is capable of development: the main theme of his finale (Ex. 13) shows that he does not know the difference between a symphonic theme and a lyric arabesque. The sequences are such as every competent teacher promptly weeds out of his pupils' first exercises. And so on, and so on. The Rubinstein tradition has never been favourable to Schumann's larger works; but Joseph's criticism is an affair of the pot and the kettle. When Nicholas Rubinstein died, Tchaikovsky dedicated to his memory a huge trio, in which every one of these faults is enormously magnified, and there is no epigrammatic vein at all. The trio ought to have been dedicated to Joseph.[1]

It is quite true that Schumann's treatment of large forms is no model for students. It presupposes a style like Macaulay's, in

[1] See Foreword to the Second Impression.

which 'it is impossible to tell the truth'. Macaulay thought his own style a very bad model for students. But a style in which it is impossible to tell the truth may be a great advance on a style in which it is impossible to express an opinion; and in any case the composer is not speaking on oath, as even the most partisan historian must be.

Schumann's antithetic sententiousness is so honestly exhibited as the rules of his game that no reasonable person ought ever to have misunderstood it. His orchestration is another matter; tragedy was latent in it from the outset, and became manifest in his pitiful failure as a conductor. The first two symphonies had the advantage of being conducted by Mendelssohn, who showed his unselfish care and consummate mastery by making a success of each performance, and his profound and instinctive respect for another artist's personality by not interfering with what must have seemed to him the incredible clumsiness of Schumann's scoring. Mendelssohn early learned the unwisdom (if he ever needed to learn it) of trying to change a grown man's habits. Perhaps he helped Schumann with more detailed advice than we know of; for the scoring of the First Symphony is not nearly as opaque as that of later works, and so perhaps it profited by as much of Mendelssohn's advice as Schumann could digest in one work. The few outstanding defects in the published score are ridiculously easy to correct, and it is a mistaken piety to leave them uncorrected. One thing must be made clear; whatever need Mendelssohn or later conductors may have found for correction, there is no room for really different orchestral ideas. When a redistribution of the mass of wood-wind is advisable in order to bring the main theme out, we need not worry about the changes in tone-colour that may result. Unlike Beethoven, Schumann has not in such cases clearly imagined a definite tone-colour that would be spoilt by any change. When obstacles to clearness have been removed, the resulting purity of tone is indeed rather new to listeners who have hitherto tried to hear Schumann's orchestra in its native fog; but the revelation is nevertheless that of Schumann's real intention. What is wholly inadmissible is the introduction of new 'beauties', which have even been known, within living memory, to include a *forte* end to the scherzo.

The need for some revision in modern performances of Schumann's works is forcibly shown by an incident in the history of the Meiningen Orchestra. When that wonderful band, with its wonderful conductor, Steinbach, visited London in 1902, the English committee begged for a Schumann symphony. In those days it was supposed that Brahms could not orchestrate much, if at all, better than Schumann; and Steinbach was, next to Joachim, the most authoritative interpreter of Brahms. Steinbach's reply

to the Committee was 'Schumann we cannot and will not play'.
Under further pressure he consented to play the overture to
Manfred.

It may safely be said that no orchestra ever earned its reputation
by its interpretation of Schumann. It is possible, with a minimum
of re-touching, to make a Schumann symphony sound normally
clear and euphonious. But it is difficult; and the difficulty is
not evident. As for a brilliant performance, that would be an
outrage on Schumann's holiest intimacy. To perform Schumann
faithfully and with a modest helpfulness in certain technical
matters is a task in which every thoughtful musician will rejoice.
The inner content of this music is a perpetual springtime of young
enthusiasm; the externals are robed in an old dressing-gown and
carpet-slippers amid thick clouds of tobacco smoke. But in this
atmosphere humbug can no more survive than in the presence
of Bach or of Beethoven. Schumann's dreams do not come from
opium. His mind at its full vigour has more kinship with Brown-
ing's than with any other artist, whether in music or verse; and
even when his health gave way, the failure of his mind appeared
in his music merely as loss of power and coherence, not as any
change of direction from its original impulse.

The opening of the First Symphony was intended to sound like
a summons from heaven, evoking the vital forces of springtime.

Ex. I.

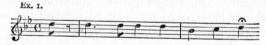

It originally began a third lower, like the theme of the following
allegro, and was given to the horns. But the valve horn was not
yet in use, and on the old natural instruments the notes G A, in
the key chosen by Schumann, were 'stopped' notes tolerable only
in a soft passage, and comically shocking in a forte. As far as this
symphony is concerned, the accident was lucky, for the opening
is much finer with trumpets, and a third higher, as it now stands.
But for a man so easily discouraged as Schumann, nothing can
have been more unlucky than that he should receive a shock at the
very beginning of the first rehearsal of his first finished orchestral
work. And it is not as if the misfortune concerned a general principle
of orchestration: within a year or two a pair of ventil horns was
to be found in every orchestra, besides a pair of natural ones.
I am inclined to ascribe much of the deterioration of Schumann's
scoring to precisely this accident. He soon followed his First
Symphony by the powerful work in D minor, which was kept back
for revision and eventually published as his Fourth Symphony,
after a re-scoring which is hardly better than a heavy process of

doubling in order to avoid risks from the composer's incapacity to conduct. It is a pious duty to use the original score of the D minor Symphony as a model for reducing all Schumann's later orchestration to its essentials. The First Symphony does not need much work of this kind; the ossification of its tissues has not gone far.

The introduction continues with a suggestion of the first stirrings of sap in the trees and awakenings of woodland life; and at last the Spring enters in full vigour.

Ex. 2.

A quieter second group begins with an admirably contrasted theme in a subtle blend of keys—

Ex. 3.

and ends with a vigorous cadential epigram difficult to bring out as Schumann scores it.

Ex. 4.

The development picks up its sequences in Schumann's way, which somewhat resembles the way of Schubert and of all young composers who have not been trained under the eye of a Rubinstein; but most especially of those who have. It combines the initial figure of the main theme with a fine episodic counterpoint.

Ex. 5.

When Shakespeare called springtime 'the only pretty ringtime', he obviously referred to Schumann's happy use of the triangle in the lighter passages of this development.

The recapitulation arrives at the top of a grand climax in which the opening phrases of the introduction blaze forth in the full

* The light syncopated echo turns the crass fifths from a blunder to a very accurate paradox.

II   E

orchestra, to be followed by the continuation of the allegro theme instead of the theme itself (Ex. 2), which, admirable in its original place, would have been prosaic here. (This is the kind of lesson the school of Rubinstein never learnt.)

The coda introduces, with the happiest effect, an entirely new spring song—

Ex. 6.

whose rhythm ousts the otherwise ubiquitous Walrus-and-Carpenter metre of the movement. Then that metre is resumed in quicker tempo, until at last the original trumpet-call to spring concludes the design.

The slow movement, unlike the short *intermezzi* that occupy its place in Schumann's later symphonies, is a spacious lyric with sustained development. Its orchestration is rich, and so successful as to indicate that Schumann had a decided talent in that category, though he afterwards stifled it. The main theme is a broad cantabile—

Ex. 7.

which alternates with a modulating theme introduced by the auxiliary inner figure (*a*) of Ex. 7.

Ex. 8.

The whole is scored for small orchestra, until in the coda the trombones enter softly with a very solemn modulating sequence. This, at first seeming to arise from Ex. 7, proves to be an anticipation of the theme of the scherzo, which follows without break.

The scherzo is in D minor, a key which it enters by the subdominant.

Ex. 9.

The first trio is a highly imaginative and picturesque design in
D major, in chords distributed between wind and strings in a
constant rhythmic figure (amphibrachic, if you prefer nice long
Greek words to simple musical ideas).

Ex. 10.

The first return of the scherzo is immediately followed by a second
trio in B flat.

Ex. 11.

The style of this is of course epigrammatic; but the theme is
rather too—shall we say—normal for an epigram : and that, perhaps,
is why Weingartner regards this second trio as 'an awful example'.
I cannot help suspecting that his point of view is slightly Rubin-
steinian. The mood of the second trio shows a bustling energy
which sets off the abbreviated da capo very well, while the
sequences do not last long enough to make us feel the substance
to be too dry. Certainly it is not a good model for students;
but to adopt Dr. Johnson's criticism in its two forms, the colloquial
and the lexicographical, it has wit enough to keep it sweet, while
a student's imitation would doubtless not have sufficient vitality
to preserve it from putrefaction. The coda, with its mysterious
fleeting vision of the first trio, is really wonderful.

The finale begins with a scale in a striking rhythm—

Ex. 12.

and proceeds to a main theme as slight as a daisy-chain (and why
not?)—

Ex. 13.

A transition-theme alternates the canzonetta of Mendelssohn's
Quartet, op. 12, or the theme of the finale of *Kreisleriana*, with
Ex. 12.

Ex. 14.

A second group turns the rhythm of Ex. 12 to girlish purposes—

Ex. 15.

and a single tonic-and-dominant cadence theme brings the exposition to a normal close, the whole being repeated from Ex. 13.

The development is a very different matter. Beginning dramatically—

Ex. 16.
Clarinet.   Strings.

it first deals gently with Ex. 15, but then, at the summons of trombones, takes that rhythm back to the original scale-figure (Ex. 12), which it builds up into an enormous and impressive sequence on the following lines—

Ex. 17.

Trombones.   Basses.   &c.

developing into a surging new figure.

Ex. 18.

The sequence rises to an ominous forte, but never to a fortissimo; and the climax is actually a decrescendo. The home dominant being at last reached, the recapitulation is ushered in by that most dangerous of unorthodoxies, something that is thoroughly old-fashioned: that is to say, an unbarred cadenza for the flute. As Wagner's Hans Sachs says, 'in springtime it must be so'.

The full energy of the finale appears in its coda, which grandly works up the thread of the development to a triumphant end.

XLV. SYMPHONY IN E FLAT MAJOR, NO. 3, OP. 97

1 *Lebhaft.* 2 SCHERZO: *Sehr mässig.* 3 *Nicht schnell.* 4 *Feierlich.*
5 *Lebhaft.*

The 'Rhenish Symphony' has suffered a neglect which is probably due mainly to the fact that Schumann's orchestration grew worse with the growth of his experience as conductor at Düsseldorf. Written in 1850, it shows no signs of the illness which a few years later invaded his mind and body; and there is no foundation for the notion, sometimes expressed, that it belongs to the sad and voluminous number of the works of his declining health, though it happens to be, in conception, the last of his symphonies.

As the Fourth Symphony shows in many points the influence of Beethoven's C minor Symphony, so does its successor, this third or 'Rhenish' Symphony, show in its first movement some kinship with the *Sinfonia Eroica.* The main theme is a grand paragraph that any pupil of Parry will recognize as a source of inspiration to his own school of British music.

Ex. 1.

A terse auxiliary theme—

Ex. 2.

effects many of the important transitions in the movement.

The second subject begins in G minor, with a wistful cantabile—

Ex. 3.

which soon gives way to more strenuous jubilation in the orthodox dominant, resuming the material of Exs. 1 and 2. The development moves on long sequential lines (distinctly like a stiffened version of those laid down in Beethoven's Eroica), making prominent use of Ex. 3 and introducing at intervals an episode, urgent in expression.

Ex. 4.

Again the influence of Beethoven's Eroica is seen (though in a way that only strengthens the evidence of Schumann's independence) in the long and exciting preparations for the return to the tonic—one of the most genuinely dramatic things Schumann ever achieved.

The recapitulation is regular, until Schumann substitutes for the short formal cadence theme of his second subject a new and broader cantabile. He is always peculiarly happy in his art of introducing new ideas at the last stage of his design, and the continuation of this cantabile—

Ex. 5.

adds greatly to the energy of the coda.

The scherzo is a slow *Ländler* with a comfortable Rhenish rusticity in its lilt.

Ex. 6.

One's first impression of the sequel is that it is trying to make a free variation of the theme—

Ex. 7.

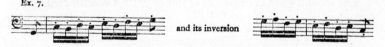

but its bustling semiquaver figure does not conform to that harmonic plan, and subsides eventually into an accompaniment to the mysterious theme of the trio, which is in A minor, while the bass quivers throughout on C; a *locus classicus* for that elusive phenomenon a 'mediant pedal'.

Ex. 8.

After the resumption of the main theme Schumann finds occasion for a new idea in his coda. Quotation is unnecessary.

The tiny slow movement is of a type invented by Schumann in his symphonies; the suggestion for its form, though not for its mood, coming from the allegretto of Beethoven's Eighth Symphony, via the andante of Mendelssohn's Italian Symphony.

Two gentle melodies, a main theme with a transition-theme, alternate with a more warmly full-toned second subject, so as to produce an *arioso* form without development.

First theme—

Ex. 9.

Transition-theme—

Ex. 10.

Second subject—

Ex 11.

If the impressive fourth movement is regarded as part of the finale, not merely as introductory, then the final quick movement will become intelligible as the natural and almost lyric reaction from the awe inspired by the Cathedral of Cologne as described in one of the finest pieces of ecclesiastical polyphony since Bach.

Ex. 12.
Solemnly.
(a)
Strings.
f (a) *diminished.*

At the end of this solemn movement Schumann again introduces a new idea, which I do not quote.

The fifth movement, if regarded as complete in itself, would seem to have no action at all. After a broad cantabile theme—

Ex. 13.

a transition (suggested by Ex. 12) seems to lead to the following second subject.

Ex. 14.

But this theme behaves merely like an incident in the main stream of melody, and the subsequent developments have a merely decorative or pattern-making effect. Even when a new idea—

Ex. 15.

leads back to a recapitulation from Ex. 13, the effect is not dramatic. But the purport of the whole, as in itself the dramatic contrast and consummation to the fourth movement, becomes manifest when the orchestra gathers itself up to a solemn climax in which a new idea is combined with a diminution of Ex. 14—

Ex. 16.

and the Cathedral-polyphony returns in triumph, to culminate in an unmistakable allusion to the theme of the first movement, Ex. 1.

XLVI. SYMPHONY IN D MINOR, NO. 4, OP. 120

INTRODUCTION (*Ziemlich langsam*), *leading to* I *Lebhaft, leading to* II ROMANZE, *leading to* III SCHERZO, *leading to* IV *Lebhaft.*

This first version of what was afterwards known as Schumann's Fourth Symphony was published in 1891, fifty years after it was written. Schumann himself withheld it for ten years and then in 1851 produced it in the revised version now known as his Fourth Symphony. The revision effected many improvements in form, and included some remarkable changes in notation which indicate that Schumann thought his original notation likely to mislead conductors. Now whenever this happens it will generally be found that the new notation misleads the conductor in the opposite direction, for it is the nature of all such cases to be on the border-line. Hence, if a composer has found that his old indication of tempo produced a tendency to drag, his new indication will certainly produce a tendency to hurry on the part of any one who does not know the history and motive for the change. The other alterations in this symphony concern the scoring; and herein lies a tragedy. The

revised version is undoubtedly at all points easier to play—after
a fashion. It has profited by experience and profited in the wrong
way. In 1851 the symphony appeared as Schumann's fourth, but
the original edition of the score explains that it was 'sketched'
shortly after the First Symphony; so that the symphonies known as
the second and third were really the third and fourth. Brahms discovered the original version of the Fourth Symphony, and caused it
(not without some demur from Frau Schumann) to be published.
The fact was revealed that Schumann's original and inexperienced
talent for orchestration was by no means contemptible, though he
evidently had had little liking for display. Professor Niecks, in his
posthumous biographical notes on Schumann, gives abundance of
interesting information as to Schumann's difficulties in orchestral
conducting; how, for instance, when the horns were completely
helpless over an important entry in a new overture by Joachim,
Schumann could give them no better help than to whisper sadly
over his shoulder to Joachim, 'They've missed it again'. The
progress in Schumann's own orchestration is set steadily in the
direction of making all entries 'fool-proof' by doubling them in
other parts and filling up the rests. That way safety lies, and the
same may be said of proclaiming Martial Law. Fortunately the
recovered early version of the Fourth Symphony can show us what
was likely to be in Schumann's mind in all types of theme and
contrast: so we have excellent guidance in the use of the billhook
on the strangling undergrowth of his wood-wind.

Schumann had in his First Symphony made some disconcerting
discoveries as to the ways in which orchestral balance may go
wrong; but the material of that triumphantly melodious work had
not presented him with many difficult problems of orchestration,
and though the final result is not without its difficulties and risky
passages, the First Symphony was probably on the whole an en-
couraging experience to him. In 1912 I was privileged to see
two movements of a yet earlier unpublished symphony which
had cost Schumann an immense amount of trouble before he left it
unfinished after making nearly two complete full scores and
innumerable sketches. If he had finished this earlier symphony he
would almost certainly have been much happier in his experience
of the orchestra; it gives every evidence that he was on the right
track; it would have proved effective and not difficult for the
orchestra, and the discouragement of his failure to finish it may
have been greater than he himself realized.

The success of what we now know as the First Symphony would
of course retrieve this set-back. But then followed a greater discouragement, and one that involved perhaps the noblest and most
ambitious inspiration that Schumann ever experienced. The D

minor Symphony is perhaps Schumann's highest achievement for
originality of form and concentration of material. In revising it he
increased the concentration in certain matters of detail; thus, for
instance, the all-pervading restless theme of the first allegro became
an accompaniment to the triumphant opening of the finale; and
again, it is only in the revised version that we are expressly told to
play the whole symphony straight through as a single movement.
But the essential differences in structure are quite inappreciable.
The whole work was from the outset fully as advanced an example
of free form and concentrated thematic continuity as any symphonic
poem that ever professed to be revolutionary. So novel a work
could not fail to be more risky in performance than its predecessor;
and when anything went wrong with a performance under Schumann's direction, all he could do was to look distressed, or try not
to look distressed, and ask the band to play it over again. Eventually he would make things safe by doubling the difficult or weak
points, and so his score would become playable but opaque. In
later works his orchestration took this final state of petrification as
its starting-point; but here in the D minor Symphony we have been
privileged to rediscover what Schumann's imagination could create
before an imperfect kind of practical experience disappointed him.
The later version contains some undoubted improvements, some of
which ought to be introduced into the original. And the ideal
version of the symphony would undoubtedly be arrived at by
taking the later version as the text and striking out all superfluous
doublings until we reach the clarity of the original. This is a very
elaborate process; but it has been executed recently in Germany.
Weingartner applies a similar process to all Schumann's scores;
and whatever qualms one may feel about it on principle, there
is no question that this original version of the D minor symphony
presents a justification perhaps not elsewhere to be found in the
fine arts.

Original as Schumann's D minor Symphony is, there is one work
which has inspired three of its most salient features, namely, the
C minor Symphony of Beethoven. Schumann's introduction, with
its broad melody—

Ex. 1.

is a new type of symphonic opening; the purely rhythmic transition
to the allegro is a simple device which in the later version is filled
out by foreshadowings of the main theme. The allegro itself—

Ex. 2.

(a)

shows unmistakably in the original notation that Schumann was
here inspired by the first movement of the Beethoven C minor
Symphony, with its exceptionally short exposition and its tendency
to broaden *ad infinitum* as it proceeds. The comparison is worth
making from Beethoven's point of view as well as from Schumann's;
it so completely proves that Beethoven, though popularly supposed
to have founded the whole movement on a single figure of four
notes, deals from the outset in huge paragraphs, whereas Schumann
never attempts to advance beyond square couplets. With these he
conveys a very pleasant impression of sonata form; nor, so long as
we do not expect anything dramatic, is there cause for cavil that his
second subject is not only (like many of the greatest in Haydn and
Beethoven) made of the same material as his first, but moves in
couplets of exactly the same type.

Ex. 3.

(a)

By degrees Schumann shows us, in his own boyish vein of slow
thought and quick expression, that he is full enough of drama after
all; but it will hardly develop on the lines of sonata form, and this
symphony is one of the few works in which Schumann has contrived to set himself free. He brings what has sounded like his
exposition to an abrupt and formal end; and then starts an
apparently orthodox line of development which goes through
enormous sequences in various keys, building up in the process a
pair of new contrasted themes, of which I reduce the first to
a generalized version.

Ex. 4.

Ex. 5.

(a)   &c.   N.B. The later version has no such thematic accompaniment.

These, though the rhythm remains rigidly square, really do make
very much longer paragraphs than anything in the exposition. The

process is repeated wholesale in another cycle of keys. There is no
sign of a return to D minor for purposes of recapitulation; nor
would such a form be effective in the circumstances. What happens
is that eventually the cycle of keys comes round to D major, and
the episodic cantabile (Ex. 5) bursts out in the full orchestra and
brings the movement to a triumphant and abrupt end.

Whereupon (according to the indications of the revised version)
we proceed straight to the next movement; a delicious little romance
in which a plaintive lyric melody in tiny couplets—

Ex. 6.

is brought into unexpected alternation with the broad melody of
the introduction (Ex. 1). By way of central episode a solo violin
embroiders the framework of this introduction with a beautiful
arabesque in D major.

Ex. 7.

This is worked out in binary form with repeats, after which a few
bars of the tiny opening couplets bring the movement to an end
which it is hard to call A minor rather than the dominant of D.

And now the scherzo bursts in; making a spirited tune play bass
to rhythms in the wood-wind which reveal themselves as the first
triumphant episodic theme (Ex. 4) in the middle of the first movement.

Ex. 8.

The trio is a transformation of the arabesques (Ex. 7) in the slow
movement.

Ex. 9.

The scherzo returns in due course and, under the influence of Beethoven, so does the trio. It dies away; and then comes a darkness before dawn which just avoids provoking comparison with that of the same point in Beethoven's C minor Symphony, inasmuch as it is a quite definite series of developments of the main allegro figure (Ex. 2) with hints of Ex. 4. It leads majestically into a finale which represents delightfully the effect of the enormous triumph of Beethoven's C minor Symphony upon this intensely thoughtful composer, who has never lost a certain boyish impulsiveness of expression. The theme is that of the scherzo and of the middle of the first movement (Ex. 4), with no allusions to other figures though in the final version Schumann added the main allegro figure in the bass, thus securing its survival in the finale.

Ex. 10.

In his simple sectional way, Schumann builds up a very effective sonata movement with an important transition-theme—

Ex. 11.

and a second subject in which that of the slow movement of Beethoven's Second Symphony sets its cap at a rakish angle.

Ex. 12.

Nothing is more characteristic in the difference between the two scores than the natural dialogue of single wood-wind instruments which Schumann wrote here, and which he afterwards turned into a thick plaster for full wind-band.

The development is broad, and, discreetly avoiding the first subject, leads straight to a recapitulation of the second; and then the movement expands with a fresh melody—

Ex. 13.

into a coda, which forms a fitting climax to the whole symphony as a single design. The pace quickens to a presto without the slightest loss of dignity or balance. In this finale, as in the first movement,

there has been a change of notation, from the 2/4 of this original
version to the common time of the later. As with the first movement, so here : information as to the change is valuable as giving the
real tempo and showing that we are much more likely to take the
final version too fast than, with it in our minds, to take this version
too slow.

CÉSAR FRANCK

XLVII. SYMPHONY IN D MINOR

1 *Lento, alternating with Allegro non troppo*. 2 *Allegretto*.
3 *Allegro non troppo*.

Nowadays the only difficulty than can come between the listener
and this great model of clarity and breadth is its misleading resemblances to the forms of older classical music. The resemblance
misled the teaching, but not the practice, of the composer, much
as it misled Bruckner both in teaching and practice. Such is the
nature of most artistic revolutions ; the conscientious revolutionaries
survive by what they preserved in spite of themselves, and the
conservatives design motor-cars with a high box-seat for the driver.
But the cars are quite efficient. When we see César Franck twice
alternating his introduction with his allegro, we instantly recognize
the influence of Beethoven's B flat Quartet, op. 130; and so, in
all probability, did Franck himself. But critics have been known
to complain that Franck's first movement drags because of this
expensive procedure. That impression comes only from expecting
something like the pace of the classical sonata from a composer
whose sense of pace, whether he knows it or not, is in process of
becoming Wagnerian. The externals of sonata form, such as the
division into self-contained movements, the balance of keys and
contrast of 'subjects', &c., are surprisingly tolerant of Wagnerian
movement; and César Franck's wonderful improvisatorial style,
often the result of endless labour, makes admirable sense of them.
But it does not make sonata style of them; it produces 'symphonic
poems' whether they call themselves Symphony in D minor, or
Éolides, or *Chasseur maudit*.

In almost every case the form is convincing, and the movement, whether slow or swift, so comfortable as to be discoverable
only by external evidence. The terms of sonata form are convenient in the four first-rate works (the Violin Sonata, Quartet,
Quintet, and Symphony), which imply an acknowledgement of
them; but in his F sharp minor Trio, op. 1, it was already
obvious that the sonata standard of movement was not in Franck's
mental gear.

The symphony begins with a group of three slow themes, of which I quote the first two.

Ex. 1 then piles itself up, harmonized chromatically in three steps of sequence rising in thirds from D minor through F sharp minor and B flat (= A sharp) minor, thus reaching home through an enharmonic circle, and leading straight to the allegro. This begins with the main figure of Ex. 1 worked into a paragraph with new figures—

and coming to a cadence-clause thus—

With a dramatic gesture the key is changed to F minor and there the whole process is repeated note for note from Ex. 1 to Ex. 4. No wonder critics are disappointed who expect anything like the athletic movement of Beethoven's op. 130. Franck's drastic simplicity belongs to quite another view of the universe. At all events, if we prefer to cling to sonata terms, we are now very comfortably landed in the proper key for a Second Subject; and here it is, in orthodox cantabile contrast and thoroughly Franckish in its way of hovering around the mediant.

Ex. 5.

It is not to be hurried; and it culminates punctually in another theme, also pivoted on the mediant and delivered exultantly.

Ex. 6.

&c.

This rises to a grand climax that disguises the final cadences of the exposition in gorgeous modulations. These expire slowly, and the theme lingers among pianissimo echoes with pauses. One of Franck's most beautiful strokes of genius is the sudden gleam of D major with which, amid these pauses, the development begins. The D major is the first descent in a key-sequence of thirds, F, D, B = C flat. This brings us to A flat minor in which remote region the themes begin to combine in energetic development. All the figures of Exs. 3, 4, and 6 are soon at work in triple fugue. A new episodic figure, of descending scales over a sustained pedal D, intervenes, and when the bass falls to D flat, leads to the resurrection of Ex. 2, pianissimo in minims approximating (without change of tempo) to the pace of the introduction. A quick change brings this to a crisis and to the next phase of the development. Now, starting in A flat minor, Ex. 4 alternates with a new episodic theme, which, with its bass descending by semitones, has a capacity for wide changes of key.

Ex. 7.

Soon Ex. 2 strides majestically over the slowly descending bass. During its third step it declines into a pianissimo, and its further course is in the bass underlying a series of pathetic efforts to resuscitate Ex. 5. These efforts persist and gain strength; the figure of Ex. 1 surges up in the deepest bass, and so this masterly and lucid development accomplishes its last climax and arrives punctually to the recapitulation.

Nothing tests a composer's sense of form more severely than a recapitulation. Where it is exact, it must not sound mechanical. Where it deviates, it must not demonstrate that the original statement was imperfect or redundant. Wagner's art depends as much on the sensitive handling of extensive recapitulations as any classical sonata; and the recapitulation of the present movement is a perfect example of such handling. To begin with, it completely justifies the rigid architecture of the opening. The main theme of the lento (Ex. 1) is given in a grand sombre fortissimo by the full orchestra, with trumpets answering in canon at the half-bar. The fifth bar is insisted upon and turned aside into B minor, a new and grand modulation upon which the six bars are repeated in that key, the whole twelve thereby forming a complete counterpoise to the exactly opposite D-minor-F-minor pair in the gigantic exposition. Another 4-bar clause, with a sudden pianissimo, suffices to lead into the allegro again. But now we find ourselves in the incalculably remote key of E flat minor. In this kind of surprise, which is often suspected of unorthodoxy, Franck's recapitulations are as classical as in his most exact transcribings. Ex. 3 starts as if it were at home in E flat minor and needs only five bars, interpolated after our quotation, to swing round to G minor, the home subdominant where (on a bass that worries around D) the theme, treated in canon, strides homeward and subsides into Ex. 4 in the home tonic, closing into an exact recapitulation of the whole second group (Exs. 5-6) therein.

The exactness of this recapitulation is entirely welcome to the listener. It includes the first expiring modulations and pauses around Ex. 6. The wonderful gleam of D major at the beginning of the development finds a dark antithesis in a change to B flat at the beginning of the coda. Few writers of symphonies can escape the influence of the awe-inspiring ground-bass at the end of the first movement of Beethoven's Ninth Symphony, especially when they write in D minor. They might as well try to escape the course of nature; and the wise composer will yield and prove his right to deal with such facts in his own way. And so Franck's coda movement combines the figures of Ex. 6 and the upper voice of Ex. 4 in a slow crescendo over the following modulating ground—

Ex. 8.

The movement ends with a grand plagal cadence upon the augmented figure of Ex. 1 in canon between treble and bass in slow tempo.

There is no slow movement: the allegretto has decidedly the

allure of a slow minuet, a dance rather than a lyric. The saintliness
of Franck shines nowhere more brightly than where his music is
most *mondaine*.

The wisdom of the serpent is foreign to the harmlessness of the
dove; and the combination has an exotic glamour all its own. The
artistic danger of the combination is that innocence may break
through in a disconcerting form of bad taste: the saint does not really
know what the world understands by its formulas. And so the exquisite main theme of this middle movement will eventually find
itself striding grandly, in its white confirmation dress, over a large
area of the finale; and the finale has a mildly sentimental second
theme of its own, which of all types of phrase is most vulgarized by
being given to red-hot brass, however softly played. I take this
opportunity of uttering these criticisms as a sop to Cerberus; they
contain all that I have to say against this wonderful and most lovable
symphony, and, uttered here, may save some listeners from shocks
of a kind that often repel persons of sensitive taste from whole
regions of art which they are best qualified to appreciate.

The middle movement is in almost unbroken 8-bar rhythm
throughout, and begins with the evident intention of, so to speak,
staking out that rhythm in 16 bars with chords of harp and pizzicato
strings. These 16 bars contain the harmonies of the two strains of
melody which now follow.

A cor anglais delivers the first strain, beginning thus—

Ex. 9.

It is repeated with a counterpoint in the violas. The second strain
is on new figures, but similar in its self-repeating epigrammatic
style. It needs more tone than a cor anglais can produce, and so it
is given to a clarinet and horn in unison. In repetition (with a flute
added in an upper octave) it ends unexpectedly in the major. Now
comes a very Schumannesque trio.

Ex. 10.

This develops with a temperature just a little high for Schumann,
and, before dying down, it has traversed the 8-bar rhythm by two
bars. Then Ex. 9 returns in the lowest register of the cor anglais.
But many things are to happen before we have a da capo. A pause
interrupts at the fourth bar, and the next phrase is turned aside

into G minor, where, after another two bars of hesitation, with another pause, we hear a whispering, fluttering, new theme—

Ex. 11.

punctuated by plaintive questions. After more hesitations and pauses this theme takes shape in regular 8-bar phrases. The shape really is a strict variation of the whole main theme in both its strains; but Franck does not let us hear the melody. He is one of the few real masters of the classical variation form; he knows his theme, and his variations can afford to be unrecognizable because they do not forget it.

Immediately upon this variation a second trio follows in E flat; again a Schumannesque warm-hearted creature.

Ex. 12.

The fluttering movement of Ex. 11 has persisted throughout this second trio as an accompaniment. Ex. 11 itself returns in its native G minor. But after eight bars we are delighted with the revelation that it is a counterpoint to the main theme (Ex. 9) with which the cor anglais now sails in. A little free development follows, breaking the rhythm with odd bars and carrying the figures quickly through a wide enharmonic circle until the home tonic is reached. Here the complete da capo of both strains (with Exs. 9 and 11 in combination) sets in without stopping the movement. Its sixteen bars re-establish the tonic firmly enough to admit of a coda which modulates further afield than any other part of the movement. The themes of the two trios, Exs. 10 and 12 are reviewed alternately in B major, and then the first trio swings round to B flat major and concludes the movement in a warm glow of quiet happiness.

The finale is festive, effective, and leisurely. You will miss much if you expect from it the energy of a Beethoven finale; the introductory first six bars ought to suffice as a warning that the ensuing pageantry is not to be hurried. They serve to show the contrast between D major and the key (B flat) of the previous movement. Then the main theme is delivered. Its first three notes are destined to resuscitate Ex. 6 from the first movement later on; but at present the theme exists in its own right. (But cf. Ex. 2, bars 3 and 4.)

Ex. 13.

&c.

Its continuation has a figure which lends itself to cumulative effects—

Ex. 14.

and so in due course effects the transition, in a grand crescendo, to B major, in which bright key the Second Group is placed. The main theme of this group is in dialogue between brass and strings.

Ex. 15.

As is not unusual in finales, it is soon rounded off; and the development begins without delay. But at first the development proceeds like a separate episode, belying the promise of modulation by letting the following opening return upon itself.

Ex. 16.

On repeating itself with an additional upper part, it drifts into triplets, which become an accompaniment to the theme of the middle movement (Ex. 9), the beats of which match the half-bars of the finale. Unperturbed, this runs its gentle course, and Ex. 15 returns in B major, high in the violins. It is then given in close canon. The whole eight bars are repeated in G major, and thus the development gradually gets under way, using more of the theme (such as Ex. 14), and moving in shorter sequences through quicker modulations. At the climax, Ex. 15 is developed fortissimo. This phase suddenly ends in a collapse. The next phase begins with a dialogue between Ex. 16 and the main figure of the middle movement (Ex. 9), broken by pauses. When it settles to continuity, it climbs very slowly to a splendid culmination, on which the main theme (Ex. 14) returns in triumph in the home tonic. I have already expressed regret that Franck should expose Ex. 9 to the strain of becoming grandiose; but this event, which now takes the place of the recapitulation, is less regrettable than if any further strain had been put upon Ex. 15, which we do not hear again.

The ensuing coda is magnificent; arising from the close of the second strain of the middle movement it begins with the resurrection of Ex. 6 from the first movement, non troppo dolce, in the dark key of B flat; and then, as the harmony returns to the home tonic, the first theme of all (Ex. 1) slowly piles itself up over another Ninth-Symphony ostinato which modulates in giant strides when it moves at all.

Ex. 17.

The figure of Ex. 6 joins in the process, and proves by juxtaposition (the only possible proof) its kinship with Ex. 13, the theme of the finale. At the end it is Ex. 13 itself which (in a new canon at two bars) is allowed the last word.

Thus the finale maintains its own integrity, and this magnificent coda has none of the weakness of so many works where the ghosts of former movements seemed to be summoned by the composer to eke out his failing resources.

BRUCKNER

XLVIII. ROMANTIC SYMPHONY IN E FLAT MAJOR, NO. 4

1 *Ruhig bewegt.* 2 *Andante.* 3 SCHERZO. *Bewegt: with* TRIO: *Gemächlich.* 4 FINALE. *Mässig bewegt, alternating with a tempo twice as slow.*

Of the childlike rustic person that Anton Bruckner was apart from his music there are anecdotes without number and without form. They should be told where his music is understood. In these British Islands Bruckner has not yet come into his own; and we had better concentrate upon his music for the present. Bruckner was a helpless person in worldly and social matters; a pious Roman Catholic humbly obedient to his priest, and at ease neither in Zion nor in the apartments the Emperor of Austria assigned to him in his palace in Vienna. But the musical party politicians who honoured Wagner with their patronage felt that *das Allkunstwerk* of Bayreuth lacked a writer of symphonies. And they found their desideratum in Bruckner, whose third symphony was dedicated to Wagner, and whose symphonies always began with Rheingold harmonic breadths and ended with Götterdämmerung climaxes.

Meanwhile Brahms was working out his own salvation, in ways
that no Wagnerian could understand. For Brahms the aesthetic
system of Bayreuth was the affair of one composer whose style had
only a special relation to the whole art of music. To be a Wagnerian
symphonist was no more an ambition of Brahms than to be an
agnostic pope or a breeder of St. Bernard dachshunds. The devout
Brucknerite, regarding Bruckner's 'pyramidal' and 'lapidary'
structures as the result of the mating of Beethoven's Ninth Symphony with *Götterdämmerung*, thought Brahms's ideas ridiculously
small. (I must specifically say *Beethoven's* Ninth Symphony, for
Bruckner's ninth is *also* in D minor, and *also* begins with a tremolo
from which rhythmic fragments build themselves up into a mighty
unison.)

The 'Brahminen', on the other hand, if they troubled to express
a printable opinion, could fairly say that size does not become
proportion until it is differentiated; and that Bruckner's proportions were not masterly. And in this matter the Brahminen had
the advantage that they knew what they were talking about;
whereas the Wagnerians evidently did not. As far as the composers
were concerned, we need not expect a fair judgement from either
of them. Brahms was never satisfied with less than complete
mastery in his own work, and destroyed fully half of what he wrote.
How then should he, who seemed to his friends to be too severe
with himself, trouble to see the merits of a style not only more
foreign to him than Wagner's, but obviously clumsy in matters
where Wagner was masterly? Bruckner, on the other hand, had
none of Brahms's capacity for overcoming all initial social dis-
advantages; he impressed people as, apart from his music, a rather
cringing and puzzle-headed man who had neither education nor
the desire for it. He tipped Richter a thaler for conducting the
Romantic Symphony, and displayed excited concern at a public
banquet when he received a telegram from a practical joker telling
him that the Bulgarians had chosen him for their king, and were
clamouring for his presence. The carrying out of his vast symphonic conceptions was quite enough occupation for him, without
the burden of understanding other kinds of art which interested
persons who were anything but kind to him.

What the two masters thought or said of each other is no more
evidence than 'what the soldier said'. It ought to be treated as
private conversation. But Hanslick, who constituted himself the
official leader of the Brahminen, saw in Bruckner fair game.
Wagner gave Hanslick only too lenient a treatment when he im-
mortalized him in Beckmesser, named Hans Lich in the first sketch
of the poem of *Meistersinger*. Beckmesser at all events knew the
rules he so humbly adored. I have read Hanslick's collected works

patiently without discovering either in his patronage of Brahms or
in his attacks on Wagner, Verdi, Bruckner, the early works of
Beethoven, Palestrina's *Stabat Mater*, or any other work a little off
the average Viennese concert-goer's track in 1880, any knowledge
of anything whatever. The general and musical culture shown in
Hanslick's writings represents one of the unlovelier forms of para-
sitism; that which, having the wealth to collect *objets d'art* and the
birth and education to talk amusingly, does not itself attempt a
stroke of artistic work, does not dream of revising a first impression,
experiences the fine arts entirely as the pleasures of a gentleman,
and then pronounces judgement as if the expression of its opinion
were a benefit and a duty to society.

All marked individuality in the fine arts can be seen from an
angle from which it seems that 'this will never do'. It is Bruckner's
misfortune that his work is put forward by himself so as to present
to us the angle of its relation to sonata form. That very relation
is a mistake: but if we are to condemn all art that contains a mistaken principle, I am not sure that *Paradise Lost* is less mistaken
than these symphonies of the old Austrian organist who dedicated
his last symphony *An meinen lieben Gott*.

Defects of form are not a justifiable ground for criticism from
listeners who profess to enjoy the bleeding chunks of butcher's
meat chopped from Wagner's operas and served up on Wagner
nights as *Waldweben* and *Walkürenritt*. If you want Wagnerian
concert-music other than the few complete overtures and the
Siegfried Idyll, why not try Bruckner? It is interesting and gratify-
ing to know that Bruckner, who made a great impression in London
and Paris by his wonderful extemporizations on the organ, told
Nawrátil that in England his music was really understood. This
was in the 'seventies or 'eighties, and I fear that he over-estimated
our general culture of music other than that of the organ. His own
orchestration reveals a state of musical culture very much wider than
anything to be found in British music of the 'seventies. His
orchestration is often said to be influenced by the organ. But that is
because it often sounds like an organ. And it could not sound thus
unless it were completely free from the mistakes of the organ-loft
composer. The scores bristle (as Weingartner says) with abnormali-
ties; but the quintessence of orchestral quality is manifest in every
line. Nothing is more astonishing than the way in which *naïvetés*
that look on paper (and sound on the pianoforte) as if they really
'will never do', become augustly romantic in the orchestra if their
execution is not hurried. We must clear our minds of other wrong
points of view than mere prejudices if we are to understand
Bruckner. It is not mere prejudice that judges Wordsworth an un-
equal poet, or Sir Charles Grandison an imperfect specimen of the

ideal gentleman. These judgements are relevant. But such truisms should not be allowed to delay us in the more important business of finding what Wordsworth and Richardson really achieved.

At the present day Bruckner's Romantic Symphony ranks in Germany and Austria as a 'best-seller' item in the orchestral repertoire; being now probably more popular than Tchaikovsky's Pathetic Symphony, which is beginning to show signs of wear. Such signs, we may be sure, Bruckner will never show; his defects are obvious on a first hearing, not as obscurities that may become clear with further knowledge, but as things that must be lived down as soon as possible. No other defects will appear; this art has no tricks. Listen to it humbly; not with the humility with which you would hope to learn music from Bach, Beethoven, and Brahms, but with the humility you would feel if you overheard a simple old soul talking to a child about sacred things. The greater masters inspire that humility too: Bruckner's helplessness is not in itself a virtue. But to despise it is to miss the main lesson of the masters, without Brahms's excuse that he was one of those masters and a severer critic of his own work than of anybody else's.

At no time ought it to have been possible not to recognize that the opening of the Romantic Symphony is a thing of extraordinary beauty and depth.

Ex. 1.

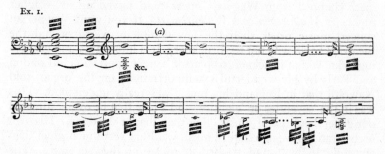

The counter-statement of this theme shows ample capacity to carry it out through modulations worthy of its solemnity. The mood is that of Schubert's *Du bist die Ruh'*. Two influences outweighed the recognized spell which Wagner exercised on Bruckner. Schubert is always ready to help Bruckner whenever Wagner will permit; and Bruckner never forgets the High Altar of his Catholic Church.

Though this opening is both broader and more four-square than any sonata-opening conceived by the classics, it is by no means impossible to follow up on an adequate scale. As with Schubert's finest openings, so here there is no evidence that this is a quick movement at all, until the first tutti bursts out.

Ex. 2.

Then for a while the action moves with classical energy. The orthodox critic has no right to complain of a shock to his habits of thought until he is confronted, not with an innovation, but with a stiff archaic pause on the dominant of B flat, the most conventional key that can be chosen for the second group of material. The stiffness is not accounted for by the fact that that group here begins in D flat instead; such evasions are as old as Cherubini's Overture to *Faniska*. And when Bruckner begins his second group and catechizes children with it in four-bar sequences ranging easily round the harmonic world, no wonder our musical Francis Jeffreys said (and in London continue to say) 'This will never do!' But this will have to do; for we are at the parting of the ways; and Bruckner has no theoretic labels with which to disguise his simplicity.

The main leitmotiv (yes, that is the magic word) of the large complex (another magic word) that now follows consists of the large-headed notes in Ex. 3.

Ex. 3.

The accompanying figures are just as distinct, and it is only in the light of later developments that we have reason to select figure (*c*) as the most important. If such phrases were obviously Wagnerian leitmotiv, that is to say, figures detached from an evidently larger whole, whether or not identifiable with poetic or dramatic elements, nobody at this time of day would have any difficulty in understanding the enormous process that now follows. The trouble is that Bruckner's mind moves no faster than in four-bar steps of moderate alla breve time. These steps the mind of the alert listener accustomed to classical symphonies takes for whole themes. We then wonder at their shortness of breath, and we marvel at the effrontery of the Brucknerite who claims that Bruckner is 'lapidary', 'pyramidal', and a master before whom Brahms dwindles to the proportions of an insect. The Brucknerite is wrong about Brahms, but he is right about Bruckner, whose four-bar phrases should be regarded as atoms, or at most as molecules. Nor should we be surprised that such giant molecules build themselves up into very simple forms; for art is not biology. We are dealing here with matters in which size is essential. Macaulay, who is only once recorded to have recognized a tune, and who certainly never heard of Bruckner, summed up the whole aesthetics of the pyramidal style by putting the simple question, 'What could be more vile than a pyramid thirty feet high?' Bruckner's following up of Ex. 3 is the right size. The opening of the symphony was huge from the sonata point of view, but not so huge as to show us that Ex. 3 is not meant for a whole statement. The storm that bursts in upon that childlike garrulity works its way, in terms of Ex. 2, with a grandeur that convinces us that the opening of the symphony is, in relation to the whole, no more than a normal passage of lyric leisure. Twice the storm dies down and mounts again. At last, upon a solemn summons from the brass, the key of B flat (the orthodox dominant) is triumphantly asserted: and in that key the accessory figures of Ex. 3 (without figure (c)) bring the exposition to a conclusion which has a very dramatic dying fall. With all its discursiveness, the movement has undoubtedly so far devoted itself, as Bruckner intends, to the business of exposition; and what follows is unquestionably a development, which the discursiveness has by no means forestalled. We must not expect Bruckner to move quickly. First the strings, putting on sordines, seem to be trying plaintively to lead back to the tonic, the wind giving hints of figure (a). But the brass rises from the home dominant to an alien dominant, on which a clarinet and flute, with plaintive diminutions of the last chromatic string figure, lead to a spacious development of Ex. 1 in combination with Ex. 2, both figures finding echoes in every region of the orchestra. In vast modulating sequences the development proceeds, alternating from quiet to climax on Schubertian lines easy to follow and enjoy. Bruckner's scores are full of echo-effects which look grotesquely crude on paper, but are so euphonious that almost the only word for them is 'comfortable'. At last we hear figure (c) from Ex. 3 in a solemn augmentation. With deep emotion this leads to the recapitulation.

Few things in orchestration are more impressive than the new depth of Ex. 1, in octaves, with a flowing figure in muted violins surrounding it as with clouds of incense. And the classical critic does not know his own favourite art-forms if he fails to acknowledge the mastery with which Bruckner composes the rest of his recapitulation and grafts on it one of his grandest codas. In this first movement there is no helplessness; though, as we have seen, there is a considerable difficulty in adjusting oneself to Bruckner's time-scale when his action really begins (at Ex. 3).

The defence of Bruckner, still necessary in this country, would defeat itself by attempting to claim that there is nothing helpless about the slow movement of the Romantic Symphony. In general, Bruckner's slow movements have been the first things that the classical critic has learnt to approach properly. Bruckner's tempo is always really slow, whatever its rate of vibration, and in the avowedly slow movement he meets the sonata style on its own ground. The plan of his adagios consists of a broad main theme, and an episode that occurs twice, each return of the main theme displaying more movement in the accompaniment and rising at the last return to a grand climax, followed by a solemn and pathetic die-away coda. The official view derives this scheme from the slow movement of Beethoven's Ninth Symphony; mistakenly, for Bruckner never has anything to do with the variation form. The slow movement of the Eroica Symphony would be nearer the mark if its two episodes were not different; and the allegretto of Beethoven's F minor Quartet would be nearest of all. Bruckner's difficulty, this time a real inherent dilemma, in even his most perfect slow movements is, first, that his natural inability to vary the size of his phrases is aggravated by the slow tempo, and secondly, that the most effective means of relief is denied him by his conscientious objection to write anything so trivial and un-Wagnerian as a symmetrical tune. Consequently his all-important contrasting episode is as slow as his vast main theme. The result is curious: the thing that is oftenest repeated and always expanded, the vast main theme, is welcomed whenever it returns; while, as Johnson would have said, 'the attention retires' from even a single return of the episode. In the Sixth Symphony Bruckner triumphed over this difficulty, and even steeled himself to cut out a beautiful passage to secure fine proportions. But in the Romantic Symphony the difficulty is almost schematically exhibited by the structure of the episode, which consists of no less than seven phrases, all ending in full closes or half-closes, all four bars long except the last but one, which is six bars, and all given to the viola with a severely simple accompaniment of pizzicato chords in slow-march time. There may, for all I know, be Brucknerites who consider this the finest thing in the symphony; and it so obviously 'will never do' that to criticize it on Jeffrey's lines will 'do' still less. However, the Brucknerites have the sense to apologize for the *Brucknersche Längen*—by which they mean *longeurs*, not that length which is essential to the size. I believe this is a case in point; and the above account goes some way towards its defence as a not unreasonable effort to deal with a genuine problem.

Here is Bruckner's main theme, of which figure (c) underlies important later developments—

And here is Sir Charles Grandison's oak-panelled room.

The final climax and coda are deeply pathetic.

The scherzo is one of Bruckner's most brilliant movements. It begins with one of his usual *Walkürenritt* scherzo openings—

continues with a more reflective theme—

and rises to Bruckner's invariable scherzo-fanfare on the dominant as the end of an exposition. The development begins in mystery, according to type, and is pensive throughout, till the exciting moment of return to the recapitulation, which ends with the invariable fanfare.

But the trio violates every Bruckner precedent by being quite frankly a tune; a slow and comfortably pinguid *Ländler*, too rustic to be called Viennese.

Ex. 8.

&c.

The da capo of the scherzo violates Bruckner's precedents in another way by taking an extremely effective short cut from the first stage of the exposition to the beginning of the development, the sudden hush being highly dramatic.

With the finale the first thing to realize is that, whatever Bruckner chooses to call it, it is really a slow movement, with all the positive qualities thereof. No Bruckner finale ever purports to 'go', nor does it attempt to sum up the whole symphony like the last act of a drama, though Bruckner's habit of reducing all his themes to terms of the common-chord and piling them up in his last bars goes far to create that impression. In the Romantic Symphony this is particularly easy, as the characteristic dip of (*a*) in Ex. 1 is present in the main themes of the slow movement and scherzo. But the listener's attention is better employed on the new themes of the finale. So long as we do not expect speed, we shall have no difficulty in following their progress through climax, reaction, combination, and final piling up.

First, then, there is the main theme; main, though delivered like an introduction. It is a single figure, (*a*), rising by tones and speeding up as it rises.

Ex. 9.

The rhythm of the scherzo (Ex. 6) is heard as the figure (*a*) begins to spin across the beats. Finally (*a*) becomes one of Bruckner's grandest ninth-symphony unison themes.

Ex. 10.

A new figure (*c*) arising from this is heard first merely as a mode of vibration—

Ex. 11.

but it becomes important hereafter. At last this first section of the movement comes to a grand tonic close in which the horns may be heard recalling Ex. 1.

After a pause an entirely new group of themes begins: at first solemn—

Ex. 12.

then as garrulous as Chaucer.

Ex. 13.

(I forbear to quote the next two bars lest the enemy blaspheme.) The garrulity increases, but with it the romance.

Ex. 14.

Other quotations are unnecessary, except for the characteristic inversion of (a), with which a section we may call the development begins.

Ex. 15.

This initiates a crescendo that leads to a solemn delivery of Ex. 13 by the brass. On paper it looks like an augmentation; but this is an optical illusion as the tempo is twice as fast.

In the last resort, the form of this movement is the same kind of three-decker arrangement as that of Brucker's slow movements, and to distinguish recapitulation from development is merely to use long words. The penultimate stage follows, a most impressive

calm after a storm upon Ex. 10, with a wonderful augmentation of
Ex. 11. Then Ex. 10, in a remote key, with mysterious throbbing
accompaniment, is inverted thus—

Ex. 16.

Muted violins ask elvish questions as to (*b*); and the rhythm of
the scherzo-theme (Ex. 6) hovers timidly in the background. Then
there is an exciting crescendo towards—No; the key of D minor
intervenes, and we have a free recapitulation of the complex of
Exs. 12-14. Then at last introduced by a combination of Exs. 13
and 10, the final climax builds itself up on the lines of Ex. 9.

XLIX. SYMPHONY IN A MAJOR, NO. 6

1 *Maestoso.* 2 *Adagio (Sehr feierlich).* 3 SCHERZO (3/4 *Ruhig bewegt*):
with Trio in slow 4/8 time. 4 FINALE, *Bewegt, doch nicht zu schnell.*

If we clear our minds, not only of prejudice but of wrong
points of view, and treat Bruckner's Sixth Symphony as a kind of
music we have never heard before, I have no doubt that its high
quality will strike us at every moment. In the slow movement I can
see no difficulty. The one redundant passage has been, though
reluctantly, excised by Bruckner himself, and the excision leaves
us with a perfectly balanced movement in classical form and of a
high order of solemn beauty.

The alarming technical difficulty of the first movement is probably the reason why this is the most neglected of Bruckner's symphonies. It begins, not with Bruckner's usual tremolo and chord
theme, but with a lively rhythmic figure below which a theme of
dark tonality stirs, Leviathan-like, in the bass.

Ex. 1.

Leviathan moves towards brighter harmonies. Soft horns, trumpets,
and clarinets rise with livelier figures. A counter-statement for full
orchestra now follows, and dies away in the direction of a new key.

The 'second subject' enters in slower time and with triplet
rhythms.

Ex. 2.

Bruckner's paragraphs are simple in form, seldom if ever deviating from four-bar or eight-bar phrases; but their inner details and harmonies are very rich. The present example is perhaps the most complex in all Bruckner's works. An inner figure in sevenths, in its second four bars, leads to much quiet rumination. In thirteen four-bar phrases this train of thought pursues its course, raising several new melodic issues by the way. At last a powerful tutti bursts out and leads through grand Wagner-Bruckner crescendos and diminuendos to a quiet close in E major, glowing as in solemn evening sunshine. The accompaniment-figure that arises from this leads to the development, which slowly drifts into other keys.

Ex. 3.

Then it sails out in full swing with one of Bruckner's characteristic free inversions of the main theme.

Ex. 4.

The enemy blasphemes when the devout Brucknerite exclaims at the wonderful contrapuntal mastery of these devices. Technically they are remarkable only for their *naïveté*; the genius of them lies in the fact that they sound thoroughly romantic. (Another curious and very effective feature is that they are always accompanied by echoes, which are always imperfect, and always scored for weaker instruments just on the border-line of audibility.) At last the livelier figures join in, also freely inverted. The music rolls on in its four-bar swing till the full orchestra thunders out the main theme in the remote key of E flat. (Note the half-heard echoes throughout.) From this it gradually swings back to the tonic A major, and so initiates the recapitulation. The livelier phrases die away; and the counter-statement is not only soft but beautifully decorated by figures in the oboe and flute, floating like clouds of incense in such Services of the Church as are never far from Bruckner's thoughts.

The recapitulation of the 'second subject' alters its key-system, starting in F sharp minor, and shortens it by twelve bars. The tutti outburst now begins *piano* and leads into the coda by a dramatic return to the tonic. The whole coda is one of the greatest passages Bruckner ever wrote; and Wagner might have been content to sign it. The first theme mounts slowly in Bruckner's favourite simultaneous direct-inverted combination, passing from key to key beneath a tumultuous surface sparkling like the Homeric seas. The trumpets join in a long-drawn cantabile, swelling and diminishing; until at last the rhythmic figure of the opening is heard, and the theme comes together in a fanfare.

The slow movement begins with a solemn theme—

Ex. 5.

to which, in the sequel, the oboe adds a pathetic counterpoint. Bruckner seldom if ever allows a theme to take shape as a lyric tune: his fundamental notion is always that of a Wagnerian leit-motiv of some four bars; and if he generally answers this stiffly by another four bars, this is only because he is building up an enormously larger whole, such as the 52 bars beginning with Ex. 2. This is, in fact, what Brucknerites mean by his 'lapidary' style. Here, however, as in the slow movements of his seventh and eighth symphonies, the slow tempo inspires him to a mastery of the big and supple paragraph such as Brahms would have been compelled to praise. The sequel of Ex. 5 does not proceed with another four bars, but with two, which are repeated in rising sequence and developed to a grand climax, after which there is no final close until, in the 24th bar of the whole, the music closes into the remote key of E. Here a 'second subject' gives us another beautiful example of quintessential Bruckner.

Ex. 6.

Listen to it with reverence; for the composer meant what he said, and he is speaking of sacred things. The music again expands enormously, and moves to a climax in C major. From this there is a slow decline till, at length, a solemn strain is heard, as of a funeral march in C minor combined with A flat.

Ex. 7.

From this the music drifts into a spacious development, based at first on the figures of Ex. 5 with the bass transferred to the treble. Then the theme is inverted and imitated, as follows—

Ex. 8.

with a wealth of new melody above it. At last it returns in the tonic with its counterpoint in the oboe and with a triplet accompaniment in growing agitation. A grand crescendo covers the whole expanse of the original first paragraph, and subsides into the recapitulation of the 'second subject' in the tonic. Reluctantly, perhaps on Bruckner's part, certainly on mine, the orthodox recapitulation which he wrote in full, with rich new details, is shortened at the composer's suggestion, and we proceed at once to Ex. 7 in F minor. The movement as a whole gains a perfection of emotional sequence by this excision, which still leaves us with adequate allusion to Ex. 6 in the exquisitely poised long-drawn coda. That allusion, moreover, has itself a power that it would have lost after a complete recapitulation.

Bruckner's scherzos are usually something like paraphrases of the *Walkürenritt* with trios consisting of quiet house-music or Church music. In the Sixth Symphony the scherzo is slower than usual and has, as Nawrátil says, a touch of *Walpurgisnacht* in its mood.

Ex. 9.

The trio is one of Bruckner's richest and most original inspirations. Strange pizzicato chords and rhythms introduce the three horns of Beethoven's Eroica Symphony into the *Urwald* of Wagner. The violins pronounce a solemn blessing in their cadences.

Ex. 10.

The finale is full of tragedy, though at last it ends in triumph.
You must not expect Bruckner to make a finale 'go' like a classical
finale. He is in no greater hurry at the end of a symphony than at
the beginning; and though his finales all begin with ample energy,
the first change of key and theme brings about a mood of argument
and meditation which will not be bothered by people who want to
catch the last train home. The finale of the Sixth Symphony is not
long; and Bruckner has himself excised the one dangerous place
towards the end.

It openes with a tragic theme in the Phrygian mode—

Ex. 11.

which leads to a tutti, marked by one of Bruckner's favourite figures
(here marked (*x*)), which pervades the *non confundar* of his *Te
Deum* and the slow movement (in memory of Wagner) of his Seventh
Symphony.

Ex. 12.

After a tremendous climax this subsides into the most naïve of
all Bruckner's 'second subjects'—

Ex. 13.

The lower figure receives the inevitable inversion during the
leisurely progress of this childlike argument all round the harmonic and orchestral universe. (Bruckner must have suffered
agonies from conductors who waded through these ruminations
in march-tempo and such intonation as occurred to the average

sight-reader.) At last it mounts to its Wagnerian climax, and so
drifts into the development. This is set in motion by a new wistful
figure—

Ex. 14.

which associates itself with the other themes and becomes lively
on its own account. The main theme returns in a slower tempo
(4/4) and, after a further discussion of Ex. 14, is inverted in F major
as bass to a consolatory melody in the style (but not the actual
shape) of Ex. 6. This inversion gives rise to some discussion, till
the brass intervenes with Ex. 12 and carries things to a grand
climax, reaching the tonic, A, and thereafter subsiding into a free
recapitulation of the 'second subject' (Ex. 13).

This is cut short by a coda which intervenes with Ex. 14. The
rhythm of Ex. 1 may also be heard in the crescendo which follows.
Wisely cutting out a page of pianissimo interruption in a foreign
key, Bruckner concludes with Ex. 12, on to which he triumphantly
grafts the figures of the beginning of the symphony (Ex. 1).

TCHAIKOVSKY

L. PATHETIC SYMPHONY IN B MINOR, NO. 6, OP. 74

1 *Adagio, leading to Allegro non troppo (alternating with Andante and
other changes of tempo).* 2 *Allegro con grazia.* 3 *Allegro molto vivace.*
4 FINALE: *Adagio lamentoso.*

It is not for merely sentimental or biographical reasons that Tchaikovsky's sixth and last symphony has become the most famous of
all his works. Nowhere else has he concentrated so great a variety
of music within so effective a scheme; and the slow finale, with its
complete simplicity of despair, is a stroke of genius which solves
all the artistic problems that have proved most baffling to symphonic writers since Beethoven. The whole work carries conviction without the slightest sense of effort; and its most celebrated
features, such as the second subject of the first movement, are
thrown into their right relief by developments far more powerful,
terse, and highly organized than Tchaikovsky has achieved in any
other work. The extreme squareness and simplicity of the phrasing
throughout the whole symphony are almost a source of power in
themselves: like the cognate limitations in Russian and French
music, they indicate the deep impression made by Schumann on

artists of widely different temperaments. Anything less like Schumann in emotional tone it would be impossible to conceive; and as
for orchestration, Tchaikovsky is as remote from the Handel of
the Crystal Palace as from Schumann. But there is no doubt about
the Schumann element in his form and style. Schumann, of
course, has different things to say, and has more leisure to say them;
consequently he speaks mainly in epigrams, and shows more relish
in making them witty. The Russian has no use for epigrams;
but the square-cut style which suits them—the cult of antithesis,
of the heroic couplet, of verse in which the sense never runs across
from line to line, of sentences which have nothing to gain by
being grouped into big paragraphs—such things suit Tchaikovsky's
methods, and are compatible with a dramatic power to which
even his operas (successful though they were) did not rise. All
Tchaikovsky's music is dramatic; and the Pathetic Symphony is
the most dramatic of all his works. Little or nothing is to be
gained by investigating it from a biographical point of view: there
are no obscurities either in the musical forms or in the emotional
contrasts; and there is not the slightest difficulty in understanding
why Tchaikovsky attached special importance to the work.

One of the most original features is the opening in a key which
turns out not to be that of the piece, but a dark outlying region
(the subdominant). Through ghost-like chords on double-basses a
bassoon foreshadows the main theme. The key shifts from E minor
to the real key of the symphony, B minor; and the allegro begins
with the first subject. I have marked (as usual) with letters those
groups of notes which are developed into other combinations.

Ex. 1.

Stated by violas, and counterstated by flutes, this theme soon
reaches a climax; and a considerable number of lively subordinate
themes follow in a long crescendo of square, Schumannesque,
antithetic dialogue. This dialogue, though excited, is by no means
tragic, but its climax, with the subsequent solemn dying-away,
indicates the advent of something important; and when, after a
pause, the second subject enters in a slow tempo, there is no doubt
that its beauty has destiny behind it. My quotation gives the
theme and the beginning of the dialogue which follows it (Ex. 2).
After the dialogue reaches its climax, the theme (Ex. 2) returns in

full harmony, and is followed by an 'envoy'—a strain with a 'dying fall'. Once more the theme returns on a clarinet, and dies away finally.

Ex. 2.

Dialogue.

&c.

The development opens with a crash, and works up the first theme (Ex. 1) in a stormy fugato, figure (*b*) settling down into a persistent figure of accompaniment to various new themes solemnly given forth by trumpets and trombones. The course of the music is easy to follow; and its finest feature, perhaps the finest passage Tchaikovsky ever wrote, is the return of the first subject, worked up in a slow crescendo starting in the extremely remote key of B flat minor, and rising step by step until, in the tonic (B minor), the whole theme (Ex. 1) is given fortissimo in dialogue between strings and wind. The tragic passage which then follows is undoubtedly the climax of Tchaikovsky's artistic career, as well as of this work: and its natural reaction, the return (in the tonic major) of the second subject, is the feature that fully reveals (perhaps even more than the despairing finale of the whole symphony) the pathetic character of the music. The dialogue, of which Ex. 2 quoted the beginning, is now omitted; and the severely simple coda, consisting of a solemn cadence for trumpets and trombones over a pizzicato descending scale, is a crowning beauty that greatly strengthens the pathos.

The second movement, an extremely simple kind of scherzo and trio, has this peculiar effect, that while it is in five-four time, which is an unsymmetrical rhythm, the bars themselves are grouped in the stiffest series of multiples of eight that have ever found room in a symphony. It is a delightful and childlike reaction from the drama of the first movement, and except for a certain wistfulness in the tone of the trio (Ex. 4), with its obstinate pedal-point in the drums, it successfully hides whatever cares it may have. My figures show how the five beats throughout the movement are really a juxtaposition of a two-four and a three-four bar. Ex. 3 gives the main theme—

Ex. 3.

and Ex. 4 the trio, which is an even more persistent mediant pedal than its prototype in the scherzo of Schumann's 'Rhenish' Symphony.

Ex. 4.

There is a short and wittily simple coda beginning with a descending scale in this rhythm in the treble, with an ascending scale of crotchets (the first bar of Ex. 3 without the triplet quavers) rising in the bass to meet it; and ending with a plaintive dialogue on the figure of Ex. 4.

The gigantic march which constitutes the third movement begins with a quiet but busy theme, the triplet motion of which lasts almost incessantly until the final stage, where the second subject stiffens the whole orchestra into march-rhythm. In Ex. 5 I give, below the first theme, the counterpoint which accompanies its second statement.

Ex. 5.
Theme.

Counterpoint.

The second subject (the main figure of which was already anticipated soon after the statement of Ex. 5) consists of a ten-bar tune beginning as follows—

Ex. 6.

and alternating with a second clause of eight bars which I need not quote.

There is no development: the first subject returns without any elaborate process; but its continuation becomes highly dramatic and is worked up to a tremendous climax crowned by the entry of Ex. 6 in G major as a rousing march for the full orchestra. The triumph is brilliant but, perhaps in consequence of the way in which it was approached, not without a certain fierceness in its tone. At all events it would, if translated into literature, be the triumph of the real hero not the story. He might share in it at the time; but his heart will be in the mood of Tchaikovsky's finale.

This experiment, unique in form and unique in success, is carried through on two themes: the desperate first subject, with its curious arrangement of crossing parts in the first four bars (the individual violin parts are quite unintelligible, but their combination gives a plain melody, as shown here in bars 3 and 4)—

Ex. 7.

and the consolatory second subject.

Ex. 8.

This second subject is worked up to a great climax, which leads, after some dramatic pauses, but without development, to the recapitulation. In this the first subject reaches a still greater climax, which dies down until a distant stroke of a gong (the most ominous sound in the orchestra, if discreetly used) brings back the second subject (Ex. 8), now in B minor and in a mood of utter despair. And so the music of the whole symphony dies away in the darkness with which it began.

DVOŘÁK

LI. SYMPHONY IN D MAJOR, NO. 1, OP. 63

1 *Allegro non tanto.* 2 *Adagio.* 3 SCHERZO, *or Furiant (a Bohemian dance). Presto.* 4 FINALE. *Allegro con spirito.*

If Dvořák's first three symphonies were of the nature of 'early indiscretions', we might acquiesce in the fate that has for the best part of a generation deprived the public of any wider knowledge of this great master of the orchestra than is given by overfamiliarity with the 'New World' Symphony and the *Carnaval* Overture. It is no disparagement of these brilliant and delightful works to say that they are popular for other than their finest features, and that Dvořák has written greater music. When Brahms and Joachim brought him to the notice of a world he did not know how to tackle, his genius was as naïve as Haydn's; and naïve it remained to the end. Unfortunately it often failed to retain that sublimity which inspired its best moments, and which Haydn never lost; that sublimity which is utterly independent of the size or range of the artist's subject; which trails clouds of glory not only with the outlook of the child but with the solemnity of the kitten running after its tail. With a loud instructive voice the world informed Dvořák that his genius was naïve; and a certain rustic craftiness, harmless perhaps in some earlier civilization, perverted his *naïveté* thenceforth. He tried to do as he thought the world bid him, and the world was the first to grumble when he wrote an oratorio expressly to suit what he understood to be the English taste. Unhappy as this result was, it was perhaps better, because more obviously unsuccessful, than the result of that most dangerous of all affectations, the affectation of qualities one actually happens to possess in abundance. Dvořák is not the only artist who injured his own originality and power by strenuously obeying the insistent clamour of the world that he should 'let himself go and be himself'. A naïve man affecting to be naïve will not often produce works like the 'New World' Symphony, which, if it has been allowed to oust its greater predecessors from their rights, is at all events full of fine things; but he will be apt to write himself down with bad and curiously ignorant imitations of his own style. Contrast this calamity with the wiser artist's fear of his own worldly

successes. The Kreutzer Sonata is not Beethoven's greatest work;
though no sensible musician has anything to say against it: but
Beethoven would have gone rapidly downhill if he had allowed
himself to increase in such easy breadth and brilliance without
deepening, enlarging, and concentrating his whole range of musical
thought.

Dvořák's First Symphony shows him at the height of his power.
It is by no means the work of a young man; its opus number is true
to the facts, and shows that Dvořák, like Brahms, had waited long
and experienced much before venturing on the publication of
a symphony. Yet the very first line presents us with those intima-
tions of immortality that make the child sublime.

Ex. 1.

No man of the world would take this theme so seriously as to make
a symphony of it, or, taking it seriously, would get so excited over
it as to swell out from pianissimo to a forte at the first top note. But
Dvořák knows what he is talking about, and the world has not yet
made him self-conscious. To the child the silver-paper stars of the
Christmas tree are really sublime: that is to say, no poet can fill
his own mind more entirely with the sublimity of the real starry
heavens. All depends on the singleness, the fullness, and the purity
of the emotion; and in works of art, also on the skill to convey it
truly. In this symphony Dvořák moves with great mastery and
freedom; the scale and proportions are throughout noble, and if
the procedure is often, like Schubert's, unorthodox and risky, it
is in this case remarkably successful.

No one can wish to disillusionize Dvořák when his first theme,
after the intervention of an energetic auxiliary, comes out *grandioso*
on the full orchestra. There is no illusion about it; the grandeur
is not that of particular styles or particular themes, it is that of life
itself; and when that grandeur is present art has little leisure
for even the most solemn questions of taste, except in so far as
the power to appreciate life is itself the one genuine matter of taste.

Dvořák's second subject is reached, as usual with him, by a
curiously long and discursive transition, one of the themes of
which must be quoted.

Ex. 2.

The second subject itself contains two great themes—

of which the second is very prominent in later developments.

The exposition is repeated, the return being brought about by a characteristically long passage, which accordingly makes it out of the question to 'cut the repeat'. Fortunately there is no temptation to do so, as the movement is by no means of unwieldy length.

The development begins with one of the most imaginative passages Dvořák ever wrote. No listener can fail to be impressed with its long-sustained chords, from the depths of which fragments of the first theme arise until the basses put them together in a dramatically mysterious sequence, which suddenly breaks off with a masterly and terse working up of the energetic auxiliary themes, including Ex. 2 and others unrepresented in my quotations. The whole development has all the ease and clearness of Dvořák's methods, with none of the flat reiterations that disfigure his weaker works: and I need not further describe its course, beyond calling attention to the dramatic stroke which leads to the return of the first subject. This stroke is easily recognized by the way in which at the climax of a full orchestral storm (based on Ex. 2) the strings are suddenly left alone, and after coming to an abrupt stop, proceed to stalk in stiff indignant crotchets to a remote chord, from whence the full orchestra plunges grandly into the main key.

The recapitulation of both first and second subjects (Exs. 1, 2, and 3) is regular, including all the accessories and the elaborate transition-passages. The climax of the second subject, however, is not allowed to subside as before, but leads immediately to a brilliant coda in which Ex. 4 is combined in free fugue with Ex. 2. This combination leads inevitably to the dramatic stroke that ended the development, and that now recurs to bring about the final triumph of the first theme, which dies away ecstatically in the height of its glory, and seems about to end in a quiet dream, when suddenly Ex. 4 (once the quietest theme of all) rouses the movement to its real end, abruptly and in full daylight.

It is a sad mystery how the man who had once written so highly organized a movement, could ever have lost the power.

The slow movement is not difficult to follow, but I know few pieces that improve more upon acquaintance. It has in perfection an artistic quality which Dvořák elsewhere unfortunately allowed to degenerate into a defect, the quality of a meandering improvisation on a recurring theme, the episodes being of the nature of ruminating digressions rather than of contrasts. This is a subtle achievement, and if Dvořák could have either left the slow movement of his First Symphony as his one example, or produced several others as perfect, we should be in no danger of missing the point of a design as peculiar as that of the slow movement of Beethoven's C minor Symphony, or as many designs of Haydn's which elude classification. At all events this movement will not fail to make its point if we dismiss from our minds any preconception that its ruminating modulations are intended to lead to something new, or that its one dramatic storm (at the beginning of the second episode) is an incident of more than fairy-tale solidity. That storm leads back to the main theme in one of Dvořák's most imaginative passages; and the whole function of all the episodes and developments in the movement is to present the most interesting possible appearance of leading back to a melody which we have really never left. Here is that melody:

Ex. 5.

The figure marked (*a*) more or less pervades the whole movement from its introductory bars (Dvořák seldom begins a slow movement without a charmingly wavering introduction) to its shy close. There is something very touching in the way the coda seems to pay homage to that supreme utterance, the end of the slow movement of Beethoven's Ninth Symphony; before which Dvořák's innocent drum figure 𝅘𝅥 𝅘𝅥𝅮𝅘𝅥𝅮 𝅘𝅥𝅮𝅘𝅥𝅮 seems to dance as the clown in the legend danced his devotions before the altar of the Virgin, to the scandal of the monks who surprised him there.

The scherzo or *Furiant* needs no quotation: nor is much wisdom to be gained from the information that the *Furiant* is a Bohemian dance. I yield to no one in my respect for folk-music and for the experts who have the tact and sympathy which alone can collect and appreciate it; but it has been noticed that the people who are loudest in saying that the *Dumky* and the *Furiant* are new and national art-forms are very apt to collect the Hunting-chorus in *Der Freischütz* as a folk-song from the whistling of a country milk-boy. Dvořák writes a lively scherzo with a picturesque trio in perfectly normal form; and some listeners may be chiefly amused by the village merry-go-round humours of the piccolo in the trio, while others may be more impressed by the poetic quality of the long-drawn phrases of the rest of the trio (very chracteristic of Dvořák and exceedingly unlike any possible folk-music) with its fine contrast to the high spirits of the scherzo.

For the finale we need at least four quotations; one for the first theme—

one for an important little figure—

and two for the second subject, the one designed for the tripping-up of the Superior Person—

and the other designed for a grand climax in the coda.

The development arises mainly from Ex. 7 and from the second bar of Ex. 8, which has the oddest ways of detaching itself from its frivolous surroundings and producing powerfully romantic passages.

In the brilliant presto coda, the onset of which may be recognized by the dramatic stroke where the violins are left to do a volplane by themselves, the listener should not fail to notice the happy effect of breaking up the first theme (Ex. 6) into this rhythm.

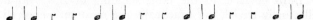

Altogether the finale, far from being, as too often with Dvořák, the
weak point, is a magnificent crown to this noble work, and is
admirably endowed with that quality that is rarest of all in post-
classical finales, the power of movement. Rapid tempo and accelera-
tion of pace can do nothing if the phrases themselves lack variety
and energy in their proportions. It is pitiful to see the *sempre più
presto* of many ambitious finales (including some of Dvořák's)
struggling vainly to make headway against the growing sluggish-
ness of their phrases. In his first symphony, however, as in a considerable volume of other neglected works, Dvořák had the classical
secret of movement, which is not a power that can be obtained at
the expense of higher qualities, for it is one of the highest.

LII. SYMPHONY IN D MINOR, NO. 2, OP. 70

1 *Allegro maestoso.* 2 *Poco Adagio.* 3 SCHERZO: *Vivace*
4 FINALE: *Allegro.*

I have no hesitation in setting Dvořák's Second Symphony along
with the C major Symphony of Schubert and the four symphonies of Brahms, as among the greatest and purest examples in
this art-form since Beethoven. There should be no difficulty at
this time of day in recognizing its greatness. It has none of the
weaknesses of form which so often spoil Dvořák's best work, except
for a certain stiffness of movement in the finale, a stiffness which is
not beyond concealing by means of such freedom of tempo as
the composer would certainly approve. There were three obstacles
to the appreciation of this symphony when it was published in
1885. First, it is powerfully tragic. Secondly, the orthodox
critics and the average musician were, as always with new works,
very anxious to prove that they were right and the composer
was wrong, whenever the composer produced a long sentence
which could not easily be phrased at sight. And this naïve and
irresponsible Dvořák, when he is at the height of his power,
happens to be a great master of the long meandering sentence
that ramifies into countless afterthoughts. The great sentences that
the unspoiled Dvořák was allowed to write, remain; and such
examples as the continuation of the second subject in the first
movement of this symphony (following Ex. 5 of our quotations)
and the trio of the scherzo (Ex. 12) would, if they were alone
preserved as fragments of nineteenth-century music, prove to
a future civilization that Dvořák was a great composer. To the
immediate contemporaries they proved that they were not easy to
remember; and, as Hans Sachs says, 'That annoys our old folks.'
The third obstacle to the understanding of this symphony is
intellectually trivial, but practically the most serious of all. The

general effect of its climaxes is somewhat shrill. Dvořák was at once recognized as a great master of the orchestra. Prout, in both of his treatises on instrumentation, always quotes him as 'the greatest living master of scoring'. And there is no page of Dvořák's orchestration which does not instantly carry conviction as eminently brilliant and orchestral. Yet his scores are almost as full of difficult problems of balance as Beethoven's, and he is anything but a correct and disciplined writer. Now if a work is loosely constructed, many a point which the scoring tends to obscure may be left in obscurity without much damage to the listener's enjoyment. The trouble comes when the composition tells such a well-constructed story that the listener cannot afford to lose a sentence. These great works of the middle of Dvořák's career demand and repay the study one expects to give to the most difficult classical masterpieces; but the composer has acquired the reputation of being masterly only in a few popular works of a somewhat lower order. It is time that this injustice should be rectified.

The first movement begins with the following sombre but energetic theme.

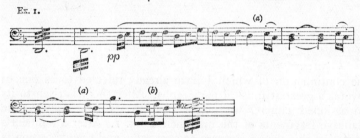

Ex. 1.

The delicate rhythmic contrast between the two figures marked (a) and (b) is of great importance in the whole scheme, and is typical of all that makes highly organized work more difficult to perform than the most elaborate technique of external effect.

From figure (a) arises an impassioned phrase.

Ex. 2.

In dramatic dialogue this passes on to a new figure with (a) in the bass.

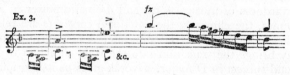

Ex. 3.

This comes quickly to a climax, and closes into a new theme—

Ex. 4.

which is taken up vigorously by several voices, and suddenly softens into a gentle dialogue between a horn and an oboe in a remote key; but the passion instantly breaks out again, and the rhythmic figure (*b*), in angry dialogue between the strings and the wind, returns through a wide range of harmony to the main key, D minor. And now the first theme blazes out on the full orchestra. (It is not very easy to hear it through the high tremolo of the strings.) Figure (*b*) brings about a fine dramatic stroke as masterly in execution as in conception, and leads through a wistful transition passage of rich harmonic interest to the second subject. This begins with a broad melody—

Ex. 5.

the continuation of which I have already referred to as one of Dvořák's greatest musical paragraphs. After this has risen to its impassioned climax, we notice through its long-drawn close plaintive fragments of the first theme, Ex. 1. After a moment's hesitation this theme emerges energetically, and the exposition is brought to a full orchestral climax with a magnificent combination of Exs. 1, 3, and 5. Just as it seems to be settling to a close, it plunges suddenly on to the dominant of D as if to return to the key of the opening. But the harmony moves far away into other regions, and the development sets out in B minor with a pathetic dialogue on the second subject, alternating with passionate outbursts of the first. It is impossible to over-praise the mastery and tragic power with which this shortest of all Dvořák's developments swiftly fetches its compass through distant keys to a recapitulation in which the first subject is represented only by its outbursts on the full orchestra immediately before the transition. There is the true inwardness of musical form and dramatic power in all this. The themes, the climaxes, the emotional contrasts are related to each other as character is related to fate. A new turn given to the harmony brings the transition into the right direction to lead to the second subject in D major. Dvořák gives us its glorious main paragraph in full, as is essential to the enjoyment of it; but when it comes to a close, and the fragments of the first theme appear, the full tragic power of the movement becomes revealed. The climax does not lead to triumph; on the contrary, the figure of Ex. 3 arises in the brass instruments like some stroke of fate, and brings the movement to a crisis of the utmost power, towards the end of which we can just catch a glimpse of one more of the themes which were so energetic in the exposition, Ex. 4. From this climax there is a still more impressive and sudden decline; and the first movement dies away in the dark mood of the opening, with the full pathos of that theme now made manifest.

The slow movement begins with one of Dvořák's finest melodies.

Ex. 6.

When the clarinet has completed its melody in two strains, the strings enter and the full orchestra surprises us within the next two bars by crowning the melody with a grand tonic chord. From this emerges a more impassioned and less naïve sequel to the tune—

Ex. 7.

which leads to one of the profoundest passages in any symphony since Beethoven.

Ex 8.

The nearest approach to this in mood and orchestration might perhaps be found in the loftiest and most characteristic moments of the symphonies of Bruckner, but it is something strange and unique in music to find an idea characteristic of that sincere but maladroit composer carried out with perfect mastery and terseness. This wonderful passage leads to another new theme in which a horn and a clarinet play the parts of a rustic Tristan and Isolde to a crowd of sympathetic orchestral witnesses.

Ex. 9.

This seems to be dying away, but it suddenly mounts to a climax in which the first notes of the main theme, Ex. 6, are heard in the brass, closing, however, into a stormy new theme in the minor. The storm dies away into D flat major, from which key a passionate dialogue sets out with several new themes which I need not quote. The modulations are rich, the orchestration is clear and varied, and the rhythms are impulsive. The return to the main key is, like every cardinal point in the forms of this symphony, a stroke of genius. Its power as such is enhanced by the fact that Dvořák does not return to the first theme, Ex. 6, but to its continuation, Ex. 7. Very few composers since Mozart have appreciated the force of a return which is made to the middle of a subject instead of to its beginning; and it is a tragic puzzle how a composer who had achieved such mastery throughout this work could ever lose it or cease to exercise it. The mysterious Bruckner-like passage follows, and leads to a much greater climax. The music seems to be dying away finally; yet we are waiting for something. At last it comes. It is the original first theme, this time upon an oboe instead of a clarinet. The oboe seems to reveal the inwardness of the melody; yet the clarinet also has its say in a final dialogue, in which the phrases are echoed on the still softer flute. Towards the end we are also shown the inwardness of that grandiose tonic chord which intervened between Exs. 6 and 7. In a new and more emotional context we have something like it started by a roll of the drums, as the wind instruments rise to one last melodious climax.

All Dvořák's scherzos are effective, but not all of them are as distinguished as the scherzo of his second symphony. Any composer who has a lively recollection of the dance-rhythms of his own province, and who is the possessor of a Czechoslovak language in which to give them names which are neither English, German, nor Italian, may easily figure in musical journalese and musical dictionaries as the inventor of a new art-form by writing quite ordinary dance music and calling it a *Furiant* or a *Trepak*. The scherzo of Dvořák's first symphony is an excellent movement, and is called a *Furiant*. The scherzo of the second symphony has no such advantage, but it is a finer movement throughout. The trio I have already mentioned as containing one of Dvořák's most beautiful musical paragraphs. From the scherzo I quote the main theme with its characteristic deux-temps rhythm—

Ex. 10.

and the cadence theme which towards the end of the movement dies away in a very impressive passage before finally flaring out.

Ex. 11.

The splendid main theme of the trio begins as follows—

Ex. 12.

but the quotation can give no idea either of the length of the paragraph, nor of the peculiar mood produced by the incessant rumbling of the basses. On the appearance of a livelier theme—

Ex. 13.

this becomes a gentle rustling on the flutes and violins. With the return of the first paragraph in a quite unexpected key, F major, the ominous rumbling again pervades the air, and at last a rapid crescendo leads to the return of the scherzo, its course shortened in some ways, but expanded emotionally in connexion with its cadence theme, Ex. 11.

The finale is no less rich in themes than the rest of the symphony. At the outset two require quotation, connected with each other by the figure marked (b).

Ex. 14.

Ex. 15.

There is no mistaking the tragic effect of the deliberate chorale-like
march of the second of the two. In quoting the first I give in
small notes the impulsive arpeggio-figure (c), with which it is
varied when the wind instruments or the full orchestra take it up
forte, as they very soon do, adding various other figures in the
course of an agitated dialogue. These other figures become gathered
up into new themes, of which the most important is the following.

Ex. 16.

This may be called the transition-theme. Dvořák's transitions,
unlike those of Schubert whom he so often resembles in his habits
of form, are almost always very discursive and elaborate; and we
need not be surprised to find yet another theme assuming importance in later developments.

Ex. 17.

After a stormy discussion of this, the second subject arrives in the
shape of a broad triumphant melody in A major.

Ex. 18.

This is brought to a full climax which ends in A minor and dies
away into the beginnings of a development on a large scale. There
is no difficulty in following its course with the aid of these quotations. Indeed the only trace of inequality in this symphony lies, as
I have already suggested, in the fact that the rhythms of this finale
are rather uniformly regular, which causes the themes and their
alternations to lie side by side rather than to build up into continuous action. Yet there is plenty of drama and plenty of coherence
in the scheme; but the task of the conductor is rather to keep the
movement flowing than to articulate what is already so clear in
the phrasing.

The development takes the themes of the first subject more or
less in their original order, and combines them with great resource
and vigour; the chief climax being produced by the sudden outburst of the two transition themes, Exs. 16 and 17, with solemn
new signals on the trombones and trumpets. When this storm has
died away there are further quiet developments on the first theme
in various remote keys; from which a rapid crescendo returns to

the tonic and brings back the first subject in the full orchestra. From this Dvořák passes rapidly to his recapitulation of the second subject without going through his transition material. This he holds in reserve for the short but powerful coda which is easily grafted on to the end of the second subject. The solemn tone of the close is amply justified by every theme and every note of this great work, which never once falls below the highest plane of tragic music, nor yet contains a line which could have been written by any composer but Dvořák.

LIII. SYMPHONY IN F MAJOR, NO. 3, OP 76

1 *Allegro ma non troppo.* 2 *Andante con moto, leading to* 3 *Allegro scherzando.* 4 FINALE. *Allegro molto.*

In 1874 and 1875 Dvořák, approaching the middle of his thirties, but still unrecognized either in his own Bohemia or abroad, wrote three symphonies. Later, in 1877, Brahms read some of Dvořák's works, and promptly wrote to Simrock, urging him to make a beginning by publishing the Moravian Duets. The works which then aroused Brahms's interest almost certainly included the symphony in F, which was originally intended to have the opus number 24, but was withheld from publication until after the great works now known as Dvořák's First and Second Symphonies. It was probably considerably improved after this delay. The other two early symphonies have now been published posthumously, and they show conclusively that Dvořák, though not the most self-critical of artists, never intended to revive them, for he has distributed their best passages in other works. The so-called Third Symphony, on the other hand, has preserved its integrity, and, while obviously and even naughtily Dvořáky, is almost as unlike his other works as it is unlike other people's music. Its nearest parallel is a later and much weaker work, the Fourth Symphony in G major, published in England, and showing traces of an effort to meet what the composer took for English musical taste. Foreign musicians have more than once supposed that the popularity of symphonic music is as wide in Great Britain as in their native land; and hence they are apt to include in their contributions to our musical festivals features that are popular only to audiences who are surprised to find that a symphony has four movements. No such audiences exist on the Continent: even the Prussian officer of pre-war caricature left the auditorium when the symphony was due, because 'das Aas hat vier Sätze!' (Translation deleted by censor.)

Dvořák's Third Symphony begins with a theme which the orthodox pedagogue would censure as being founded entirely on a triad, with no other notes until the very end.

Ex. 1.

It is true that the young composer will either find such a theme difficult to develop or fail to see the difficulty; and that to get into the difficulty is more promising than not to see it. Moreover, it is impossible to maintain that this chord-theme and its nearest classical parallel, the theme of Weber's Sonata in A flat, are the openings of orthodox models of form. But they are unquestionably the openings of works that have a right to be taken on their own terms. A revival of Weber's sonatas is by no means out of the question, though their romantic solemnity is almost more out of fashion than their gold-lace brilliance. But Haydn himself is not more unvexed by matters of fashion than the light-hearted, inexhaustibly inventive and discursive Dvořák of the Third Symphony. And fashion itself has never found much difficulty in lionizing rustics.

As to the difficulty of developing a chord-theme, the reason why Dvořák fails to see it is because he never grasped the difference between development and exposition at all. His mind is like the mind of Jean Paul, who complained that 'it is rather inconvenient that everything reminds one of everything else'. For the rest, it matters almost as little whether Dvořák's expositions are expositions as whether Shaw's plays are plays. Not quite as little; for in the days when the question was asked about Shaw's plays, a play 'within the meaning of the act' meant a clockwork story that exacted far more attention than any of Shaw's arguments; whereas musical exposition is really a much more general and less technical matter.

The above essay is very like the exposition of Dvořák's Third Symphony. After that delightful chord-theme, the lightest symphonic opening since Beethoven's Pastoral Symphony, there is a certain amount of discussion; not too much for an exposition, but enough to show that there is no hurry. The chuckling clarinet triplets of the Pastoral Symphony do not fail to make their point here. Eventually one of Dvořák's *grandioso* themes takes shape. And when Dvořák says 'grandioso', he means, as I have suggested in another essay, the grandeur of a Christmas tree.

Ex. 2.

Grandioso.

After some time we find ourselves on the threshold of a bright foreign key, D major; and in this key a well-contrasted new theme appears, in the guise of a quite orthodox 'second subject'.

Ex. 3.

But nothing could be less orthodox than the discussion which follows, and which even returns to the tonic for a while, with such emphasis as to suggest that the establishment of the new key was a casual incident. However another accessory figure, by asserting a much remoter key, saves the whole story from premature marriage-and-living-happily-ever-afterward.

Ex. 4.

8va

The claims of orthodox form being to this extent met, Dvořák, like Swift at each paragraph in his *Tritical Essay on the Faculties of the Mind*, says 'but, to return from this digression'—and repeats the exposition.

And, after all this unorthodoxy, the development, the recapitulation, and coda prove the whole movement to be a masterpiece! The development begins by taking up Ex. 4 in a series of keys that are new contrasts in the harmonic scheme. Soon all the themes are discussed in turn. The last to join the argument is Ex. 2, which leads by poetic dying modulations to a thrilling return to the main theme in the tonic. After this the recapitulation is for a while both full and regular. The curious result of its regularity is that the passage which in the exposition so unscrupulously returned to the tonic, now inevitably moves far elsewhere. Accordingly there is no further need for Ex. 4, which was active enough in the development. And so the recapitulation drifts into a peaceful coda, at the end of which we hear a combination of Ex. 1 on the surface, with Ex. 3 in the bass.

The first sentence of the prettily plaintive slow movement shows the power of a master of composition not only in its unexpected extra last bar, but in the overlapping of its answer by the violins in a higher octave.

Ex. 5.

Very characteristic of Dvořák is the way in which its opening figure becomes an accompaniment to other statements and to new themes.

Ex. 6.

Brahms's way of stating and using such devices is quite different: they are a feature of his most concentrated style; whereas with Dvořák the manner is that of Lewis Carroll's Dormouse continuing to say 'Twinkle-twinkle' until pinched or put into the tea-pot.

The central episode is a series of broad sequences on a new figure—

Ex. 7.

punctuated by pathetic ejaculations from Ex. 5. It is very picturesque; and with Dvořák, as with Schubert, the step from the picturesque to something serious, if not sublime, is always imminent. Certainly the two climaxes of this slow movement, that which leads to the return and that which constitutes something like a dramatic catastrophe near the end, amply suffice to make the whole movement sound important enough for any symphony. The movement is complete. But after a short pause an epilogue on the dominant of its flat supertonic leads to the scherzo. Simply and apparently naïvely as this link is made, it is one of the many unique master-strokes in this symphony—unique, though many, for they are all different.

Experts in folk-music tell us that Dvořák has enriched the art with two new and national forms, the Furiant and the Dumky.

I must own that I have never been able to tell a Furiant from any
other kind of scherzo that is too fast for a waltz; and that when an
elegiac slow movement suddenly shows an uncontrollable impulse
to dance on its grandmother's grave, I have sometimes been wrong
in supposing that it was a Dumky, since such impulses have been
yielded to by composers who knew of no such excuse. For all I
know, the present scherzo may be a Furiant. While it has none
of the fierceness of the Furiant of the First Symphony, it is not
unlike that of the Pianoforte Quintet in tempo and rhythm. But
Dvořák has given it no special title; possibly because nobody had
told him that it was his duty to prophesy the future glories of
Czechoslovakia.

Here is his Furiantic-corybantic scherzo-theme—

Ex. 8.

and here is the theme of the quieter trio.

Ex. 9.

(Dvořák's habit of writing *Tempo I* after a mere ritardando is apt
to produce a dangerous misunderstanding here, where *Tempo I*
looks like a return to the tempo of the andante.)

None of the movements of this symphony is very long; but
the habit of beginning discussion before exposition has taken shape
makes the listener feel as if he had come into a theatre during the
third act of the play; and his estimate of the length thus becomes
magnified by an indefinite factor. This is especially true of the
present finale. Beethoven, Schubert, and Brahms are masters of
the possibilities of finales that begin in foreign keys; whether by
way of introduction, or by means of a theme which, beginning and
obstinately returning in a foreign key, swings no less persistently
to the proper key within its own length. Dvořák, however, has
no such concern here. His main theme, beginning in A minor
(which has this point, that it was the key of the slow movement),
is at first little more than such a text for discussion as a fugue-
subject might give.

Ex. 10.

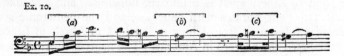

All the figures here indicated by letters are used in various combinations. The proper key, F major, is reached in triumph, after some dramatic discussion. It might as well have been any other key, for all its power to suggest that it is the harmonic centre of the symphony. But, as in the first movement, this unorthodoxy does not matter. A second theme, full of Dvořák's Bohemian-Italian lyric passion, asserts a new key, with a colour not hitherto exploited—

Ex. 11.

and a seraphic passage, in the style of the Gretchen-angelic theme in Wagner's Faust Overture, completes the material. The end of the development is marked by an impressive incident in which a bass clarinet gives out Ex. 10 in expiring tones; after which a crescendo leads to the recapitulation. As the coda approaches, Dvořák shows that he had no reason to worry about establishing F major as the true key of this finale, for he rounds off his whole work by other means altogether. The angelic Faust-Overture chords drift into a clear reminiscence of bars 9–11 of the first movement (see Ex. 1). Soon the other figures of that most original and unmistakable opening reappear; and so, when the themes of the finale gather themselves up for a final climax, we are not surprised to find the first figure of Ex. 1 forming part of the last fanfares.

LIV. SYMPHONY IN E MINOR, 'FROM THE NEW WORLD', OP. 95

1 *Adagio, leading to* 2 *Allegro molto.* 3 *Largo.* 4 SCHERZO: *Molto Vivace* 5 *Allegro con fuoco.*

This, the most famous of Dvořák's symphonies, has a high place in his art independently of its reputation. Whether the composer has adopted melodies from the negroes, or whether the negroes, finding Dvořák's style congenial, have taken up themes from this symphony and sung *Massa dear* to them, is a matter for historians. Dvořák's phrasing was primitive, Bohemian, and childlike before he went to America. It is primitive, Bohemian, and childlike to punctuate your phrases with chuckles; and the pentatonic scale pervades folk-music from China to Peru. And Abraham Lincoln emancipated the negroes in America The negroes in America are very musical. Last of all, Dvořák had a great success on that continent. This paragraph is my exhaustive *magnum opus* on Racial Characteristics in Music.

Now let us examine Dvořák's fifth symphony. It begins with a very slow introduction, of which the melancholy hesitating opening theme may speak for itself. Ominous dramatic developments include a surging figure which eventually takes shape as the main theme of the first movement.

Ex. 1.

When the whole orchestra has taken this up, its second figure (*b*) is developed into a transition-passage leading to the 'second subject'. This contains two main themes, one in G minor (Doric, note the F natural)—

Ex. 2.

and the other, reached after a climax, in G major.

Ex. 3.

When this bursts out fortissimo in the basses as a climax we notice, what was not so evident in its calm first statement, that its rhythm resembles that of Ex. 1. This is a good reason for obeying Dvořák's direction to repeat the exposition. After that the development, which is occupied mainly by sequences on Ex. 3 treated twice as fast, stands out in higher relief. At first it seems short as well as straightforward, for in a few bold steps it reaches a grand climax with Ex. 1, bursting out in E minor, our tonic. But this proves deceptive, like some of Haydn's forestalled returns; for several more dramatic modulations are needed before this climax can subside far enough for the real recapitulation to begin. When it arrives, it begins in the same scoring as at the outset of the Allegro. But its further course embodies another stroke of genius, for in a few bars it reaches the remote key of G sharp minor, just a semitone higher than the key of the 'second subject'. And in this G-sharp-A-flat key it recapitulates the whole second subject from Ex. 2 to the climax after Ex. 3. But this climax necessarily takes a more dramatic form, for only a vigorous dramatic action can restore our tonic key.

Accordingly the pitch rises from G sharp to A, the main figures of
Ex. 1 and Ex. 2 are combined, and E minor is restored in a climax
of tragic fury which brings the movement to an end.

Dvořák, like Haydn, Beethoven, Schubert, and Brahms, likes
now and then to put his middle movements into remote keys. But,
unlike those masters, he is not very willing to allow the remote key
to assert itself without explanation. The wonderful opening chords
of the slow movement are there simply for the purpose of ex-
plaining the connexion between E and D flat (*alias* C sharp).
But, as Dvořák is a man of genius, the explanation, like the con-
juror's offer to show 'how it is done', is more mysterious than the
mystery itself.

Ex. 4.

These glorious harmonies usher in the beautiful negro song
which, in its wonderful setting here, has become a glory of
Western art.

Ex. 5.

After the dying fall has been echoed, the chords of Ex. 4 in a new
position make as if for action, but culminate in the same tonic
again. Action is impossible. The melody itself takes a more
declining tendency, and dies away into a plaintive episode in the
minor. This episode, though highly emotional, has no power of
action; like the terror of dreams it remains rooted to the spot, sometimes in agitated rhythms, sometimes held in suspense, but always
meandering, always distressed, and always helpless. At last, like
fireflies dancing, a strange ghost of the main theme (Ex. 5) appears.

Ex. 6.

It soon fills the orchestra; but terror grows with it, and the figure of
the first movement (Ex. 1) bursts out like a menace. This is
answered solemnly by the slow first figure of Ex. 5, the whole
melody of which then returns, and, fading away into almost nothing,

leads to the opening chords (Ex. 4), and so to an end on a ghostly pianissimo chord of four double basses.

The scherzo, after promising to build a triad from the top downwards, in the rhythm ♪♪ ♩, solemnly arrives at a wrong note. With this wrong note in its chord it proceeds cheerfully with negroid persistence in the reiteration of its main theme (freely canonic; note the discrepancies marked **).

Ex. 7.

A contrasted outpouring in Dvořák's most enthusiastic vein of sentiment—

Ex. 8.

turns out not to be the trio, but a mere interlude in the scherzo. Dvořák thinks that to lead into a trio is a much more serious business. The Ghost of the first movement must be summoned. Then the three notes marked (x) in Ex. 1 may furnish a figure of accompaniment for a trio, which may then proceed cheerfully enough.

Ex. 9.

The finale has powerful themes of its own; first the great melody to which its nine stormy bars of introduction lead;

Ex. 10.

secondly (after transitional accessories) an impassioned 'second subject', punctuated by irreverent negroid chuckles;

Ex. 11.

and thirdly a thoroughly negroid outburst of which the three blind
mice at the end become persistent, refusing to run.

Ex. 12.

Other accessories might be quoted, and the 'diminutions' of bars
1–4 of Ex. 10 are very effective. But these materials are not enough
for Dvořák. As the development proceeds the themes of the Largo
(Ex. 5) and of the scherzo (Ex. 7) intervene. A climax is marked by
the appearance of Ex. 1, soon after which a pathetic recapitulation,
giving Ex. 10 in a mood of exhaustion, assigns Ex. 11 to the fourth
string of the violins, and afterwards to the 'cellos. Then the rowdy
theme of Ex. 12 surprises us by assuming a quiet sentimental tone.
The horns take it up, after combining it with Ex. 1. Suddenly there
is a tragic catastrophe, almost grotesque in its violence. The main
theme (Ex. 10), heralded by Ex. 1, bursts out in full fury and leads
to a climax in which the chords of Ex. 4 stride over the world like
Wagner's Wotan when he rides the storm. After this, fragments
of all four movements die away in tragic despair, until cut short by
a final storm, with a combination of Ex. 1 and Ex. 10. Even so, the
composer is reluctant to close; and the last chord, violently struck,
dies away to pianissimo.

JULIUS RÖNTGEN

LV. SYMPHONY IN F MINOR
(Dedicated to the University of Edinburgh)

1 *Un poco sostenuto.* 2 *Allegro molto ed agitato.* 3 *Andante tranquillo,*
leading to 4 *Allegro assai e passionato.*

At the end of March 1930 the University of Edinburgh gave
Julius Röntgen the degree of Doctor of Music *honoris causa.* On
receiving from the University the intimation of this intention,
Röntgen immediately sat down at his writing-desk and expressed
his sentiments in the present symphony. In due course he came
to Edinburgh and played a couple of new concertos of his own
at the last Reid Concert of the season, received his honorary degree,
and was entertained by the Principal at lunch in the hall of the
Senatus. At the lunch, in the course of replying to the toast of

his health, he produced (from beneath his chair) the score of this symphony and presented it to the University.

The Edinburgh Symphony is a typical example of Röntgen's genius and temper. Its numerous themes look as if anybody could have thought of them—but, like Schumann's, they are all viewed from an angle inaccessible to ordinary people; and, without affectation or artificiality, they all have the ring of epigrams. The enemy may blaspheme when he sees them in writing; but their simplicity is as dangerous as that of a Chinese philosopher. They have something in common with the Dutch folk-tunes which have become so famous in Röntgen's delightful settings; and your Dutchman is never so thorough a *bon vivant* as when he devotes himself to the things of the mind. Röntgen is not a Dutchman except by domicile; and his interest in folk-music is an interest in music and folk, not in archaeology and propaganda. With his Schumannesque wit he unites a Glazounov-like facility in transforming and combining his themes; and like Glazounov he has the temper of Hans Sachs in his relations to younger musicians, who have always found in him a friend who knows nothing of the weaknesses of jealousy or sentimentality.

The forms of the Edinburgh Symphony are remarkably terse, while at the same time their polyphonic development gives an impression of abundant leisure. The first movement begins by building a kind of round on the following tune:

Ex. 1.

When this round has closed with a climax, a new pair of themes enter, in contrary motion and in a new time.

Ex. 2.

This leads to a well-developed fugue, in slightly quicker time, on the following subject, which gradually rises to a storm.

Ex. 3.

The storm culminates in a Bruckner-like simultaneous combination of the theme with its inversion—

Ex. 4.

after which the fugue suddenly dies away, and a brief summary of Ex. 1 and Ex. 2 brings the movement to a quiet and pathetic end.

The second movement is a short and stormy scherzo without trio. Its first part begins with a theme of which the opening quaver figure becomes a refrain at the rhythmic joins of subsequent themes.

Ex. 5.

The second part adds a new theme to the three or four themes of the first part.

Ex. 6.

A coda in quicker tempo ends with a sudden gleam of sunshine through the storm. The quaver-figure (a), augmented to crotchets and slower notes, dies away romantically into a silence broken by an abrupt and loud unison cadence.

Solemn chords modulate in two steps from the key of the scherzo to that of the slow movement—

Ex. 7.

and a simple figure in the bass confirms the new key in a sententious manner explained by its importance in future developments.

Ex. 8.

A plaintive song is crooned by a high oboe over an accompaniment like the ticking of a clock.

Ex. 9.

It alternates with a broad cantabile, in soft full harmony, based on the sententious figure of Ex. 8.

Ex. 10.

Ex. 10a.

The figure of Ex. 10 a, which arises in immediate connexion, proves to be derived from Ex. 7, and becomes very important in the finale. The whole slow movement is formed by the alternation of these two contrasted themes, the recapitulations of which are compressed and brought into a key-sequence ending in the tonic (C sharp major) of the movement.

The finale follows without pause; the figure of Ex. 8, in rapid triplets, rushing in four bars, thus—

Ex. 11.

into the vigorous main theme:

Ex. 12.

An impassioned version of Exs. 10 and 10 a makes a second group in the dominant. Those who knew the man and know his work know that when Röntgen is passionate he is very unlike Coleridge. Lamb spoilt Coleridge's most cogent expostulation by saying to the admiring auditor, 'You m-m-mustn't mind C-C-Coleridge, it's only his f-f-fun.' Such an indiscretion would leave Röntgen's withers unwrung: his fun is as serious as Haydn's, and his passion, unlike Dr. Johnson's, is not to be deflated even by royalty. As with Haydn, so with Röntgen, you may be quite sure that the storm will yield to a burst of sunshine, and that whatever pathos may inhere in that effect will be entirely free from any tendency of the music to talk about itself instead of being itself. Thus there is abundant poetry and no sentimentality in the crisis when, after the opening theme of the symphony (Ex. 1) has appeared thunderously in the brass at the climax of the finale, the themes of the slow movement reappear in the richest and loveliest colours. (Exs. 9, 8, 10, 10 a, in that order.) Even so, there is nothing to encourage a feeble optimism, and the symphony ends in terms of Exs. 11, 12, with a major third but a flat supertonic; or, if you prefer the language of the poet to the jargon of the musical grammarian, with head bloody but unbowed, and captain of its soul.

ELGAR

LVI. SYMPHONY IN E FLAT, NO. 2, OP. 63

1 *Allegro vivace e nobilmente.* 2 *Larghetto.* 3 RONDO: *Presto.*
4 *Moderato e maestoso.*

On the fly-leaf of this work stands the following inscription: 'Dedicated to the Memory of His Late Majesty King Edward VII. This Symphony designed early in 1910 to be a loyal tribute, bears its present dedication with the gracious approval of His Majesty the King. March 16th 1911.'

Besides this, the symphony takes from Shelley its motto:

> Rarely, rarely, comest thou,
> Spirit of Delight.

The second figure (*b*) of the main theme—

Ex. 1.

may be taken as representing this motto, for it occurs elsewhere than in the first movement, and generally with a wistfulness as if it referred to something no longer, or not yet, present in the impetuous strength displayed here.

Readers who have followed my essay on Elgar's *Falstaff* (vol. iv) may find it interesting to note how much easier is the analysis of a work of similar calibre that proceeds on the lines of classical sonata form. This is not because classical forms are simpler. On the whole they are more complex than those of *Falstaff*. Nor are the forms of *Falstaff* non-classical. The only conception of form that has any truth in it is that according to which the form represents the natural growth of the matter so intimately that, in the last resort, form and matter are interchangeable terms. But it saves an immense amount of trouble in analysis if the matter happens to grow into forms which have enough family likeness to those of many other works of art to have produced a number of technical terms by which they can be named. Thanks to the very complexity and richness of the forms of a classical symphony, I am saved the trouble of trying to identify this or that feature, structural or emotional, of the present work with the glories and sorrows of the reign of Edward VII. It is perhaps permissible to say that no one who has met the composer or studied this symphony can possibly fail to see that it is animated by no mere official imperialism, but by a deep glow of personal and affectionate loyalty.

The first movement begins at once with its main theme, containing, as I have said before, in figure (*b*), the musical representation of its motto. This is the beginning of a long paragraph which builds into large sequences a number of other themes, from which I quote three.

Ex. 2.

Ex. 3.

Ex. 4.

As in the Violin Concerto and other large works of Elgar, the sequential structure and the shortness of the figures built up therein are apt to produce an analysis like that of the Wagnerian *motiv-hunter*, according to which the music would appear lamentably short of breath and still more lamentably long of procedure. As a matter of fact, Elgar's paragraphs are big and his action is swift. I have not quoted all the themes of the first group. The tonic, E flat, stands firm at the outset and the drift towards another key is sudden and decisive. But when that other key appears it proves an iridescent mixture of several keys, remote enough for the home tonic itself to appear foreign in its new surrounding as one of the chords of the main theme in the second group.

Ex. 5.

The orthodox dominant is more nearly concerned in the following accessory theme—

Ex. 6.

and various sequences that arise on the materials of Exs. 5 and 4 tend more and more to establish it.

I leave the double climax, at first brilliant and hereafter solemn, to speak for itself, and I quote only the quiet cadence theme into which the exposition subsides.

Ex. 7.

From this it passes without perceptible break into the development, which begins by alternating the expiring strains of Ex. 7 with a new figure—

Ex. 8.

in a series of remote modulations. These lead to E major, in which remote key the development takes action by using a combination of Exs. 8 and 1 as accompaniment to an important new episodic theme.

Ex. 9.

This falls in sequence, descending by semitones in bold dissonance over a persistent E natural, until at last the E gives way and both figures of the first theme (Ex. 1) appear in C major, associated with a new figure.

Ex. 9 a (compare Ex. 5).

   The development is chiefly concerned with these materials, alternating with developments of Exs. 4, 2, and 3.

   As soon as the quiet episode dies away, the action becomes rapid; and the last stage of the development, in which the figures (a) (b) of Ex. 1 reappear, moves swiftly to a grandiose return prepared for by a solemn summons from the horns and trombones. The recapitulation of both groups is regular, though the handling of the mixed tonalities of the second group has a classical subtlety and freedom.

   The coda arises naturally from the expiring of the cadence group (Ex. 7) and, without alluding either to Exs. 8 or 9, proceeds to give Ex. 9 a, augmented to twice its size, pianissimo in the tonic, after which it builds up a quick crescendo on Ex. 3, and ends with an appeal to the Spirit of Delight (Ex. 1, figure (b)).

   The slow movement is elegiac, with something of the character of a funeral march. Its first seven bars are an introduction, which I do not quote, on a figure somewhat reminiscent of Ex. 2. It is the main theme—

Ex. 10.

to which this movement chiefly owes its suggestiveness of a funeral march; and that characteristic is perhaps more inherent in the accompaniment than in the melody. (Note the figure (a), common to Exs. 1 and 10. With Elgar such points are significant.)

   A modulating transition-theme—

Ex. 11.

leads towards F major, and in a tonal region compounded of that key and of A minor, one of the main themes of the middle section appears.

Ex. 12.

Moving in broad lines and with free rhythm, as if Bruckner had become a master of phrasing, this passes through an agitated sequence on a new figure which I do not quote, to a grand and simple climax fully in F major, with another important theme which completes the exposition.

Ex. 13.

This dies away, and Ex. 11 effects a mournful return to C minor and to the main theme, which is given in full with the addition of a beautiful ruminating counterpoint on an oboe. The whole of the sequel is recapitulated in due order, Exs. 12–13 being given in and around E flat.

The coda arises from a dramatic return to the dominant of C, upon which is heard an appeal to the Spirit of Delight (Ex. 1), alternating with Ex. 11, after which the movement expires in a mournful allusion to the first phrase of its main theme (Ex. 10), which closes into another allusion to the unquoted introductory bars.

The scherzo is, as its title shows, in rondo form. A mystery underlies its playful opening theme.

Ex. 14.

The meaning of the portion marked *x* in this quotation will appear later.

The first episode is in the tonic minor.

Ex. 15.

Considerable development of the figures of the main theme, at first
in cross accents and then in combination with a new figure—

Ex. 15 a.

follows before the main theme is allowed to return in full. The
second episode is in an unorthodox key or tonal region, that of the
major supertonic, D.

A wistful introductory figure—

Ex. 16.

is delivered and echoed by several wood-wind instruments, and
afterwards worked into paragraphs together with the swinging
theme of the episode itself.

Ex. 17.

The second return of the main theme is a quiet affair, and the
strings have a tendency to adorn the outline of the group x with a
halo. This halo becomes gradually clearer until, in the key of E
flat, it takes solid shape as the important episodic theme (Ex. 9)
with which the development of the first movement had begun. On
a long tonic pedal this episode now grows to a mighty cantabile,
which eventually passes, via the trombones, into the bass, while the
scherzo-theme just contrives to penetrate the mass of tone above.
As the mass of tone dies away, another origin of the theme, Ex. 8,
becomes audible. It is always an interesting problem in aesthetics
how, when a lively movement has mounted on to a sublime pedestal,
it can come off it again. Elgar's solution of this dangerous problem
is Schumannesque and classical. Without any preaching or tub-
thumping, the music resumes the first episode (Ex. 15) quietly, as
Schumann's Florestan, or any other nice young undergraduate,
might relight his pipe after he had allowed it to go out during an
outburst of enthusiasm. As before, steps towards a return to the
main theme are taken by a development of Ex. 14, with cross
accents; but what is reached is Ex. 15 a in a grand climax without

the semiquaver figure. When this has died away, the rest of the
coda piles itself up in brilliant cross-rhythmed sequences.

The finale seems to be, as the directions for its tempo imply, a
comparatively slow movement; but this is rather an illusion of
notation, for it is in reality remarkably swift, with an irresistible
momentum in the strength of its current. No stronger contrast
could be found than that between it and the standard difficulty of
the clever composers whose finales and thematic transformations
call themselves prestissimo in a vain struggle against the flaccid
uniformity of their phrase-lengths.

The finale moves on the lines of a broad sonata form with the
following tune as its main theme:

Ex. 18.

A transition theme, starting in the subdominant—

Ex. 19.

leads in massive sequences to a second group consisting of a single
new theme in the dominant—

Ex. 20.

closing with a four-bar allusion to Ex. 18. This plunges into a
development consisting mainly of a fugue on the figures of Ex. 19
combined with new counterpoint. The tendency of fugues is not
to modulate widely. They are arguments rather than actions, or
they are actions at law rather than at large. Accordingly the venue
of this development remains in the tonal region around D major and
B minor, in which latter key the first figure of the main theme (Ex.
18) begins to assert itself obstinately.

A new figure—

Ex. 21.

brings a persuasively pacifying note into the discussion, and soon
combines with larger portions of the main theme. Eventually a
return to E flat is effected, and the more or less regular recapitulation of all the material builds itself up into a grand climax and leads

to a peaceful coda. From the quiet heights into which it recedes, this coda is dominated by the Spirit of Delight (figure (*b*) of Ex. 1 in very slow tempo) and the symphony ends in solemn calm.

SIBELIUS

LVII. SYMPHONY IN C MAJOR, NO. 3, OP. 52

1 *Allegro moderato.* 2 *Andantino con moto quasi allegretto.*
3 *Moderato, leading to* 4 *Allegro.*

The symphonies and other large orchestral works of Sibelius would, if they had no other merits, command the attention of every lover of music who is interested in the problem which baffled Bruckner and eluded Liszt: the problem of achieving the vast movement of Wagnerian music-drama in purely instrumental music. Liszt achieved at best, as in *Orpheus*, a large orchestral lyric, or, as in *Mazeppa*, an enlarged *Étude d'exécution transcendante*: at worst, as in *Ce qu'on entend sur la montagne*, forty minutes of impressive introductions to introductions. Bruckner conceived magnificent openings and Götterdämmerung climaxes, but dragged along with him throughout his life an apparatus of classical sonata forms as understood by a village organist. His was the fallacy of the popular natural-history writer who tells us that a flea magnified to the size of a dog could jump over Mount Everest, whereas the poor creature could not support its own weight without a vertebrate anatomy. Your pocket working model has—I forget what inverse-geometrically greater power than the full-sized machine.

Most of the later solutions of the problem of instrumental music on the Wagnerian scale of movement have continued to use and to extend the Wagnerian apparatus, especially in harmonic range and polyphony. Much of the resulting complexity is apparent rather than real, for the problem is subtle rather than complex, and modern composers have more common sense than is indicated by modern methods of high-art advertising. False simplification is a more menacing danger to the arts nowadays than over-elaboration; as we can easily discover when our analysis has distinguished the apparatus from the work.

The simplicity of Sibelius is not a simplification, and his art is neither revolutionary nor negative. His latest symphonies retain something like the classical division into three or four movements, for the true classical reason that his designs complete themselves sooner than the emotional reactions they demand, so that these reactions must be expressed in separate designs. He does not share the superstition of many modern composers that a work in sonata form *must* have four movements, including an adagio and a scherzo:

a superstition only apparently originating in the classics. They arrived at the custom of writing in four movements whenever they used more than three players, because it seemed expensive to collect more players for a work of less than full size. No modern composer, whether on classical or revolutionary lines, has achieved anything like the variety of forms shown in the sonatas, duets, and trios of Haydn, Mozart, and Beethoven. Those three masters worked out their own salvation, and in due time learnt from each other in spite of differences of age. They learnt by experiencing the necessities of each individual work; and the accumulation of such experience leads to a knowledge of universals, and has no concern with averages. Beethoven produces his C sharp minor Quartet, with its apparently improvised form, by the same creative process as that of his Sonata in B flat, op. 22, the most diplomatically regular of all his works. The diplomatic regularity was not imposed on him by precedent, and the free form was not troubled by any wish to 'get away from' old formulas and restraints. Beethoven's movement was equally unhampered in both.

By its movement you may know when music is free. Pioneers may be free from human tyranny, but it is idle to call men free when their minds have never had leisure for other interests than the bare necessaries of life. The enjoyment of 'roughing it' begins after the technique of desert life or polar exploration has been mastered. Sibelius, standing on the shoulders of the late nineteenth-century masters of 'symphonic poems', moves with perfect ease in his least convincing works, and the ease is strengthened into freedom in his masterpieces. Although his designs complete themselves so quickly that his symphonies (except the Seventh) break up into three or four movements, they have little real analogy with the sonata forms. In his First Symphony the sonata forms are easily traced, but even there they are neither a necessity nor a convention, but a convenience which may not be convenient another time. With the Fifth Symphony nothing whatever is gained by thinking of them at all; and, even without thinking of them, much criticism has been directed to Sibelius for his neglect of qualities which those forms imply. His intention and achievement are entirely different: instead of working out groups of complete themes on various principles of alternate exposition, development, and recapitulation, with essentially dramatic and narrative effects throughout, he makes his scheme build itself up out of fragments until a full-sized theme arrives as a supreme climax. Two such processes will cover the ground of one of his largest movements, and sometimes, as in the finale of his Third Symphony, one will suffice. The result is that, in works of no inordinate length, Sibelius achieves climaxes on the biggest Wagnerian scale without any redundancies, hesitations, or confusions from the habits of older art-forms. A Bach toccata is perhaps the most recent precedent for this order of musical architecture.

Sibelius's Third Symphony is dedicated to his friend Bantock. The long passages that arise out of Ex. 5 are said to represent the composer's impression of fog-banks drifting along the English coast. The quality of the themes, especially of Ex. 1, is such as we would be glad to think distinctly English. If this work should come to be known as Sibelius's English Symphony, we might come to consider ourselves not so anti-musical after all.

The first movement is more like a normal classic than any other in Sibelius's symphonies. The splendid opening theme—

Ex. 1.

Allegro moderato.

swings into a crowd of accessories, such as—

Ex. 2.

and as the transition-theme—

Ex. 3.

with a power of movement that takes us into the heart of the classical symphonic style. Three slow rising notes on trumpets and trombones lead, like the abrupt attitudinizing transitions of Schubert, to a 'second subject'.

Ex. 4.

A very typical feature of Sibelius's style is the emergence of a long-drawn melody from a sustained note that began no one can say exactly when. Another characteristic point is the way in which one theme gradually shows a kinship with another. The continuation of Ex. 4 thus tends to resemble the opening of Ex. 1 reduced to sustained instead of repeated notes. At present, however, this is not shown, but the theme passes naturally into the rolling figure of Ex. 5—

Ex. 5.

which from this point pervades the movement as fog-banks pervade our shores.

The development is indeed almost one single extended passage arising out of Ex. 5. Fragments of other themes, notably from the second bar of Ex. 3, together with the 'conflation' of Ex. 4 and Ex. 1, loom through the fog and grow to a climax, on the top of which the recapitulation sails in with glorious vigour. The second subject is brilliantly re-scored.

The coda is of a kind peculiar to Sibelius. The music suddenly becomes almost ecclesiastical in tone. A new hymn-like theme appears—

Ex. 6.

and the movement ends in solemn calm.

The second movement is an intermezzo combining the functions of slow movement and scherzo: the lyric function of a slow movement with a gentle dance-rhythm for a quiet and slightly pathetic scherzo.

The key is remote: G sharp minor stands to C, as Beethoven's F sharp minor stands to B flat in his Sonata, op. 106. The rhythm revives an ancient ambiguity of triple time. In ancient days the notion of triple time was by no means so rigid as it is in modern music. To the modern musician twice three is not only different from thrice two but hard to reconcile with it. Once you have established the system ONE-two-three-FOUR-five-six, you will find it hard to change casually into ONE-two-THREE-four-FIVE-six. A poetic ear has no such difficulty; for poetic stresses are much lighter and less rigid than the powerful muscular energies of musical rhythm. Nevertheless, in the sixteenth century the musical triple times were as vague as the poetic. In all Palestrina you will find no sustained passage on a six-beat basis that does not shift from twice three to thrice two. In the eighteenth century the shift from thrice two to twice three is a regular characteristic of the French courante; and in every cadence in triple time in Handel's works you will see the opposite shift, the majestic broadening from twice three to thrice two. 'The glory of the Lord shall be re-veal-ed.'

$$1 \quad ^2 3 \quad 1 \quad ^2 \quad 3 \quad ^4 \quad 5^6 \quad 1$$

Prout quotes a whole series of such cases as examples of Handel's faulty declamation.

Sibelius has erected 'Handel's faulty declamation' into a system throughout the charming intermezzo of his Third Symphony; and, as Bantock tells me, he requires the conductor to beat the time in such a way as to emphasize these shifting accents.

Ex. 7.

Ex. 8.

Towards the end of the movement a ruminating passage introduces other figures of curling runs; but no further quotations are needed.

The finale is in a form invented by Sibelius. At first only fragments of themes are heard; of which I quote two.

Ex. 9.
Moderato.

Ex. 10.

Several others might be added, but their bustling movement in a crescendo will suffice to mark them. The essence of the whole is just this, that nothing takes shape until the end. Then comes the one and all-sufficing climax. All threads are gathered up in one tune that pounds its way to the end with the strokes of Thor's hammer.

Ex. 11.

LVIII SYMPHONY IN E FLAT MAJOR, NO. 5, OP. 82

1 *Tempo molto moderato, leading to* 2 *Allegro moderato.*
3 *Andante mosso, quasi allegretto.* 4 *Allegro molto.*

This symphony is easily followed with the aid of enough quotations to show how one element of a theme leads to another. Here are the six main elements with which the opening section (almost a slow movement) builds itself up from its dawn-like beginning. They show several features of Sibelius's style; most obviously his love of letting the first note of a phrase begin at the obscurest point of the measure and swell out; also his austerely diatonic or modal harmony, varied, as in Ex. 4, by collisions severely logical in origin and consequence.

The climax attained with Ex. 6 is followed by a resumption of the whole process, beginning with figure (*a*) of Ex. 1, which leads to the continuation of Ex. 2, and thence to Ex. 3; the key having returned from the bright region of G major to the environs of E flat. Ex. 4 does not follow on here, but the pair of themes, Exs. 5 and 6, are recapitulated in E flat, the tonic. Symmetry being thus established, Ex. 4 is worked up into a wonderful mysterious kind of fugue which quickens (by 'diminution') into a cloudy chromatic trembling, through which its original figure moans in the clarinet and bassoon. An impassioned development of Ex. 5 (largamente)

intervenes, and, with a new version of Ex. 2, moves to B major,
then, without real change of tempo, breaks into a dance-measure
(allegro moderato). This might be regarded as the real first movement, to which the rest was introduction, if the classical terminology
had any real application here. But the very fact that there is no
change of tempo (the crotchets of the allegro being equal to the
quavers of the moderato, so that four 3/4 bars are equal to one 12/8)
shows that we ought not to expect the remotest connexion with
sonata ways of moving. In the sonata style the composition moves
like an athlete; its movements are voluntary muscular actions, and
its changes of key are not merely architectural but dramatic events.
This is all quite compatible with a sublime sense of cosmic movement, controlling the whole, and making the persons of the drama
automatic contrivers of their own fate in all that they think to be
their free action: but it depends on keeping the cosmic movement
in the background until the actors' movement is finished. Here we
are not dealing with the actors' movement at all; nor has any music
dubbed 'modern' attempted either to recover that classical sense of
movement last recovered by Brahms, or to make a synthesis of it
with the purely cosmic movement which is almost the only modern
escape from stagnation.

Beginning in B major with a dance-tune in which figure (a) is
embodied with other figures—

Ex. 7.

this allegro moderato moves back to E flat, where a trumpet joins
the dance with a tune of its own.

Ex. 8.

This returns to B major, and, after developments in a more
plaintive mood, Ex. 8 extends itself in a mysterious staccato
labyrinth, beginning thus—

Ex. 9.

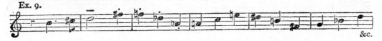

In due course the trumpets point to the key of E flat with figure
(*a*), followed by hints of Ex. 6. This (which, you will remember,
was recapitulated with a symmetrical effect in the moderato) now
unifies the whole design by bursting out in full force, and leads to a
presto final climax, pervaded by the notes of figure (*a*) chimed
simultaneously as a chord.

The little middle movement (*Andante mosso quasi allegretto*)
produces the effect of a primitive set of variations, such as those in
the allegretto of Beethoven's Seventh Symphony, where the theme
is not varied at all, but merely scored in a progressive series of
different ways with a counterpoint. But it produces this effect in
a paradoxical way, inasmuch as it is not a theme preserving its
identity (melodic, harmonic, or structural) through variations, but
a rhythm—

built up into a number of by no means identical tunes; e.g.—

Ex. 10.

As the tunes proceed, quaver motion confirms the sense of progressive variation. After this sense has been established, an unquestionably independent episode (più tranquillo, around E flat)
sounds a more sonorous note, and thus makes a return to the
G major material dramatically welcome. Towards the end there
are mysterious gestures and modulations, but the little movement
resolves them with its own childlike calm.

Huge as is the effect of the finale, it can all be summed up with
the help of two quotations. The bustling introduction—

Ex. 11.

provides a rushing wind, through which Thor can enjoy swinging
his hammer.

Ex. 12.

While he swings it there are sounds of a cantabile trying to take
form. Thor's hammer swings us into C, in the minor of which key
Ex. 11 develops itself.

In due course we reach the key of G flat. In this dark region the
whole process represented by Exs. 11–12 is resumed, but pianissimo.
And so we eventually come to E flat, where, without change of
tempo, Thor swings his hammer in 3/2 time, the cantabile attains
full form and glory, and the symphony ends with the finality of a
work that knew from the outset exactly when its last note was due.

VAUGHAN WILLIAMS

LIX. PASTORAL SYMPHONY

1 *Molto moderato.* 2 *Lento moderato.* 3 *Moderato pesante.*
4 *Lento, leading to* 5 *Moderato maestoso.*

In his Pastoral Symphony Vaughan Williams has set his imagination
at work on lines which at no point traverse the ground covered by
Beethoven. The very title of Beethoven's first movement shows
that Beethoven is a town-dweller who is glad of a holiday in the
country; and the other scenes, by the brook, at the country-dance,
and during and after the thunder-storm, are all conceived as
interesting to the visitor who has left town for the sake of the
experience. The experience is deep and poetic; but Beethoven
never thought of describing any of his compositions as a 'town'
sonata or symphony. One does not describe what has never been
conceived otherwise. Now Vaughan Williams's Pastoral Symphony
is born and bred in the English countryside as thoroughly as the
paintings of Constable. If he had not given us his London
Symphony we should have no artistic evidence that this composer
had ever thought of town in his life. But whether in town or in
the country, this music is contemplative in a way that was not
possible a century ago. Beethoven's nature-worship has much in
common with Wordsworth's; but since that time pantheism and
mysticism have gone a long way further towards Nirvana.

Beethoven's touch, in his Pastoral Symphony, is so light that,
as with Mozart *passim*, the listener forgets the power. In Vaughan
Williams's Pastoral Symphony the listener cannot miss the sense
of power behind all this massive quietness; it is as manifest in the
music as in a bright sky with towering, sunlit, cumulus clouds—and
as little likely to rouse us to action. Across this landscape of
saturated colours there float the sounds of melodies older than
any folk-song. These melodies are harmonized on the plan first
reduced to formula by Debussy: whatever chord the melody begins
with is treated as a mere sensation, and the chord follows the

melody up and down the scale, instead of dissolving into threads of independent melodic line. But Vaughan Williams adds to this principle another, which is that two or even three melodic threads may run simultaneously, each loaded with its own chord, utterly regardless of how their chords collide. The collisions will not offend the naïve listener if they occur only between sounds on planes of tone so different that they do not blend. As applied to classical counterpoint this principle is as old as Bach; but the systematic application of it to the anti-contrapuntal method of Debussy is new. Bi-planar or tri-planar harmony is what the theorists call it; and it is both more schematic and more free in this work than in most of the examples that have been discussed and quoted during the last twenty years. Earlier examples have generally had one of the parts standing comparatively still, like an ornamented organ-point; but such a passage as Ex. 3 shows rigid chords moving quite freely in three planes of harmony.

The symphony begins with a soft, waving figure below which a theme appears in the bass:

Ex. 1.

The harp supplies a full chord to each note. A solo violin, imitated by an oboe, answers with another figure.

Ex. 2.

The first theme is then given in imitation between treble and bass. I quote in order to show the 'tri-planar' harmony.

Ex. 3.

Other themes, some less serene, follow; of which it will suffice to quote two: the one a mysterious pair of chords, to which a cor anglais adds a plaintive question—

Ex. 4.

and the other a salient example of the pentatonic melodies with which the whole symphony abounds.

Ex. 5.

These and similar materials are worked up quietly and combined, coming at last to a climax from which the movement descends to a pianissimo end on the first notes of Ex. 1.

The second movement is built from two pentatonic melodies—

Ex. 6.

and—

Ex. 7.

both of which stand out against the dark background of a chord of F minor.

Later on a trumpet is heard, playing in the natural harmonic series of E flat. This natural series, which is that of the overtones of a pipe, extends of course *ad infinitum*, but before it has reached its tenth note it has already included one note which has never been absorbed in the classical system of harmony.

Ex. 8

    1   2   3   4   5   6   7   8   9   10

The seventh note of this series is flatter than any B flat recognizable either in mathematically pure classical harmony or in the mechanical average embodied in our tempered scale. But to call it unnatural would be like calling a Frenchman a foreigner in Paris because he did not speak English.

The ninth note of the natural series is, again, not the same as the corresponding tempered note; but its exact intonation is thoroughly realized in the classical system, as Helmholtz found when he tested Joachim's intonation on the violin. Obviously the pianoforte, which is obliged to make the interval from C to D equal to that from D to E cannot distinguish the ratio 8 : 9 from the ratio 9 : 10. A trumpet, however, that renounces the use of modern valves and relies entirely on lip-pressure, is not only able to distinguish these ratios and to add to them the musically unknown ratio 7 : 8, but it cannot possibly get them wrong. Accordingly in this passage the trumpet declaims in free rhythm on these natural sounds. This is the central feature of the movement. At the end a natural horn in F repeats this trumpet-passage in combination with Ex. 6.

In the scherzo a rustic human element seems present, rather at work than at play. (The composer tells me that the element is not human: the music was sketched for a ballet of oafs and fairies.)

Ex. 9.

This alternates with another theme in livelier time.

Ex. 10.

A warbling figure, given out by the flute, follows and combines with these. Later a spirited tune in a Mixolydian scale dances its way in the brass and the full orchestra, constituting the trio of the scherzo.

Ex. 11.

The scherzo returns, rescored; and likewise, for a few lines, the theme of the trio. Patient beasts of burden are manifest as well as human (or oafish) labourers. But the movement unexpectedly subsides in a mysterious fugue—

Ex. 12.

which explains itself by combining first with a variant of the
(unquoted) warbling theme, and then with it and Ex. 10. And so
the gnats (or the fairies) have it all their own way.

The finale is a slow movement. It begins with a deep soft roll of
the drum, over which a distant human voice (or, if necessary, a
clarinet) sings a wordless rhapsody in a pentatonic scale.

Then, after some introductory bars, the following tune is
announced:

Ex. 13.

An agitated utterance of the cor anglais, taken up by the solo violin,
gives rise eventually to one of the serenest passages in the whole
work. It is the shape towards which the phrases of the distant
voice were tending at the outset.

Ex. 14.

The solo violin intervenes passionately, and leads to a climax in
which all the strings declaim the vocal opening. They die away
into a figure of accompaniment below which Ex. 13 returns in all
its solemnity. Eventually, the symphony ends with the distant
voice no longer over a drum-roll, but under a high note sustained
like the clear sky.

LX–LXIII. VARIATIONS

BEETHOVEN

LX. CHORAL FANTASIA, OP. 80

1 *Adagio.* (Pianoforte Solo.) C minor.
2 FINALE: *Allegro* (Introductory dialogue with orchestra).
3 *Meno allegro.* C major (Statement of theme, with group of variations
  and coda).
4 *Molto allegro.* C minor (Variation followed by development).
5 *Adagio.* A major (Slow variation with coda), *leading to*
6 *Alla Marcia: assai vivace.* F major (Variation followed by development).
7 *Allegro.* C minor (the first introductory dialogue resumed).
8 *Allegretto moderato quasi Andante con moto.* C major (Vocal statement
  of the theme to a poem by Kuffner).
9 *Presto* (Coda).

There are certain works of Beethoven that seem foreign to his
style; yet they are historically among the landmarks in his art.

They are the works in which he is really breaking fresh ground. The great works which fully reveal his conquests come later, and show no more violence than these almost quaintly conciliatory forerunners which legitimate his claims. The Choral Fantasia is the herald, many years in advance, of the Choral Symphony. It is in a light vein which admits of little cadenzas in a style Beethoven had elsewhere long ago regarded as inadmissible, except perhaps when he was extemporizing. It has also a touch of the insolent bravado of an 'academic' masterpiece: and if we ask how the result can be anything but insufferable, we shall soon find where Beethoven's spirit parts company with 'academicism'. It is just because the mood is naïvely gay and the form conspicuously new that the result is so delightful as to put to shame the long faces which solemn Beethoven-lovers sometimes pull over such lapses. The insolence of 'academicism' is always standing on its dignity, and its forms are neither new nor old, but purely diplomatic.

A glance at the list of movements given above will make the plan of Beethoven's work clear. The introductory pianoforte solo is the finest written record we have (except one cadenza to the early C major Concerto) of what Beethoven's manner must have been in one of his many styles of extempore playing. It was not written down until long after the disastrous first performance of the work.[1]

The orchestra enters with the tread of conspirators; then there are horn-calls, with oboe echoes, in a rhythmic figure that foreshadows figure (a) of the theme, which the pianoforte states in full.

Ex. 1.

Cadenza;
then bars
5–8 as finish.

Few things in Beethoven's art are more curious than the family likeness of this soft-limbed, childlike tune (an earlier song of Beethoven's) to that consummation of manhood in melody, the

[1] December 22, 1808, in a hall where the heating apparatus failed and the orchestra broke down in the A major adagio. The Fantasia came at the end of a programme in which the Fifth and Sixth Symphonies, the Fourth Concerto, an aria, and about half of the C major Mass were performed, all for the first time! Beethoven also extemporized another fantasia (possibly op. 77) as well as the introduction to this work. The concert can hardly have taken less than 3½ hours.

choral theme of the Ninth Symphony. The comparison, as the
present statement and group of variations get more and more
playful, is so quaint as to inspire affection for the Fantasia rather
than contempt. Why should one not feel kindly to the child who
is father to such a man? The plan of the work obviously follows
the lines of an ode to St. Cecilia: the characters of various instruments and groups (the flute, oboe, clarinet, and bassoon, and
solo string-quartet) are exhibited in turn, and then various styles
of music are passed in review on a larger scale. But first the full
orchestra bursts out with the theme, and appends to it a codetta—

which has the same function as the similar codetta at just the same
point in the Ninth Symphony. The pianoforte takes it up and
soars aloft into a cheerful cadenza from which it bursts into a
violent temper with the variation in C minor (molto allegro 2/2).
To this it appends a cadence-phrase on the harmonic lines of the
codetta, and continues it in a gradual modulation to a very distant
key, where it begins another variation of the theme. Three bars
(5, 6, 7) of this are promptly taken up by the violins in a gently
ruminating passage in three-bar rhythm, which suddenly flares
up in A minor and eventually leads to the adagio variation in
A major 6/8 (in dialogue with clarinets), gentle, pleading, and
ornate. Here, too, the codetta is used to bring about the slow
dramatic change to the March, in F major.

The March-variation is again followed by a codetta phrase; and
then comes a passage of great poetic power, in which the pianoforte
moves in a dream of solemn concords, while pizzicato strings in
subdued agitation feel for the first notes of the theme (figure (a)).
Suddenly there is a crash: the orchestral introduction is resumed,
and leads to the return of the original theme, a little slower. Solo
voices bring it in, with the following poem, which the chorus takes
up at the third stanza. The codetta follows ('receive the gifts of
Art divine') and leads to triumphant final developments.

> Soft and sweet thro' ether winging
>   Sound the harmonies of life;
> Their immortal flowers springing
>   Where the soul is free from strife.
>
> Peace and joy are sweetly blended,
>   Like the waves' alternate play;
> What for mastery contended
>   Learns to yield and to obey.

When on Music's mighty pinion
 Souls of men to heaven rise,
Then doth vanish earth's dominion,
 Man is native to the skies.

Calm without and joy within us
 Is the bliss for which we long,
If of Art the magic win us,
 Joy and calm are turned to song.

With its tide of joy unbroken
 Music's flood our life surrounds;
What a master mind hath spoken
 Through eternity resounds.

Oh! receive, ye joy-invited,[1]
 All the gifts of Art divine:
When to love is power united
 Music makes the Gods benign.

BRAHMS

LXI. VARIATIONS FOR ORCHESTRA ON A THEME BY HAYDN, OP. 56*a*

The theme of this work comes from an unpublished Diverti-
mento by Haydn for wind-band. The theme is inscribed *Corale
St. Antonii*, a fact which tells us nothing, but which has led that
otherwise attractively enthusiastic and well-informed biographer,
Kalbeck, to read into Brahms's variations a musical description of
the temptation of St. Anthony. Brahms did not live to see this
outrage on one of his most serenely beautiful monuments to the
joy of sanity. But if intimacy with a diamond so true and so
rough as Brahms could not scarify the nonsense out of his accredited
biographer, we can at least give an independent listening to the
music. It is quite as imaginative as any masterpiece that ever dealt
with St. Anthony's trials; but whatever the temptations it deals with
they never endangered the soul or the reason of saint or sinner.

It is difficult to describe in words the shape of a beautiful
vase or building; but nobody would think worse of the object
because the description is necessarily statistical and dry. Now it so
happens that, apart from what instinct can give, by far the best
way to obtain definite musical insight into the variations of
Beethoven and Brahms is to grasp the form and proportions of

---

[1] The translator evidently intends by this phrase to introduce an
allusion to the Ninth Symphony and Schiller's Ode to Joy. The rest of the
stanza I have been compelled to change on account of the tangle of vocal
impossibilities it involved. The whole question of musical translation is
full of difficulties that make it a duty to sacrifice both elegance and ease.
For permission to print this revised version of Lady Macfarren's translation I am indebted to Novello & Co.

their themes. Form and proportion are dull things to describe,
but in music they produce such important subjects of instinctive
enjoyment as tunefulness and swing. And in such sets of
variations as Beethoven and Brahms delighted in, the swing of
the theme, as conveyed in its rhythmic form, is all-important.
The tunefulness is important in another and somewhat paradoxical way. If the theme happens (as in the present case) to be
a specially beautiful melody, well and good; but mere embroidery
of the most beautiful melody will soon become more tiresome than
any number of plain repetitions, if the melody has no such 'swing'
as repetition or variation may enhance. On the other hand, the
most grotesque bare bass may make an ideal theme for variations,
when the composer has Beethoven's grasp of form; as we may see
in the finale of the Eroica Symphony. And one effect of this grasp
of form is to set the 'tunefulness' free in the variations; there is no
more need for them to keep on reminding us of the original melodic
surface of the theme, than there is for birds of paradise to remind
us of crows because the anatomist knows that that is what they are.

The listener need not try to recognize Haydn's melody throughout Brahms's variations: he will have no difficulty in doing so
wherever Brahms wishes; and an elaborate analysis would show
something like a nervous system of melodic connexions. But the
best way to enjoy these is to become familiar with the whole work.
To begin with the finishing touches is not the best way to enjoy the
whole. In music, as in all art that moves in time, the listener should
fix his attention on some element that pervades the whole, not upon
some guess as to the course of events. In a set of classical variations
the all-pervading element is the shape of the whole theme. How its
external details may be treated is a matter of decoration and wit.
The promise of life is not there, but in the Vision of Dry Bones.

No musical quotations are needed here beyond Haydn's theme,
the bones of which I give completely, as follows:

Ex. 1.

Like a bell the solemn last five notes of this coda toll from beginning to end throughout the first variation (poco più animato). This
does not mean that the real order of events in the theme is altered;
it simply shows that the surface-melody is now completely free to
discuss in any order whatever topics are suggested by Haydn's
theme, or added to it by the variations; meanwhile, in each
variation you will still be borne irresistibly along by the same
peculiar momentum of the three strains: the first, of five bars ending in a half-close repeated with the substitution of a full-close;
second, of four rising bars answered by four falling bars ending
on a half-close; the third, of the last half of the first strain closing
into a coda consisting of twice two bars and the five tolling chords.
This description is as dry as the description of the Spenserian
stanza, but the forms themselves are among the loveliest resources
in music and poetry.

The second variation (più vivace, in the minor mode) discusses
the details of the first with some temper; the third variation (con
moto) is peaceful and flowing.

With the fourth variation (andante con moto; 3/8 time, in the
minor), we have a pair of new melodies, melancholy, simple, and
smooth. No one would guess that their combination is of an order
of counterpoint which, at the beginning of the second strain,
reaches to a development which the severest scholastic theorists
have declared to be unattainable. It *is* unattainable by conscious
calculation; but in great art these things happen, and the art is at
no pains to conceal them—on the contrary, it owes its apparent
simplicity to the fact that they are effective where less highly
organized processes would be awkward. The fifth and sixth
variations (vivace 6/8, and vivace 2/4) are brilliant from the outset
of the fifth to the rousing close of the sixth. The seventh variation
(grazioso 6/8) is the crowning point of new melody and new
lusciousness. Those who play this work in what is better called
its co-equal form rather than its arrangement for two pianofortes,
will know more of its gorgeous wealth of detail than any one
orchestral performance will ever bring out; but it is characteristic
of all classical polyphony, as we may see in the Eroica and Jupiter
Symphonies, that while no two performances will bring out the
same set of details, no performance need sound obscure or in-
complete. Nature herself has more details than one aspect of
light reveals in a scene, but the scene may be complete in any
aspect.

The eighth variation (presto non troppo 3/4) is again in the
minor, and strikes the only dark and mysterious note in the work.
When it has hurried by in whispering awe, we hear the first five
bars of Haydn's theme as a solemn ground-bass harmonized in

ecclesiastical style; and in this charmed five-bar circle the finale
(andante ₵) moves—

Ex. 2.

through various phases of triumph and meditation, until suddenly
(as in Schumann's first symphony) the sound of a triangle and the
stirring of busy life throughout the orchestra remind us of 'the
spring-time, the only pretty ring-time'. Then the charmed circle
expands into the full sweep of Haydn's third strain, and the
glorious tune crowns everything until the last bell-strokes toll high
and deep.

DVOŘÁK

LXII. SYMPHONIC VARIATIONS ON AN ORIGINAL THEME, FOR FULL ORCHESTRA, OP. 78

There is evidence in the fine arts for a paradoxical law by which
persons notoriously slack and irrelevant in their treatment of
matters and forms that are popularly supposed to be 'free', become
remarkably shrewd in their handling of forms which are obviously
more strict and of specially intellectual interest. There are in
music few things more obviously intellectual than the variation
form. This does not prevent variations from being, next to the
concerto form, the most misunderstood and mishandled form in
music, nor does it mean that there are many great sets of variations
in existence. If great groups of variations were as numerous as
great sonata movements, of course the form would be better
understood. Current ideas of the nature of the form have been
derived, as in the case of concertos, not from the few masterpieces,
but from the enormous majority of plausible works on false lines.
But it is wonderful to see how the superb instinct of a naïve genius,
such as Schubert or Dvořák, grasps the essentials of this eminently
scholarly problem in music, though the patience is lacking which
can bring the same concentration of mind to bear upon the apparently more free, but really more complex, problems of other
instrumental forms. Neither Schubert nor Dvořák has left many
sets of variations; but those which they have produced are, with
a few trivial exceptions, perfect. They are also of types peculiar to
their composers. In discussing variation works elsewhere, I have
ventured to lay down a basis for a strictly scientific classification
of the form. The basis of my classification is the teaching of Sir
Hubert Parry. Variations may be classified into (*a*) those which
show that the composer knows his theme, and (*b*) those which

show that he does not. Dvořák certainly knows his themes; and indeed he invented a rather peculiar type of theme for variations. At all events, his three outstanding variation-movements, the wonderfully clever finale of the Terzet for violin and viola, the brilliant and poetic finale of the otherwise unsatisfactory Sextet for strings, and the present orchestral work, are all on themes of this peculiar type, which has since been made more familiar to the public in Elgar's Enigma Variations. Instead of relying upon any solid rhythmic or harmonic structure, the composer takes two alternating strains as full of different melodic figures as possible, and states them in the order A, B, A. It will be seen from my quotation—

Ex. I.

that every pair of bars of this whimsically severe theme contains a very recognizable melodic figure (like (a), (b), (c), (d)); and that the second strain B groups its new figure (d) on steps of a rising scale reaching to a climax. These melodic facts are solid enough to allow Dvořák in some of his later variations to break away from the original rhythmic limits of the theme, and to indulge in considerable passages of development without seeming to break the backbone of his variation.

The theme having been stated in harmony of portentous bareness, the first three variations simply clothe it in all sorts of bright counterpoints.

The 4th variation disguises the first strain of the melody, although retaining its harmonic outline; but the second strain, with its rising scale, is easily enough recognized.

The 5th variation has brilliant running figures.

In the 6th variation there are symptoms that the theme is able to stretch itself, for the first strain begins by taking two bars for one of the original theme. The second strain, however, moves at the old pace.

In variation 7 the freedom of rhythm grows as the colouring becomes more dramatic, and in variation 8 it is possible for the strings to add a little introduction on a diminished version of figure (b) before the winds enter mysteriously with the theme.

Variation 9 again spreads out the first strain, and, apropos of the F sharp in its second bar, enriches the harmony throughout more boldly than hitherto.

Variation 10 is vivace in a springing rhythm.

Variation 11 returns to a meditative tempo, in dialogue with the lower strings and the wood-wind, the modulations becoming richer as it proceeds; and it expands into a dreamy cadenza for the violins, which leads to variation 12 poco andante, a highly expressive violin solo.

Variation 13 is again lively, and of almost the same length as the original theme.

Variation 14 (lento) is wrapped in mystery, which is not revealed until the third strain, where the bassoon shows that the palpitating harmonies are a beautiful and natural accompaniment to the first strain.

Variation 15, maestoso at the same pace, arises in its wrath, and after an attempt to expostulate gently in the second strain, broadens out into an interlude in which the pace accelerates, until in variation 16 the orchestra storms through the theme at double quick time.

So far the variations have remained in the original duple time. Now a new epoch begins with the scherzo (variation 17). This is a somewhat expanded statement in the tempo of a triple-time scherzo. Beginning quietly enough, it flutters away mysteriously into variation 18, a larghetto, in which we have the original melody in a very unexpected harmonic position. Imagine the theme as quoted above, with no alteration but the presence of two sharps in the signature, the notes remaining the same; and imagine the bass-note of the whole to be A. Thus this whole variation is in D major, a key very contradictory to that of C. It leads straight to the other contradictory key, on the other side, B flat.

In this key variation 19 appears in tempo di valse, with a transformation of the theme so ingenious that I must quote it.

Ex. 2.

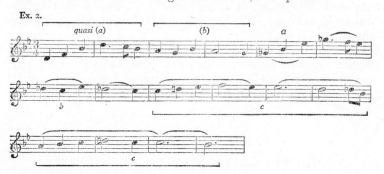

Variations 20 and 21 continue in B flat minor, with livelier transformations.

In variation 22 a horn climbs up from the depths by way of throwing the first strain to the higher wind instruments. The second strain is of the nature of a hilarious pillow-fight between the basses and the full orchestra.

In variation 23, still in B flat minor with the same type of rhythm, the original melody is much more easily recognized, and in variation 24 the orchestra settles solemnly down to a broad and gloomy treatment of the figures in a 12/8 andante. This brings the B flat section to a close.

In variation 25 we find ourselves in the extremely distant key of G flat minor. The outlook is serene, with the peculiar naïve, almost Italian sentiment, which Dvořák commands in his romantic mood.

From G flat (or F sharp) to D major is a natural step, and variation 26 begins in D major with the melody of variation 25 in the bass. It turns plaintively into the minor, and so moves round to C major, where with some wistful questionings it leads to variation 27.

Here, in the original key and in a tempo near to that of the original theme, the figures of the first strain are repeated dryly one at a time by the strings and wind alternating. There is a decrescendo and a ritardando until the violins break away dramatically and bring down the whole string orchestra with a solemn cadential shake, closing into a fugue. This fugue is the finale, allegro maestoso. Dvořák simply takes strain A as his fugue subject, with a shake on the last note but one, and he amuses himself and us by storming along at it with the greatest vigour and any amount of resource. There are quieter passages, and passages which are no more in strict fugue than similar things in Beethoven; but the whole is thoroughly solid and quite easy to follow, until at the end it culminates in what would be a unison statement of its subject if the trumpets and drums did not insist on playing only one note. The tempo is considerably quickened by the time this unison is reached, and after one of Dvořák's grandioso climaxes the work ends più animato in 2/2 time. Why it is not better known passes the comprehension of any one who can recognize good music. Sir Charles Stanford places it *non longo intervallo* after the *Études Symphoniques* of Schumann; and it is so far unlike all other variation-works in existence that it cannot suffer by comparisons.

C. HUBERT H. PARRY

LXIII. SYMPHONIC VARIATIONS FOR ORCHESTRA

To the pupils of this great English master these symphonic variations will vividly recall the man. To others the work will assuredly reveal him; not perhaps in such detail as his choral works with their unsurpassable truth and depth in the setting of words; but

certainly as pure instrumental music can reveal a character that
grounded optimism on a brave recognition of facts, that lost all
sense of duty and self-sacrifice in the simple pleasure of goodness,
and unconsciously destroyed conceit and priggishness as sunlight
destroys germs.

Parry never pretended to found or foster a 'distinctively English'
style of music—as if it were a smaller thing to be English than to be
a musician. He could no more help writing an English style than
he could help being a musician. An English style ought, if English
music were comparable to English literature, to be the most
universal and resourceful of all styles. That is one reason why the
best English art can never afford to be provincial and uneducated.
An English Berlioz is simply out of the question. The unteachable
Berlioz grew up surrounded by artistic logicians and disciplinarians.
The unteachable Englishman grows up among people and in-
stitutions as chaotically instinctive as himself, with dullness ever at
hand as a safe solution of the problems of life. An unlearned
British composer trying to write in an English style will, of course,
write in the style the average Englishman likes: that is to say, he will
write in a style compounded of the religious and theatrical idioms
of French, Italian, and Jewish music of the mid-nineteenth century.
That compound is English in so far as the genuine recipe for it is
not to be found in any other country. The way to attain a true
English style is Parry's way: the way of knowledge. That is also
the way of instinct; for adequate knowledge allows for instinct and
uses it, whereas the man who says too loudly that he 'trusts his
instinct' is not always able to discriminate between the nest-
building instincts of birds and of mares. Besides, instincts often
improve with their surroundings and the resources they have to
deal with. An instinct for musical form is more often acquired
than innate; yet without it an instinct for melody is mere self-
indulgence. For instance, no two melodies could be more unlike
each other in all aspects of sentiment and style, except in their
innate nobility and simplicity, than the theme of the slow movement of Beethoven's last Quartet (op. 135) and Parry's theme.

Yet the structure of the two themes is nearly identical; viz. a short

opening phrase (bar 1), repeated with an added detail (bar 2); then
two bars of sequence (bars 3 and 4) rising to a climax (bar 5), which
leads to an expanded cadence (bar 6) closing into the beginning of
the next variation. No pupil of Parry can forget how directly his
teaching aimed at the solid musical facts in all their meaning and
capacity. The British composer who merely trusts in what he
believes to be instinct, is quite capable of thinking *Home, Sweet
Home* a good theme for variations. A theme like this of Parry's is
the perfection of English instinct directed to wise purpose by a
knowledge which is never irrelevant.

The variations are grouped on a plan of Parry's own, which he
has also followed in a remarkable set of pianoforte variations in
D minor. The grouping suggests four symphonic movements—
an analogy which must not be pressed too far, for it would require
a bigger finale, and there would be some difficulty in deciding
whether the first two groups should not represent two movements rather than one. If we regard them as the first movement
(E minor, followed by E major), we shall have no hesitation in
calling the lively C major group the scherzo. The slow movement in A minor (triple time) strikes a tragic note, while the finale
is not so much a new movement as a cheerful return to the beginning, in the major mode, with a triumphant amplification of the
theme to end with.

The individual variations, as they arise one out of the other, are
easily followed from the theme, which I have quoted in its entirety,
except as to harmonies. The first gives the melody to the violas,
the second to the basses, with a new melody in the winds. At the
third the violins come striding in, and soon stir up the orchestra to
a rousing measure in the style of a sailor's chanty, with the theme
in the bass. Then they settle down to an agitated figure, broken
off from the closing notes of a variation, while all the horns and
bassoons in unison give a version of the theme. The violin-figure
flutters down and away in a beautiful little cadenza for the flute,
which leads to the second or tonic-major group of variations
(allegretto). This begins with a cheerful duet between a clarinet
and a bassoon; then the basses take the clarinet part, while the
violas have a version of the original theme. Next, the violins have
a soaring figure that reaches and descends from a calm climax into
a graceful antiphonal variation—wind answering strings in broken
phrases. Soon afterwards the minor mode returns with a version
of the theme at half the pace (two bars equal to one of the original)
for the solemn quiet mass of brass instruments.

Upon this the scherzo group, in C major, comes dancing in with
a playful variation for the flute. The strings follow: then there is a
lively game between the strings and the wind, with the theme in

staccato syncopations, punctuated by a snapping figure in the wood-wind. The tackling (if a Rugby technicality be admissible at Eton) is excellent. The trumpets next have their say; after which the strings and drums stir up a whirlwind, which finally settles down into a long shake for the clarinets (a very difficult shake too), while the strings have a slow and broken pizzicato version of the theme.

The shake changes towards A minor, and suddenly the slow-movement group bursts in with tragic pomp. It contains four powerful variations, the last of which is expanded, with an increase of pace, to a dramatic climax. The solemn catastrophic collapse from this leads to nothing more than a perfectly nonchalant return to a version of the original theme in the original tempo, but in the tonic major. A pupil of Parry can almost hear his laugh as he asks, 'What's old Tchaikovsky making all this fuss about?' Then the clarinets start a merry variation at twice the pace. The violins come running in, and soon, with but little expansion, the work marches to a brilliant close in terms of its own theme—spacious, adequate, and final—with no preaching or tub-thumping to make it seem too small for all that has been devoted to it. Not only the battle of Waterloo was won upon the playing-fields of Eton, but this battle against the Philistines also.

MENDELSSOHN

LXIV. SCHERZO IN G MINOR, FOR ORCHESTRA

Mendelssohn's thirteenth symphony was written in 1824, when he was fifteen years of age. It now figures as his First Symphony, and is a clever piece of work, though hardly presenting any striking features that would make a revival interesting now. In the same year he produced his Octet for 4 violins, 2 violas, and 2 violoncellos. There are not many string octets in existence; and where the necessary eight players find themselves together they would be tempted to do even a mediocre work that was decently written for the combination. They would, for instance, gladly attack anything as good as Mendelssohn's First (or thirteenth) Symphony. But it so happens that his Octet is unmistakably a work of genius. Its first movement is an admirable specimen of Mendelssohn's most spirited and energetic style; and if sometimes the inner parts degenerate into orchestral tremolo, Mendelssohn as the first offender has received the whole blame for a vice which is cheer-fully condoned when later composers indulge in it far more unscrupulously. The slow movement is rather vague in structure and theme, but extraordinarily beautiful in scoring and colour. I have no reason to doubt that, if produced under the name of a later composer, it would be regarded as notably original and romantic. The finale is very boyish, but so amusing that it wears a good deal better than many a more responsible utterance. As to the scherzo, it is as far beyond praise as any classic can be. It is not quite the first of Mendelssohn's visits to his own fairy kingdom. There are two or three almost uncannily romantic scenes from that country in pianoforte works which he wrote at the age of fourteen, and they are by no means very like each other. The scherzo of the Octet is their archetype, and eight string players might easily practise it for a lifetime without coming to an end of their delight in producing its marvels of tone-colour. But now the humour of the situation begins. On 25 May 1829, Mendelssohn, being then twenty years of age, conducted his thirteenth-first symphony at a concert of the Philharmonic Society in London. He dedicated the work to the Society, but, before producing it, came to the conclusion that its minuet was perhaps not very interesting, and so he swiftly arranged the scherzo of the Octet for orchestra to take its place. This was neither the first nor the last time that this scherzo proved a favourite piece. There is one occasion recorded in Mendelssohn's letters where it was performed, and very well performed too, in a Roman Catholic Church at a service, to Mendelssohn's own scandalized amusement. Be this as it may, the orchestral version is quite as wonderful as the original, and it would be impossible to guess that it had ever existed in another form. Mendelssohn has drastically altered a great deal of the movement and has considerably shortened its by no means long development. We must not hastily jump to the conclusion that all the alterations are in the nature of criticism of the earlier work. The new orchestral medium has inspired Mendelssohn with sharper contrasts and broader effects; and this has had the paradoxical result of compelling him to spend less time over gradual changes of colour and wealth of special detail for eight individual players. Wagner has told us that he found it easier to start our orchestral sight-readers than to stop them. And this state of things he maliciously dubbed 'the Mendelssohn tradition'. The real Mendelssohn tradition consisted in doing precisely what Wagner himself was driven to do: teaching the orchestra to play a quarter of the programme really well, in the hope that thus an improvement might be manifest in those items which there was no time to rehearse. From the very first note the orchestral version of this scherzo is full of practical devices.

The whole piece drifts by in an intense pianissimo and the lightest of staccatos. Its first theme is a mere formula asserting the key after the manner of Scarlatti.

The second subject (the movement is in tiny but highly organized sonata form) is a very definite theme starting in B flat, but gradually shifting to D major.

It ends in a staccato cadence figure, which becomes important in the development and coda.

A great deal might be written about the two versions of this movement, and it would be interesting some day to hear them together. I am not, however, so historical-minded as to think that the orchestral scherzo has anything to gain by being swamped in the rest of the early symphony in which Mendelssohn inserted it. The only reason I can see for its neglect as an item in our orchestral repertories is the singular fact that it was first published in 1911.

DVOŘÁK

LXV. SCHERZO CAPRICCIOSO, OP. 66

It is surprising that this great and most brilliant orchestral work should ever have fallen into neglect. It is obviously one of Dvořák's most important movements, and in it all his characteristics are summed up with complete strength and mastery. The title describes it admirably. The work is a scherzo worthy of Beethoven: it is also a capriccio worthy of the author of *The Shaving of Shagpat*. It is a masterpiece of form and especially of the imaginative handling of remote key relationships. Finally its humour,

---

* In the orchestral version Mendelssohn facilitates the start by giving the first violin an inaudible bottom G instead of the quaver rest.

ranging from riotous high spirits and mock tragedy to luxurious pathetic sentiment, is as true as its form. There is no great music whose company it need fear.

The aesthetic value of a system of key relationships is not a thing that can be explained in untechnical language; and I must be allowed to leave it as a dogmatic statement that in this piece every harmonic effect and especially every change of key throw into highest relief the contrasts and the perfect balance of the whole composition. Nobody except Schubert was less conscious of any responsibility in these matters than Dvořák, and accordingly both Schubert and Dvořák have produced weak works in which a riot of gay modulations produces no better effect than the modulations in any operatic pot-pourri. But when Schubert and Dvořák are writing with inspiration their imaginative power shows itself nowhere more vividly than in their use of rich and remote contrasts of key. In this they rank with Beethoven, Brahms, and Wagner as masters whose modulations are always true, always prepared so as to carry the utmost weight, never weakened in ultimate result by appearing in response to insufficient need, and never cramped by mannerism or by the discipline of the inadequate theories that have driven so many composers into complete scepticism as to any aesthetic principles whatever in this matter.

Dvořák's Scherzo Capriccioso begins with a theme cheerfully thrown forward by the horns in the key of B flat major.

Ex. 1.

The strings, as we see, are far from convinced that this is the right key. Nevertheless they ruminate about and about its dominant; and a flute answers the theme thereon. Other instruments, however, continue to take a pessimistic view. The first figure (*a*) is tossed up agitatedly on this dominant of B flat, and suddenly, in a short crescendo, the whole orchestra realizes that of course (but why 'of course'?) the right key is D flat. In this key, then, they all burst out with the figures of Ex. 1 in four-bar phrases, *fortissimo* with big drum and cymbals, and *piano* with harp and triangle. Soon it goes in an orthodox manner, though in none too regular a rhythm, to A flat, the dominant of D flat, thus clearly proving that D flat is the real harmonic centre of the composition. (From

B flat the key of A flat would be a direct contradiction.) Now on this dominant the second stage of the design opens, with a note of interrogation.

Ex. 2.

The answer is a miracle. We have been convinced that D flat is our main key to which this note of interrogation demands our return; and now there appears a glorious waltz beginning in G major, the one key that sounds infinitely remote from D flat.

Ex. 3.

In irregularly expanding rhythms this sweeps through four changes of key until it reaches F sharp major, which, could we but recognize our whereabouts after these magic-carpet journeys, is really G flat, the safe and comfortable subdominant of our D flat. Here, at all events, we settle down with a derivative of the main theme.

Ex. 4.

When this has come to its formal close there is a bustling return to the key of—what? Of the opening, B flat major. The orchestra sets about repeating this whole exposition from the beginning. The scepticism as to B flat being the right key is, however, far more pronounced now, and the passages that express doubt are greatly developed and enriched. The establishing of D flat is all the more triumphant, and from this point the repetition is varied only by richer scoring and by a slightly longer and much angrier version of the note of interrogation (Ex. 2). And so we again pass through the glorious sequences of the waltz (Ex. 3) to the cadence-group in the subdominant (Ex. 4). This cadence-group is now allowed to subside slowly into silence. Then in another unexpected key, D major, the trio begins. The system of keys is now complete. The mystery of the effect of these keys, G and D, is that they are unfathomably distant from D flat, but they are in a clear and brilliant relation to B flat, the key of the opening.

The main melody of the trio is one of Dvořák's great passages of naïve Italian sentiment, given at first to the cor anglais—

and repeated higher with a halo above it. Another theme appears in B minor, a key equally remote from B flat and D flat.

As the quotation shows, it soon bursts into a forte in F sharp minor, whence it passes triumphantly to A, where, with trumpet and trombone signals, it comes to a grandiose close. Then it solemnly, slowly, and quietly returns to repeat the trio from the beginning. After the repeat the figures of Ex. 6 are vigorously developed in combination with those of Ex. 1, which is given in comic forcible-feeble rage by various small groups of wind instruments. Soon the opening key of B flat is reached. This time there is no longer any pretence of believing in it; the bass clarinet and the flute cheerfully blow the theme away into B natural and thence into G; after which many further developments follow in a steady progress. Here, for instance, is a combination of Exs. 1, 3, and 6, with a new counterpoint (Ex. 7).

Before long the key of D flat is reached in triumph and the main theme comes out *grandioso* in a higher position than ever before. It is continued in a regular recapitulation which passes through Ex. 2, in its simple version, to Ex. 3. Here a simple change of harmony makes the waltz-tune lead to Ex. 4 in D flat. The cadence dies away plaintively, mysteriously, and slower and slower. There is now no longer the slightest doubt that D flat is the key of the composition; and the coda begins peacefully swinging the themes of Exs. 1 and 3 on its tonic and dominant. Suddenly the tempo revives; the horns put the theme in the form of a question; the harp seconds them with a cadenza; and then the orchestra builds up an excited stretto, and brings this great movement to a brilliant *presto* end.

BRAHMS

LXVI. TRAGIC OVERTURE, OP. 81

For one reason and another, the popular musical judgements of the last thirty or forty years seem often to show less grasp of the nature of tragedy than might be expected where the fine arts are taken seriously. It is to be hoped that the day is not distant when it will be thought strange that so thorough a musician as Weingartner should endorse the once widespread doubt whether Brahms's Tragic Overture deserves its name, and when Tchaikovsky shall be duly applauded for his wisdom in calling his last symphony *pathetic*, though it was at first universally acclaimed as tragic.

Without troubling to go as far back as Aristotle, we may safely say that if there is any use in the special term 'tragedy', the term implies something more sublime than pathos. When we try to define this sublime element, we instantly run counter to a large current of prejudice, which every age has regarded as its own modern unconventionality, though it belongs to the childhood of every human mind. This prejudice impels us to talk of the classic dignity and reserve of a truly tragic work of art when we wish to do it justice, and to talk of classical (or even of 'academic') coldness when we are out of temper with it. The truth would seem to be that the word 'reserve' already indicates far too negative a view of the whole matter. It is not academic coldness that makes Shakespeare close the tragedy of *Hamlet* in the triumph of Fortinbras; nor is it warmth of feeling that makes Garrick bring down the curtain on the moment of Hamlet's death. Shakespeare is far from despising the interests of the actor; he writes well for his instruments; but they are not going to prevent him from giving us the one final proof that the Hamlet whom we have been privileged to see in self-confessed weakness was not a successful actor-manager, but a man whose foes knew him for a soldier who as king would have 'proved right royally'.

Impressions of formality, and even of anti-climax, whether in music or in tragedy, are often by no means frigid in their ultimate results. We have been taken into an idealized world, and before we leave it we are made to understand that what we have been shown in it was really true. We have not been regaled by a mere feast of effects with 'no dull moments, and the best reserved for the end'; still less have we had a story told us by a narrator who stands outside and points the moral or tells us what to admire. The story, the music, the art, each is made to convince us of its own reality, and the means by which it so convinces us are not merely those which rouse our emotion, but also those which show that we were justly moved. True art gives us more than the artist's word for his capacity to understand or believe in his own sentiments.

Brahms's Tragic Overture is certainly not written at the dictation of any one tragedy, either in literature or in his own experience; and any tragic characters of which it may remind us can be safely regarded only as our own illustrations of its meaning. On this understanding, we may legitimately compare Brahms's energetic but severely formal conclusion with Shakespeare's Fortinbras, not as a course of events, but as an aesthetic fact; and there is no harm in comparing the mysterious and pathetic development (molto più moderato, in the middle of the work) with the Fool in *King Lear*, or perhaps with some frightened child, the burden of whose grief is not 'what will become of me?' but 'what ought I to be doing?'

The order of events in this overture is as follows. After two powerful chords which embody one of the principal figures of the themes, a noble subject is stated by the strings, rising swiftly to an uprush of energy, and followed by a counter-statement in the full orchestra.

(All groups of notes bracketed under a letter, as [a], [b], are separately used in new developments and derivatives of the main themes.)

Ex. 1.

A procession of energetic and terse new themes follows, including one that has an important formal function, playing, as it were, the part of Fortinbras.

Ex. 2.

Soon there is a dramatic crescendo, in which the basses, giving a fragment (*b*) of the first theme in a rising series of questions, are passionately answered by the wind-instruments (*c*). This culminates in a decisive close to the first subject, a close which will eventually prove to be at the root of the whole tragedy.

Ex. 3.

Then comes a sustained passage beginning in utter dejection, the broken utterances of an isolated oboe being sternly answered by the horns. The oboe nevertheless rises into the upper light while the clouds darken below. We are now in an extremely remote major key; and through the solemn darkness a message of peace comes from the trombones while the glow brightens above.

Ex. 4.

And so we reach what is commonly called the second subject. This begins with an aspiring melody, full of passion and comfort.

Ex. 5.

It rises to a magnificent climax of pride, and ends defiantly with some of the terse sequels of the first subject, notably Ex. 2. Then we return to the opening: the powerful short chords and the first theme (Ex. 1). The continuation of this, however, turns into a passage of solemn mystery, and leads to the long più moderato (already described), which has the musical function of the development, and the dramatic function of throwing an unexpectedly pathetic light on those traits of the first theme which have hitherto been liveliest.

Ex. 6.

Upon this descends, in muted violins, the solemn message of peace which we have once before heard from the trombones (Ex. 4). It is now in the tonic major instead of in a remote key. The impassioned second subject (Ex. 5) follows, in accordance with principles of form which are no scholastic conventions to hamper an inspired composer, but are to this music what the laws of human probability are to the dramatist. The proud climax and defiant close of the second subject are a natural preparation for the coda, which gathers up the remaining threads of the story in a catastrophe clearly represented by the solemn emphasis with which the trombones bring in the 'decisive close to the first subject' (Ex. 3). As the trombones have played so personal a part throughout the work, Brahms is not going to degrade them to the conventional function of adding more volume of tone to the last chords. Hence they are silent in the conclusion, where the most formal of the energetic accessory themes (Ex. 2) shows us the poet's conviction that tragedy is more deeply pathetic in daylight than in limelight.

LXVII. AKADEMISCHE FESTOUVERTÜRE, OP. 80

A student-song intimately associated with beer-mugs—

Ex. 1.

leads to mysterious stratagems and spoils—

until with the dawn of major harmony the mischief shows itself to be unadulterated high spirits with the promise of dignity when occasion shall demand it.

For the moment, however, dignity is not encouraged; the strutting theme is turned into mock-mystery again, and the first theme is resumed. But now it dies away into real solemnity; and the spirit of Alma Mater is manifested in the old student-song, *Wir haben gebauet ein stattliches Haus.*

And out of this the high spirits of youth arise in their full athletic dignity in the following triumphant derivative of the mysterious first theme, which builds itself into the phrases of the solemn song.

Though the time-signature is changed from 2/2 to 4/4 there is no decided change of tempo; Brahms's intention is merely that the accents should be heavier and more frequent.

The first figure of this derivative then settles down to calm activity and modulates with dignity to the bright key of E major, where another old student-song swings in with an aristocratic energy and grace imparted to it by Brahms's invention of holding its top note in a higher octave while the tune continues below.

This, which we may call the second subject, drifts towards
G major, where, with the aid of the Great Bassoon Joke, the
song *Was kommt dort von der Höh'* inaugurates the harmless rag-
ging of the guileless freshman.

Ex. 7.

The tune is allowed to continue for one odd bar, when it is run
away with by other instruments. Soon the fat is in the fire. Conciliatory strains nevertheless indicate that all is essentially peace—

Ex. 8.

followed by

but the ribald song, like the cheerfulness of Dr. Johnson's friend
Edwards,[1] breaks into the philosophy and leads to a catastrophic
irruption of Ex. 2 in full fury. From this point the overture recapitulates everything in the tonic, dealing freely and tempestuously
with Exs. 2, 3, 4, and 5. This recapitulation makes a great mock-
mystification of its dealings with the claims of Ex. 3 to self-respect,
and it does not repeat the solemn entry of Ex. 4. The second
subject (Ex. 6) is given in C major, unaltered except that its
modulations are not allowed to drift away. The Great Bassoon Joke
is omitted as a thing that cannot work a second time; so the peaceful
phrases of Ex. 8 now have no mockery behind them, though, as
before, cheerfulness breaks in. This time it leads to a tune which
every audience presumably knows, and so with a solemn full
orchestration of *Gaudeamus igitur* the overture ends.

LXVIII–LXXXIII. ORCHESTRAL POLYPHONY

BEETHOVEN

LXVIII. OVERTURE: ZUR WEIHE DES HAUSES, OP. 124

This overture, written to inaugurate a new theatre in Vienna, is
unique in form. It consists of a solemn slow march, followed by
a passage of squarely rhythmic fanfares for trumpets, through
which bassoons may be faintly heard in a sound suggestive of
hurrying footsteps; then there is the tread of some concourse not
less excited, but more certain of its goal; a moment of solemn calm;
silence, and the first faint stirring of a movement impelled from some

---

[1] Edwards has broken into these essays already some five times, and
will break in again. The reader has been warned that these volumes are
not designed for continuous reading.

vast distance by a mighty rushing wind, which then seizes us in the career of a great orchestral fugue, rising from climax to climax in a world which is beyond that of action or drama because all that has been done and suffered is now accomplished and proved not in vain.

The above paragraph has been the only account I have hitherto given of the *Weihe des Hauses* Overture. I retain it because its conciseness is more immediately effective than a point-to-point analysis in putting before the listener the sublime combination of energy and immobility which characterizes this overture. But I cannot leave without further illustration one of Beethoven's grandest and least understood works, especially as its forms and procedures have never been anticipated or imitated either by Beethoven or anybody else.

An instinct, which the event proves to be well grounded, has prevented me from attempting an extended analysis on the numerous occasions on which I have performed this work; for a more indescribable piece of music I have never yet encountered. Even précis-writing gives but little help, for none of the incidents can be summed up in technical terms. Beethoven's fugues have always been considered such debatable ground that for many amateurs and critics the mere statement that the allegro of this overture is a fugue suffices to bar all further inquiry. But this prejudice is now a little old-fashioned. Fugues are coming into their own; and in this overture it is probably the introduction which most takes listeners, conductors, and critics by surprise. Beethoven has never written anything that is quite so unlike everything else. This would cause no difficulty if the unusual features were obviously strokes of genius. But they are mostly formulas; only we have never met them elsewhere.

The first four bars consist of introductory chords.

Ex. 1.

If we compare these with the introductory chords of two of Beethoven's most cautious early works, his first symphony, and his first overture, that of *Prometheus*, we find that those early works begin with a stroke of genius, which did in fact shock the contemporary critics.

Ex. 1 a.
1st Symphony.

Ex. 1 b.
Prometheus Overture.

It is the same stroke of genius in both cases, and is far more powerful in the relatively unimportant *Prometheus* Overture than in the
symphony. The *Prometheus* Overture anticipates the *Weihe des
Hauses* in the tone and scoring of the solemn tune which follows
the introductory chords. But the first four bars of the *Weihe des
Hauses* Overture are plain tonics, dominants, and subdominants,
with no systematic interest in the bass. Their purpose is, of course,
to define the key, but they also have the more important purpose
of measuring out the rhythm, from the broad end foremost. They
stimulate the listener to do what he should always do with music,
to listen from point to point and allow each musical fact to enter the
mind without letting gratified anticipation degenerate into information received. Thus, it is not until the third bar that we can know
that the long intervals of silence are not unmeasured pauses. During
the third bar the intervals are halved, and in the fourth bar the
quarter beats and the rhythm of the trumpets have set us in step with
a slow march. Elementary as all this may seem, it has surprisingly
few parallels in other music. Mozart separated the opening chords
of the *Zauberflöte* Overture by unmeasured pauses; but Beethoven
is here contriving his chords so that in the course of the third bar we
discover not only what the rhythm is but that it has been in swing
from the beginning. For this purpose it is essential that the opening
chords should not be monotonous. If they were mere reiterations we
should in the retrospect feel as if the rhythm had begun before the
music. On the other hand, it is equally important that they should
not contain a stroke of genius, nor, as in the *Prometheus* Overture,
a systematic feature such as a bass descending by steps. Lastly, there
must be no air of mystery about them. I have not seen any sketches
of this overture; but Beethoven's sketches often show elsewhere
(as in those for the Eroica Symphony) that these architectural for-
malities give him endless trouble. It is worth while seeing what
happens when they go wrong or lack necessity, as in the following
Awful Example from the adagio of Spohr's ninth concerto, where
the rhythmic angularities of slow 6/8 time are as unsuited to this
kind of solemn exposition as limericks for a tragic chorus.

Ex. 1 c.

Beethoven follows his chords by a big tune, given out first by soft winds and then by the whole orchestra. It is full of harmonic subtleties, such as the sudden bare octaves at the end of its first clause.

Ex. 2.

Trombones.

The trombones, though intimately associated with the trumpets, have a symbolical meaning of their own, for they are confined to the introductory chords and to the echoing of each cadence in this great tune in both its soft and its loud statements. When the loud statement is finished the echo-cadence of the trombones marks their final exit from the overture. Then (un poco più vivace) the trumpets erect a series of typical flourishes into a symmetrical theme of two 4-bar sections, each repeated, the rest of the orchestra marking the time in big tonic and dominant chords. At the repetition of the first section, it is the bassoons which supply what I have above described as the sound of hurrying feet. This gives occasion to remark that there is no doubt that the overture was calculated for performance with at least double wind. Financial restrictions do not often allow me to give it fair play in this matter in my concerts; but in the course of many performances my astonishment has steadily grown at the ease with which its fine details may be made to penetrate even with single wind, in a work written at a time when Beethoven's deafness already made him quite unable to test his orchestration in matters of balance. With this trumpet theme, however, the 'hurrying footsteps' certainly need four bassoons to make them audible, unless the trumpets and drums are weakened below Beethoven's manifest intention. Beethoven probably quite understood that even a Handelian proportion of bassoons would not make these runs more than a background effect. The suspicion that there is any miscalculation here seems to be quite out of the question, although I must admit that in the previous loud scoring of the big tune the bassoons have been given some independent quaver movement which I see no prospect of ever making more audible than the independent low flutes of Haydn's tuttis.

The opening chords I have shown to be unusual in spite of their commonplace appearance. The big tune is obviously impressive, and its restatement with full orchestra deepens its impressiveness.

But this fanfare-theme, with its square repeats and its eccentric scoring, throws the orthodox Beethoven-lover completely out of his step. Nevertheless, I find myself enjoying it as a convincing item in one of Beethoven's greatest inspirations, and it certainly throws into high relief the more dramatic passage that follows. The close of the fanfare-theme has been echoed; and the horns, relapsing into slower time, fix the echo on to the dominant. Now throughout this overture the dominant is kept, so to speak, out of office. The main modulation of the big opening tune was to the mediant, E minor; and this re-echo of the last fanfare is the first moment in which the dominant is emphasized. It is now promptly treated as a key, G major, but that key will never be established until we hear its own dominant, and this Beethoven does not allow.

Musical philologists may enjoy the suggestion that in what follows Beethoven has a mild attack of the Rossini fever which about this time was devastating Vienna, inciting Schubert to write overtures in parody of the Italian style, and putting Weber's nose the more out of joint because he confessed that he was himself 'beginning to like this rubbish'. The suggestion is my own, and all I beg is that it should not be taken as a criticism, for I have the greatest horror of the imbecilities which these philological discoveries generate when they are applied without sense of the composition as a whole. Rossini himself, if not the Rossinians, may have intended some dramatic thrill in the tramp-tramp-tramp of his favourite accompaniment of monotonous staccato chords, though I find the earlier and Mozartean Cimarosa already using it with the vulgarest inanity in the overture to a tragic opera. To Beethoven it is evidently, when taken in the right tempo, an intensely dramatic thing, whether he got it from Rossini or invented it himself. Here it accompanies a fugato at the octave on a staccato theme, which for all its fugal treatment is almost as Rossinian as the accompaniment. A bassoon and the violoncellos bring the fugato into the home tonic, and soon afterwards all the strings take it up, massed four octaves deep on the dominant, which is now maintained as a long pedal-point. The strings rise in cross-rhythmed sequences to a climax where the Beethoven lover may find himself on more familiar ground. Yet both the climax and the decline from it are as unique as everything else in this work, and are typical of its drastic severity. The sure way to misunderstand the whole work is to regard its features as deviations from Beethoven's style. The most Beethovenish thing about it is the composer's grasp of the fact that a deviation *into* Beethoven's normal style would be a fatal lapse. Nobody but Beethoven could have written a line of it, for nobody but Beethoven could have maintained its style consistently. If I were less afraid of the musical philologists

I should say that it realizes what Beethoven saw in his beloved Cherubini; the sublimity which that unresponsive master always intended but missed because he lacked that which could cast out his fear.

A sudden diminuendo leads to a passage of the most halcyon calm, of which the first faint stirrings give rise to a lyric turn of melody which moves into the key of the dominant and almost comes to a close therein. The first faint stirrings might be by Cherubini, but are much more sublime in a music that does not consist wholly of inhibitions; the lyric turn is pure Beethoven.

Ex. 3.

But, as the quotation shows, the cadence is interrupted. Harmonically the interruption is a drastic example of the subtleties with which this overture is full; for the quite unaccented first note of the following short upward runs disclaims any intention to bear the strain of resolving the previous leading note. The sweet concession to lyric melody has simply been disavowed by a moment of silence, followed by the first stirrings of a pentecostal wind. Notice again the extreme simplicity and originality of the crescendo and stringendo that lead from the introduction to the fugue. The stringendo is no exception to the rule that Beethoven does not accelerate his pace except in approaching the last section of a finale, for, as my short summary has indicated, the essence of this whole composition is finality.

With all its audacious simplicity, this uprush is ingeniously calculated to avoid accent on the previously emphasized dominant; and just before the tempo has reached allegro con brio the lower octaves have deviated and ended on the tonic, leaving the violins alone to find their way into the first note of the double fugue (Ex. 4). I have some reason to believe that the thrice three quaver chords (*e*) that accompany figures (*c*) and (*d*) are a Masonic symbol, like the *Dreimaliger Akkord* in Mozart's *Zauberflöte*. The structure of the subjects would in any case enable Beethoven to preserve these chords as thrice three more often than

to repeat them indefinitely or to cut them short; so they may be an
accidental feature. But I doubt whether anything is accidental in
this very solemn *Weihe*; and there are several places where the thrice
three is preserved without being associated with the subjects.

Ex. 4.

The two subjects are duly answered in the dominant; and the
third entry, giving the first subject to the bass and the second to
the treble, returns to the tonic. Another entry follows in the
dominant, with the first subject in the violins and the second in the
basses. All this has been delivered apparently with full strength,
but Beethoven is able to make still more powerful fifth and sixth
entries by giving one subject to the united winds and the other to
the strings.

The sixth entry shows that the fugue has passed beyond the
stage of exposition, for the first subject is now definitely in G major
by its own right, instead of entering as a tonal answer to C. By
this time it ought to be clear why the dominant has not hitherto
been more definitely asserted as a key. The swing from tonic to
dominant is so essential a part of the exposition of a fugue that, if
the subject is long enough to make it a matter of alternating keys
instead of non-committal chords, there is no sense in treating the
dominant as an important centre of contrast. I have used the term
'exposition' rather loosely here, for the exposition of a fugue means
the initial portion which brings in all the voices one by one; and
Bach and Handel realized, as well-meaning arrangers of their
works have not, that it is folly to conceive an orchestral fugue, or
any orchestral music, as written for a definite number of parts.
The notion of a four-part fugue for orchestra is, despite the pious
efforts of arrangers, nonsense; and neither Bach nor Handel ever
perpetrated any such thing. For them, as for the pioneer monodists

and the modern orchestrator, the orchestra consists of a top, a bottom, and a *tertium quid* to hold them together. Any third or fourth part will belong aesthetically to the top, however independent its behaviour. Bach and Handel differ from the later masters of the orchestra only in the fact that they shelved the whole problem of the *tertium quid* (in other words, of orchestral domestic service) by relegating it to the continuo, the gentleman at the harpsichord who filled in the background from a figured bass, or the organist who could provide a background when the orchestra was adequate and drown the orchestra when it was not.

The counterpoint of this overture gives neither Beethoven nor the listener the slightest difficulty, its whole material being contained in its classically simple and formal combination of fugue-subjects. When Beethoven's polyphony deals with themes that are less conformable to old fugue-types, the harshness of his counterpoint becomes open to criticism, though not to disrespect. Apart from this, objections to Beethoven's fugues are based mainly on the widespread notion that all fugues since Bach are bound to be hybrid and pedantic. The dangers implied by the word 'hybrid' are precisely those into which Beethoven is least likely to fall. If students need a warning against them, the safest advice is to take the forms of Beethoven's fugues as models if they can ascertain them. The difficulties of Beethoven's counterpoint in general are quite another matter. Therein he is obviously no model for students, and the main mistake of his critics has been in supposing that the highest art lies only in the safest models. But the idea that Beethoven's fugues are concerned either to propitiate or to annoy the academic musician is worthy of the proverbial backwoods millionaire who urbanely took leave of the Professor of Latin in the words: 'And now I will leave you to the study of your irregular verbs.'

Let us return to the study of Beethoven's irregular fugues. So far we have had six entries of the pair of subjects, and the sixth entry, by being definitely *in* the dominant instead of *on* it, has begun to make us feel that the fugue has passed beyond the stage of exposition. Accordingly, events now begin to move more rapidly, and this is where the difficulties of fugue-writing begin. The difficulties are not matters of counterpoint, but of composition. The first question is: does the composer intend the whole piece to be a fugue? Or (as in Mozart's *Zauberflöte* Overture and the finale of Beethoven's C major Quartet, op. 59, no. 3) has he merely stated his first theme in the form of a fugue exposition? Many critics, and even some composers, see red at the sight of a fugue exposition, for the same reason that Byron saw red at the mention of Horace. Yet Horace was a most gentlemanly writer, and the

only difference between a fugue exposition and other ways of
stating a theme is that the fugue exposition takes up more room
than most ways of stating a theme, and has a decidedly argumentative effect. In the sonata forms there is neither more nor less
difficulty in passing from such argument to action than there is in
drama. The difficulty begins when you determine *not* to abandon
the argumentative fugue style. This is partly inherent in the nature
of the orchestra. When Bach and Handel begin an orchestral
movement with a fugue exposition, they soon take to alternating
the fugue with matter in the style of a concerto. Really the problem
of an overture so consistently fugal as the *Weihe des Hauses* is
essentially new. The orchestral aspect of it Beethoven has mastered
in his stride. Here, as in all his fugues, the themes are at once
contrapuntal, rhetorical, and magnificently instrumental. Their
distribution in the orchestra is entirely unhampered by irrelevant
notions of choral style with a definite number of voices. Beethoven
knows very well how far anything is to be gained by applying such
notions to keyboard music, and in the fugue of the Sonata, op. 106,
he is justifiably proud of the fact that the *alcune licenze* consist in so
few departures from three-part writing. But such questions of
licence are mere grammatical trivialities compared to the difficulties
and dangers that arise at the point when Beethoven's instrumental
fugues have irrevocably committed themselves to continue beyond
the stage of exposition. Quite apart from 'real' part-writing, the
scoring, whether it be for pianoforte alone, for string quartet, or
full orchestra, is inseparably associated with a dramatic style. This
in itself is not incompatible with maintaining the fugal argument
style. It merely enhances the elements of drama proper to all
rhetoric. The trouble is that it is also inveterately associated with
sonata-like methods of phrasing, of modulation, and of establishing
keys. And here we have Beethoven at the height of his powers
taking up the problems of fugue, when he has already summed up
and transcended the whole experience of Haydn and Mozart in the
totally opposite system and habits of the sonata style.

Consider the matter for a moment in the light of the things
which Beethoven must not do. The most obvious Don't is that
which every student has to learn: he must not make sectional full-
closes. Like most Don'ts, this rule is much more accurate and
helpful when it is turned into a Do. Anybody can avoid full-closes
by simply not having enough meaning to distinguish a grammatical
subject from a predicate: your music and your philosophy will
sound learned enough if nobody can make head or tail of them.
The true advice is to think as clearly as you can from one full-close
to the next, and to undermine your full-closes after you have drafted
and arranged your propositions. Much the most serious difficulty

for fugue-writing in Beethoven's style is that you must not prepare
and establish your keys in the sonata fashion. Your home tonic
must be like the horses of the Red and White Knights in *Alice
Through the Looking-Glass*: however wide the range of modulation,
the tonic must allow the fugue to get off it and on again as if it were
a table. There is thus no scope for a dramatic return to the tonic,
and the necessary architectural preponderance of the home tonic
at the end must be, as with Bach and Handel, unaided by any such
interest. Similarly, anything like the process of firmly establishing
other keys will tend to be associated with a dropping-away from
fugue-writing. In plenty of classical fugues some such licence has
proved a welcome diversion; but the strictest fugue-writing in the
world could not digest such a process as harping on the dominant
of a new key by way of establishing that key.

Let us see how Beethoven modulates now that his fugue is in
full swing. His sixth entry having been definitely in the dominant,
he annuls the effect of that key by passing quickly through the
tonic into the subdominant; and at the same time he indicates a
nuance which is one of the most impressive characteristics of his
fugues, and significantly related to their whole aesthetic system.
The all-pervading fortissimo quickly subsides into a whispering
piano. Just as the tonic is not allowed to assert the 'here and now'
aspect of the music with undue pride, so the dynamics of the sound
have a way of receding abruptly into illimitable space, and of bursting upon us in full strength, not as dramatic surprises, but as
thunders and lightnings too unconcerned with our little temporali-
ties to warn us to get out of their way. Beethoven, having now
retired into the subdominant, takes occasion to show us that this
fugue is not concerned with contrapuntal paraphernalia in themselves. Stretto, the overlapping of subject and answer, is a device
usually explained to students as an effective and ingenious means of
producing climaxes in the later stages of a fugue. The orthodox
teaching on this point goes so far as to assume that it is the main
means of climax and a positive necessity, so that a rule is laid down
that 'every fugue subject must be capable of at least one harmonious
and effective stretto'. Of this doctrine it is enough to say that it
wipes out thirty of the fugues in Bach's Forty-Eight, besides at
least seven in the *Kunst der Fuge*. Where Bach does use stretti
his habit is to bring them on at an early stage of his fugue, and only
in a minority of cases does he rely upon them as a means of climax.
Beethoven knew his Bach well enough to give little weight to the
already orthodox doctrine that the stretto is necessarily a method
of climax; and he takes early opportunity deliberately to minimize
its effect by making this first soft passage begin with a perfunctory
indication of a stretto in the subdominant before the full-sized

subject enters. The first subject is then allowed to complete itself in F major, the second having lost emphasis by being disguised in tremolo. Then figures (c) and (d) move easily through related keys back through the tonic to the unexpectedly bright region of A major, where in another adumbration of stretto Beethoven perfunctorily inverts the first figure of the main theme. The momentary gleam of A major is the first excursion beyond the key-relationships of Bach and Handel. It is a mere natural adddition to the harmonic vocabulary, but its effect is as accurately calculated as every other subtlety in this extraordinary composition.

The impression of stretto now becomes more serious, though the device remains rigorously debarred from dealing with complete themes. But the following sequence—

shows a strong drift towards E minor, and on the dominant of this key there is enough pause with a short crescendo to produce a moment's feeling of sonata-like preparation, as if the key had some dramatic meaning. It has, and the meaning exactly shows how far such plotting and preparation are admissible as a means of reconciling the fugue style with that of the symphonic orchestra.

The pair of subjects now bursts out in the full orchestra in E minor and leads to a magnificent dispute between E minor and the home tonic of which the following is the outline (Ex. 6). I do not know a finer stroke of genius in musical architecture and accurate delimitation of style. The key (E minor, the mediant) is that of the only modulation in the big tune of the introduction (Ex. 1). That is its precise dramatic meaning; it has a just perceptible association with a memorable melody. Not with any event that could have interrupted the flow of that melody or made its tonic vanish below the horizon. Had the dominant, or any major key, such

as the bright A major which we have already heard, been chosen
either in that tune or in this place, the magnificent effrontery of
Ex. 6 would have been impossible, with its obstinate attempt of the
home tonic chord to overbalance the key of E minor and its
contemptuous yielding to the E minor cadence at the last crotchet.

Ex. 6.

Moreover, any major key, related or remote, would here have had
the wrong kind of dramatic importance. Thus emphasized, it
would have definitely looked forward to actions and excursions in
sonata style. And such things have already long ceased to be
possible to this music. Beethoven is still as free to abandon polyphony as Bach is to let his orchestral fugues drop into concerto
passages; and he does at this point need to mark that the fugue has
reached its middle stage and closed an epoch in its course. Accordingly, Beethoven allows himself a drop into sonata style in its most
inactive phase, that of a tonic and dominant winding-up process,
which, beginning by playing with figure (c), answers the paradoxical
effrontery of Ex. 6 with the more drastic effrontery of ordinary
tonic and dominant chords ending with unisons on the tonic.

Upon this mundane conclusion fugal wisdom suddenly descends
as from the heavens, and the chord of E minor changes in Beethoven's most characteristic way into that of the home tonic, each
descending interval being an allusion to figure (a).

Ex. 7.

The fugue is resumed pianissimo, the second subject being still more disguised with semiquaver ornament. The entries are crowded closer together with a more serious effect of stretto. Suddenly the sequences begin to rise instead of falling—

Ex. 8.

and in four bars of crescendo the full orchestra is ablaze over a dominant pedal, figure (*a*, *b*) of the theme swinging to and fro in the middle part, while the rhythmic figure which I believe to be Masonic assists as accompaniment. The Beethoven-lover is now on more familiar ground. For, while the sonata-like dramatic treatment of keys, themes, returns, and recapitulations is inadmissible to an orchestral fugue, sonata-like methods of emphasizing the home tonic in the coda will, however unknown to Bach and Handel, always be welcome as soon as the fugue has reached its final stages. And now, with no physical conditions to fatigue us, we can enjoy climbing the last stages of a mountain with a series of surprises at discovering again and again that there is yet another stretch before the summit. With all its symphonic resources, this coda never lapses into a merely symphonic style. It never implies that the return to the home tonic has been a return from a long journey. The first deceptive cadence, without dropping into a Handelian idiom, uses Handel's device of being an ordinary full-close played very slowly.

Ex. 9.

As will be seen, this close is interrupted by Bach's characteristic flattened seventh on the tonic, which brings us into the subdominant regions associated with plagal cadences. Beethoven, having rounded off into a brisk four bars the phrase begun in Ex. 9, proceeds to repeat it, and the repetition drifts mysteriously into dark modulations, climbing up through the flat supertonic. These dark modulations are the accurately timed counterpoise to the momentary flash of A major which occurred early in the fugue. The home tonic is again reached in a two-bar crescendo, and we again have an ordinary tonic and dominant swing on figure (*c*) with the Masonic rhythm. We have often heard it descend in sequences, but it is a new thing to have it brought to a cadence on the last beat of the bar. By means of this behaviour, it leads to a quite new four-

bar phrase as unexpected as the little notch in the last ridge of the
Matterhorn which Edward Whymper feared might block his way
at the last moment, but which turned out to be an easy change of
slope when he came to it.

Ex. 10.

And so figure (*c*) begins climbing again, this time on a tonic pedal.
Suddenly, on the fourth beat of the bar, the subdominant appears
in its grandest solemnity, and the main theme is given a new
epigrammatic turn as a two-bar phrase repeated and leading once
more to the tonic. Then the whole first theme is given in the tonic,
and its close is insisted upon in a new way, on the tonic without
the dominant, until a passage of scales with strings and wind in
antiphony seems to be leading us towards the summit. But again
there is an obstacle. At first the sudden dark intervening A flat
seems to be merely alternating with the tonic, but on repetition it
becomes a serious dark modulation.

Ex. 11.

When this has yielded, nothing interferes with the final tonic and
dominant cadential climaxes, which Beethoven keeps spinning with
all his astronomical momentum. He knows a good deal about the
music of the spheres, and is not afraid in his Ninth Symphony to

make the stars march to the Turkish music of big drum, cymbals, and triangle, and the singing of a tenor whose rollicking and broken rhythms suggest that, at all events for humanity, the sublime spectacle is almost too intoxicating. Whatever the difficulties of the *Weihe des Hauses* Overture, it does not shock decorum; but, though it does not use the big drum, it agrees with the Ninth Symphony that the stars in their courses do not thump on tubs.

LXIX. GRAND FUGUE, IN B FLAT, FOR STRINGS (OP. 133)

This movement is incomparably the most gigantic Fugue in existence. It was written as the finale to the String Quartet in B flat, op. 130. That work is in six movements, and in spite of its enormous difficulty, made a great impression on the highly intelligent group of music-lovers who heard its first performances in Vienna a hundred years ago. But the finale was regarded as quite beyond the bounds of endurable effort, whether for players or for listeners. Beethoven himself came to the conclusion that the quartet did not need so enormous a finale. He accordingly numbered the fugue as a separate opus, and, when already on the verge of a fatal illness, wrote for the B flat Quartet a delightfully playful and clear-cut sonata-form finale, his last composition. It is significant that the key-system of this finale includes an opening on the dominant of C minor (chord of G), and a prominent and long episode in A flat; both of which are unusual features similarly conspicuous in the fugue.

The fugue remains to this day an extremely difficult task for a solo quartet. And, as a rule, nothing could be worse than to play a string quartet on a full string band. But this fugue is the exception which proves the rule. Bülow discovered long ago, what Weingartner has demonstrated more recently, that the technical difficulty of the huge first section of the piece arises merely from the fact that the players have to maintain for at least five minutes a quasi-orchestral fortissimo. The style is such that the orchestral string-players of Beethoven's day would never have attempted any of its passages; but there are no technical difficulties in it that are beyond the daily experience of modern orchestras. On the other hand, there is no passage (not even in the wonderful G flat moderato) which demands that intimate string-quartet tone which it would be blasphemy to dissolve in a chorus of players. The fugue is full of long passages of stormy energy in which the listener has nothing to gain by any sense of effort on the part of four solo players; and the writing is not, like typical string-quartet style, dependent on suggestion. It is not in the nature of a fugue to be impressionistic; we hear where every note comes from and whither it goes. Every-

thing that is material to the aesthetic system of this fugue will gain
enormously by appearing under effortless conditions; and I frankly
own that I was astonished at the ease, mellowness, and clearness of
the most strenuous parts of the work at the very first orchestra
practice of it. In my first performance I did not follow Weingartner
in adding double basses. That is a procedure which materially alters
the aesthetic scheme; and though many hints for such an addition
might be gathered from Beethoven's own arrangement of the work
for pianoforte duet (op. 134), that remarkable document [1] also shows
that Beethoven, if he once began to add anything at all, would have
gone far beyond the range of anybody's conjecture. Meantime,
I was glad to prove from Beethoven what Wagner was the first to
demonstrate—that violoncellos make a perfectly adequate bass even
to a full orchestra, and that the double-basses are in a totally different
category from all other stringed instruments. But a splendid performance by the Berlin Philharmonic orchestra under Furtwängler
has now convinced me that a discreet use of the double basses in
this fugue can be exactly right.

The Introduction is called by Beethoven *Overtura*. It introduces
four versions of the main theme.

The third version I give in the form in which it occurs later, with
its companion-subject as a slow movement (*Meno mosso e moderato*)
in G flat.

The fourth (syncopated) version, announced mysteriously without
its companion-subject, I give as it is proclaimed—fortissimo—at
the outset of the enormous double fugue which now begins, and
remains fortissimo for ten pages (or forty lines) of score.

---

[1] Doubts have been raised whether it really is Beethoven's arrangement; but the late Mr. Edward Speyer possessed the last pages of the
autograph, which contain a wonderful device in pianoforte tone-colour.

Ex. 4.

Some time after the exposition of this pair of themes, Beethoven adds triplet counterpoint to the combination. This enables him to develop on an enormous scale; and by ceasing the triplet motion he obtains a high relief for the mighty climax of an episode in which the leaping iambic figure of the upper theme of Ex. 4 is the only topic. This episode comes to the first full close in the piece (in D minor); and now a new combination appears (in the tonic). The main theme has its syncopations shifted across the crotchet beats; the other theme is divided (in two-bar portions) between two voices, and a new rhythmic type of counterpoint is added. Ex. 5 (generalized from several entries)—

Ex. 5.

shows the type of the treatment. There is now but little change of key; and the last stage of this movement works out a brilliant and ingenious 'diminution' of both themes.

Ex. 6.

(All these methods of transformation are peculiar to Beethoven, and, though to some extent anticipated by Bach and Bach's predecessors, they represent in their general range a new aesthetic system for fugues.)

Suddenly there is a pause on the chord of a dark and rather remote key, G flat; which, by the way, had a cardinal function in the first movement of the quartet to which this fugue originally belonged. Beethoven's fugues never fail to listen to the voice that came after the fire and the whirlwind. A movement, headed *meno mosso e moderato*, but certainly slower than those words imply, now develops the combination shown in Ex. 3. Its sublime calm and euphony stamp this work as a fit companion to such sacred music as the Missa Solemnis, which had occupied Beethoven for the three or four years before the period of these last quartets. This movement, though short, is as vast as the sky. We follow it down to the horizon; and suddenly we are in the every-day world. The ensuing allegro molto e con brio begins by stating Ex. 2 in the tonic (B flat), and proceeds to give out a passage of formal assertion of key, like a prosaic piece of sonata business.

Ex. 7.

There can be no greater mistake than to think this a lapse on Beethoven's part. Only artists who are afraid of life neglect these opportunities for proving the truth of their work. By the way, it is these formal passages which Beethoven intended to designate by the word *libre* when he called the work *Grand Fugue, tantôt libre, tantôt recherché*. Here *recherché* is a technical term derived from Italian usage; a *Ricercare* being simply a piece written in fugue.

The formal passage (Ex. 7) proceeds to repeat itself, as if to close the whole discussion; but the inner harmonies press forward; and suddenly, in a key (A flat) fundamentally contradictory to the tonic (compare here the key-system of Beethoven's new finale to the B flat Quartet), new developments burst out. First there is the 'augmented' version of the theme given at the very beginning of the Introduction, as in Ex. 1, with a countersubject made from its first three notes inverted and diminished.

Ex. 8.

That diminution turns into a bustling quaver figure, while the group marked (*b*) in Ex. 1 is treated as the main subject, until its trill (anticipating Verdi's Falstaff under the restorative influence of sack) 'pervades the world'. Meanwhile the main theme is telescoped into the following figure which, in dialogue between 'cello and viola, stamps its way up the scale.

Ex. 9.

At last the storm comes to a point of repose; the key is the subdominant, not so very far from home. In the moment of quiet we are suddenly reminded of the iambic counter-theme of Ex. 4. The fugue flares again fiercely on the following weird combination. The upper theme, after its prefix of quavers, is an inversion, in a strange rhythm, of the main figure (*a*).

Ex. 10.

The key darkens again to A flat; the inverted figure dominates majestically, while the iambic leaping theme of Ex. 4 persists, in combination with the countersubject of Ex. 8 and reminiscences of the syncopations of Ex. 5; until the tempo unexpectedly broadens into that of the meno mosso e moderato. This now sails in with superb fullness, the main theme being heard in two of the parts in contrary motion, while the other two parts give the countersubject of Ex. 3 and an adaptation of the leaping figure of Ex. 4. This passage culminates in what appears to be a grand close in A flat; but a trill in the bass of the penultimate chord rumbles echoing into mysterious distances.

Ex. 11.

The harmony drifts irresistibly to the dominant of B flat; and suddenly we are again in the workaday light of Ex. 7. And now the coda blossoms out in all the sweetness and light of Beethoven's full sense of achievement. There are many new features, ranging from the luscious formal crescendo beginning thus—

Ex. 12.

to the mysterious, but equally formal (*libre*, not *recherché*) division
of the theme (and of its inversion) among pairs of voices.

Ex. 13.

At last, after a pause, fragmentary reminiscences of the two main
movements (Ex. 4 and Ex. 3) are followed by a triumphant outburst in the manner of Ex. 1, expanded to majestic finality. Once
more the music dies away in vast spaces; and then the iambic
leaping theme of Ex. 4 assumes a seraphic sweetness as it hovers
(note the slurs and ties) over the augmented main theme in the final
crescendo.

Ex. 14.

BACH

LXX. ORCHESTRAL SUITE IN D MAJOR, NO. 3

1 *Ouverture*: *Grave, leading to Allegro*. 2 *Air*. 3 *Gavotte I and II*.
4 *Bourrée*. 5 *Gigue*.

Bach's own title for his orchestral suites is 'Ouverture'. They are,
in fact, French Overtures, which earn the title Suite or Partita
inasmuch as they consist of an overture proper followed by a suite
of dances.

Immensely as Bach transfigured every art form that he used, he
left its essential character more clearly defined than it had ever been
before; and in the French Overtures of Bach we can see, even more
vividly than in their models, the appropriate music of the solemn
introduction in iambic marching rhythm as the nobility and gentry
enter to take their seats; the lively movement paying perfunctory
homage to the art of fugue, but really more concerned to give the
concertino an opportunity for showing off individual players; and,
with the rise of the curtain, a display of the *corps de ballet* before
the (less?) serious business of the drama begins.

In none of Bach's orchestral overtures are the suite movements anything like as numerous as those in the Suites and Partitas for clavier and for solo violin and violoncello. In the present case, there is no allemande, no courante, and no sarabande; that is to say, with the exception of the gigue, the staple dance-movements of the suite are absent, and only the 'Galanterien', which we may call the movable feasts, are represented.

The orchestra consists of strings, two oboes, three trumpets, and kettle-drums. The first and second trumpets are Bach's usual 'clarino' parts, such as my unregenerate soul loves, though some fastidious modern ears, trained to the most drastic contemporary discords, find them too shrill.

In the solemn introduction of the overture, the iambic dotted rhythm is at first buried in the inner parts, being overlaid by another figure in the main melody—

This quotation displays the treatment by inversion of the over-lying figure (*a*) and the close canonic presentation of the iambic figure (*b*).

Throughout the introduction the oboes are in unison with the first violins; and the trumpets, after punctuating the first two bars with chords, mark the iambic figure (*b*) during those bars in which the music is in the tonic.

The vivace, indicated by Bach's archaic French instruction in the first violin part, 'viste', begins with a solid fugato, of which I quote the subject and its three countersubjects as we hear them all together at the bass entry.

Ex. 2.

Of the three countersubjects, the last and topmost one with its ringing monotone is by no means the least effective. The working out of this fugue-material is given to the full orchestra, with the

oboes in unison with the strings, and with punctuating parts for
the trumpets, except where the first trumpet can, by a *tour de force*,
produce the main theme. Immediately after this event, the theme
enters in the basses and is brought in a few bars to a full close. Here
follow what may be called the solo episodes of the movement.
There is no reason for segregating a solo quartet from the rest of
the strings, but there is no doubt that the following theme is in the
character of a solo; and it is confined to the first violins.

Ex. 3.

It retains its character when the second violin and viola proceed
to combine the main theme (Ex. 2) with it, in a passage which occurs
twice in the movement, and which is distinguished by the independence of the oboes, who contribute an exquisite series of
slow suspensions over the throbbing rhythm of the trumpets.

The materials now accumulated revolve twice in their cycle, and
close into a resumption of the opening *Grave*.

The second movement is Bach's famous Air *not* on the G string.
At my concerts it will be heard as Bach wrote it, in its original D
major as an angelic soprano strain, and not in C major as a display
of contralto depths. The last time I heard this Air I did expect,
since it occurred in a performance of the whole Suite, that I should
for once in my life hear it as Bach wrote it. Unfortunately the
conductor had discovered that it makes a beautiful oboe solo. It
does, and it was beautifully played, but this does not alter the fact
that what Bach wrote is incomparably more beautiful than any
such arrangement. Early eighteenth-century string scoring suffers
in modern presentation if it is attempted without an adequate
rendering of the continuo part on a harpsichord or (with all respect
to other scholars, preferably) a pianoforte. But, except in a very
few notes, this Air happens to be more independent of the continuo
than most things in Bach's orchestration; and when the continuo
correctly fills up the very few hollow moments, the result is one of
the classical touchstones of string orchestration. As for Wilhelmj's
discovery that the melody sounds magnificent a ninth lower on the
fourth string, we need not doubt that Bach would have thought
this quite interesting. But imagination boggles at the idea of Bach's
reception of Wilhelmj's piety in leaving the inner parts undisturbed
and in crassly ungrammatical relation to the melody in its new
position; and it is no very simple task to correct the four or five
gross blunders that have thus been foisted upon Bach in one of the
most impressive examples of his purest style. Recently, a conductor who combines in the highest degree his own sense of humour

with a reverence for the classics has managed to extract a useful
lesson even from Wilhelmj's devastating derangement. Weingartner allows a full string orchestra to play this Air in C major on
the G string, but avoids all grammatical blunders by leaving out
the inner parts altogether! The result demonstrates, as nothing
else could, the amazing power of Bach's harmony as tested by
Brahms's method of criticism. Brahms, when asked his opinion of
a new composition, was accustomed to place his hand over everything except the top and the bottom of the score, saying: 'Now let's
see what your melody and bass come to: all the rest is trimmings.'

I am not likely to forget the impression Weingartner's demonstra-
tion of this Air made upon me, and I shall not scruple to repeat it
on some occasion when I am not doing the whole Suite. Otherwise,
I can only devoutly wish that everybody who insists on playing this
Air on the G string will have the goodness also to play it with one
finger: the result can add but little to the sloppiness of the popular
arrangement.

The Gavotte is again one of Bach's best known tunes, both in
its first and its second sections. It may be as well to point out the
witty inversion of the opening figure in the course of the first
gavotte—

The scoring of both gavottes is again as in the tuttis of the overture; namely, the oboes are in unison with the violins, and the
trumpets partly double the theme and partly punctuate.

The same scoring prevails in the bourrée and is disguised in the
final gigue only by the fact that the trumpets transfer the actual
theme to the topmost octave and so mask the tone of oboes and
strings below. Thus in the whole overture the notes of the 'solo'
episode in the vivace have been the only passages in which the
oboes have had an independent part.

LXXI. OVERTURE IN B MINOR FOR FLUTE AND STRINGS

1 OVERTURE (*Grave, Allegro, Lentement*). 2 *Rondeau* (*Gavotte*).
3 *Sarabande*. 4 *Bourrée I, II*. 5 *Polonaise, Double*.
6 *Minuet*. 7 *Badinerie*.

The term Overture applies formally to the long first movement of
a suite of this type, and means a design such as Lulli established as
the orthodox introduction to an opera. A grave movement in slow
but jerky iambic rhythms—

Ex. 1.

leads to a fugato, allegro—

Ex. 2.

in which the orchestral fugue passages alternate with florid solos. In the present instance Bach follows the procedure of resuming the slow iambic movement at the end, but ingeniously transforms it to triple time.

Now follows a suite of dances. The first is a gavotte in rhythm, and in form a *rondeau en couplets*, which, on this small scale, corresponds obviously and almost exactly to the rondeau in verse.

Ex. 3.

Next we have a solemn sarabande, with the bass following the melody in canon.

Ex. 4.

A lively bourrée (note the obstinate bass)—

Ex. 5.

alternates with a second bourrée in which the flute has something of its own to say.

Ex. 6.

The polonaise is a more gentle and indolent affair than the
brilliant things which go by that name in the nineteenth century.

Its *double* consists of a florid counterpoint by the flute while the
basses play the original tune.

Bach's minuets are short, sturdy little tunes, neither runaway
like Haydn's nor stately like the dance in *Don Giovanni*.

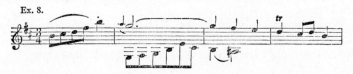

The finale is called by Bach a *Badinerie*, and in it the flute and
violins play in a humorous disguised unison throughout.

LXXII. CONCERTO IN D MINOR FOR CLAVIER AND STRINGS

1 *Allegro.* 2 *Adagio.* 3 *Allegro.*

The making of many of Bach's works is a wonderful history; but
the making of this D minor concerto is perhaps the most wonderful
of all. Unfortunately the original composition is lost, and this
clavier version is one of Bach's adaptations of it. Evidently he was
very fond of it (and no wonder), for he adapted it to many occasions. A single glance at the solo passages will show that, like most
of Bach's clavier concertos, the work was originally a violin concerto: in this case the greatest and most difficult violin concerto
before the time of Beethoven. With the aid of Bach's two earlier
extant keyboard versions it is easy to restore the original text with
complete certainty, even in the very bold and difficult unaccompanied passage at the climax of the first movement. A restored
text of the work as a violin concerto is published, but unfortunately

it was done in the Dark Ages as regards Bach-scholarship, and it is demonstrably wrong in every possible way besides several impossible ways. Meanwhile Bach's own wonderful arrangement for clavier is full of magnificent features which the original could not possess; and these may well outweigh the undeniable fact that the solo passages, though much easier to play on the keyboard than on a violin, have none of the points which passages really imagined for the keyboard would have, while they would vividly bring out all the qualities of a violin. This is especially the case with those passages in which one hand is kept repeating a single note, A, E, or D, while the other hand dovetails neighbouring notes around it. On the violin the notes A, E, and D are open strings with more resonance than the other notes, and a special effect is thus produced spontaneously. A pianist can produce something analogous, but he needs to know these facts before he can see the point of the passage. On a harpsichord with two manuals, or an organ, this type of passage can produce a special effect more automatically, and can of course produce it around any note—not only around A, D, and E. (The magnificent harpsichords which Mr. Dolmetsch now makes might even reveal the effects Bach had in mind to a large audience in a large hall: it is unlikely that the best-preserved ancient harpsichord, delightful though it still can be, is quite what it was in its youth; and Mr. Dolmetsch's new harpsichords are probably finer than any instrument of Bach's time. I have seen one of his spinets which has fully the sustaining power of a large pianoforte.) Against the disadvantage, such as it is, of these violin idioms, we may set the wonderful new material Bach has given to the left hand of the clavier player. In the three extant versions of the work we can see this new part (for it is nothing less) in all stages of its growth, beginning with a mere adaptation of the orchestral bass and ending in a rich contrapuntal fabric which it is impossible to conceive as other than an integral part of the whole conception.

So far, however, we are on comparatively technical ground; though I cannot admit that the imaginative treatment of instruments is a merely academic matter. But there is a more significant history to this work than its origin in a violin concerto. One day Bach had occasion to write a church cantata beginning with the text, 'We must pass through much tribulation into the kingdom of God'. Here was an opportunity for doing justice to his favourite and greatest concerto. He arranged the violin part of the first movement for the organ *an octave lower*. This gave it an unusual and impressive darkness of tone, which he threw into relief by adding to the orchestra three new parts for two oboes and a taille (or cor anglais). The cantata, then, begins thus with a great instrumental overture, chosen and arranged as a fit representation of the

heroic progress of the souls of the faithful through the valley of
tribulation. Then comes one of the most stupendous *tours de force*
in all musical history. The slow movement is arranged in the same
way, with the same transposing of the solo part an octave lower and
the same additional wind-parts; but all this is the mere accompaniment to a totally independent four-part chorus! If the result were
confused or unnatural there would be little more to be said for it
than for Raimondi's four complete simultaneous fugues in four
different keys, or for his three simultaneous oratorios, or for many
other scholastic tomfooleries which may be played backwards and
upside down without sounding noticeably more sensible than when
played right-end foremost. But Bach's result is of the same Greek
simplicity, for all its ornamentation, as his original: in fact, it is
just as much an original inspiration as if no earlier or simpler version had existed. The chief interest of comparing these versions
is aesthetic. With works of a transition period, it might be mainly
historical; but here we are dealing with maturity. The composition
and its arrangements can teach us how different elements of the
art are on different planes; and how the great artist, by keeping
these planes distinct, preserves clearness and simplicity in his
whole results, where lesser artists would produce confusion and
pedantry.

Bach's concerto form is easy to follow, so long as we are not
misled by the popular fallacy which supposes that an artistic
contrast becomes less real when it is made less violent. In the
concerto styles from Mozart onwards the contrast between the
solo and the orchestra is greater than that between any other
members of any musical combination; but the more level texture
of Bach's music should not delude us into thinking that he knows
of no contrast between solo and tutti at all. On the contrary, his
whole concerto style depends on it, just as the almost identical
style of the vocal arias of the period depends on the power of the
voice to arrest attention and to thrust the most elaborate instrumental accompaniment into the background. Hence the concerto,
like the aria, naturally begins with a paragraph for the orchestra,
giving the main themes on which the solo is to be developed. And
perhaps the solo will take up these themes at once, or perhaps (as
in the first movement of this concerto and in many other cases) it
will begin with something quite new. My first quotation gives the
opening paragraph (the shortest and most powerful of all Bach's
ritornellos) together with the first notes of the solo. In the solo
theme the demisemiquavers are a detail Bach has added to what we
know to be his original version—an addition typical of the way in
which he transforms violin-figures into a keyboard style (Ex. 1).
The plan of the movement is that of all such concertos: the solo

passages become richer and bigger as the work proceeds, and
from time to time the orchestra crowns a climax by breaking in
with the ritornello, each time appearing in some different related
key, as buttresses appear at suitable points as you walk round a
cathedral.

Ex. 1.

The slow movement is in a form which only Bach has brought to
perfection, though many an earlier composer used it in a less concentrated way. We may call it the modulating ground bass. The
orchestral ritornello consists of the bass of Ex. 2. Upon the last bar
of this enters the dialogue between the solo and the upper strings,
which I give in the other staves of the quotation.

Ex. 2.

The ritornello becomes a ground bass to this dialogue throughout
the movement, but it differs from an ordinary ground bass in this,
that its final cadence shifts to a different key each time, and that
before each recurrence a connecting link of three bars (modelled on
bars 3-6 of Ex. 2) establishes yet another key for it to start from.
At last, of course, it comes round to the tonic; the final cadence is
expanded (in the church cantata there is a crowning stroke of
genius in the chorus here), and the movement closes, as it began,
with the bare ground bass. Part of the unique grandeur and
solemnity of this concerto lies in the fact that the slow movement
is in the minor mode, and still darker than the other movements.
In all Bach's other concertos and sonatas in the minor mode the
slow movement is in a major key.

The finale, though in no obvious outward contrast to the rest of
this powerful work, is distinctly brighter in tone. Bach has proved
that he meant it to be so, by arranging it for organ as a prelude to
a cantata on the text 'In the Lord have I put my trust' (*Ich habe
meine Zuversicht*). Unfortunately, though we possess the cantata
itself, only one page of this arrangement is extant. It shows that
Bach has added the same extra instruments, but has not, so far
as we can see, transposed the solo part to a lower octave.

I give the ritornello, numbering with roman figures those clauses
which the orchestra sometimes brings in separately. It is also necessary to quote the bass of clause 1, because it is in 'double counterpoint' with the treble; that is to say, in some of the later returns
of the theme the treble becomes bass and the bass treble.

Ex. 3.

The solo is as full of remarkable violin passages as in the first movement, and the extant fragment of its arrangement as a church cantata prelude throws valuable light on the original form of the final cadenza. The design is on almost the same vast scale as the first movement, so that this movement, though not the longest movement in this concerto, is the most important of all Bach's instrumental finales; a fitting climax to this monumental work.

The preface to the miniature score of this concerto asserts, on the authority of recent musicologists, that the composition is not only arranged from a lost violin work, but that its style shows it to be one of Bach's transcriptions from Vivaldi or some obscurer writer. If any predecessor of Bach could have designed the whole of a single paragraph of this concerto, Bach's position would not have been unique. He has the same kind of scholarship as Milton, and the same power to assimilate his material, no matter where it comes from. But when he arranges Vivaldi, Telemann, or even the best work of his own uncles, every patch added by him annihilates the rest. My disrespect is unparliamentary for a musicology that has no sense of composition. The only composer who could have planned this concerto is John Sebastian Bach.

LXXIII. CONCERTO IN D MINOR FOR TWO VIOLINS AND STRINGS

1 *Allegro*. 2 *Largo ma non tanto*. 3 *Allegro*.

Bach is known to have written two double concertos on similar lines. The well-known one we possess in its original form, and also in one of Bach's own wonderful arrangements for two harpsichords. The arrangement is lowered a tone, as in most similar cases; and, though it loses much with the loss of the violin qualities, it gains some fine detail for the left-hand parts of the two claviers. The slow movement, however, is obviously only a makeshift in this clavier version. The other concerto exists only in the clavier version. It was originally (as technical details prove) in C minor, and has not been transposed. As a concerto for two claviers it is very well known; but it is obviously twin-brother to the famous work now before us, and loses very nearly as much in its arrangement for claviers. Seiffert has shown that it is for violin and oboe.

Nearly all Bach's concertos are exceptionally highly finished; that is to say, we possess them in forms which record a large proportion of what Bach usually left unwritten because he was at the keyboard himself and needed no guidance. An astonishing amount of fine detail in phrasing is given by Bach himself; so that it is no mere purist prejudice to say that performances from modernized editions are more remarkable for what they leave out than for what they put in. Who, for instance, could pick out from a crowd of fussy editorial details the authentic fact that in Ex. 4 it is Bach himself who wishes one violin to play the figures detached while the other plays them slurred? But the main and most misleading omission of modernized productions of Bach comes in the ignoring or the wrongly conceived execution of the continuo, or filling out of the figured bass on a keyed instrument. This device was the eighteenth-century composer's standardized method for settling all that most troublesome class of problems in modern orchestra: the problems of securing that all necessary harmonic filling-out should be at once present and unobtrusive. The details of a really fully figured bass by Bach are almost a complete system of what may be called interior instrumentation—though they concern only a scarcely audible keyed instrument and are written in a kind of musical shorthand. Without their careful execution nobody, for instance, will ever hear the consummate final effect at the end of the slow movement of this concerto when Ex. 4, which has hitherto always been filled out, is left *tasto solo*, that is to say, with the bare bass.

For analysis it will suffice to give the main themes. There are always, in the first and last movements of a Bach concerto, two themes or groups of themes; a tutti ritornello—

Ex. 1.

and a solo theme—

Ex. 2.

which, if independent, as here, is destined to be combined in counterpoint with the tutti. These groups of material are built up into an architectural design, in which portions of the ritornello intervene in different keys like buttresses at the corners of a building. The designs throughout this concerto and its lost twin-brother are remarkably terse without any loss of breadth. For instance, the end of the first movement with no more than four bars of final ritornello ought theoretically to sound abrupt: but it does not.

The slow movements of Bach's concertos leave more to the solo players; and this slow movement has no tuttis at all. Nevertheless its main theme—

Ex. 3.

&c.

stands out like a ritornello, alternating with short and more conversational themes, such as—

Ex. 4.

Nowhere has Bach written music with a more irresistible appeal to personal affection.

In the finale Bach takes advantage of the transparency of his string orchestra and of his rhythms, and gives his unmistakable tutti theme to the solo violins, leaving the orchestra to supply merely the accented figures. Hence a special liveliness in the opening, which is entirely lost when the work is played merely with pianoforte accompaniment.

Ex. 5.

&c.

The solo themes are in graceful contrast.

Ex. 6.

Twice later on in the movement comes another lyric episode.

Ex. 7.

Everybody will remember with delight the other episode, in which the solo violins give a Handelian mass of four-part harmony in slashing chords.

LXXIV. CONCERTO IN C MINOR, FOR VIOLIN AND OBOE (RESTORED FROM THE CLAVIER VERSION)

1 *Allegro.* 2 *Adagio, leading to* 3 *Allegro.*

Bach's extant works include eight clavier concertos, three concertos for two claviers, and two for three claviers, besides a transcription for four claviers of a concerto by Vivaldi. On the other hand, only three violin concertos and one concerto for two violins have been preserved. Yet the study of all these concertos in connexion with each other and with the rest of Bach's work reveals that as a matter of fact only three of the clavier concertos (the C major Double Concerto, the D major Brandenburg Concerto, and the A minor Concerto) are originally clavier music at all, that all the rest are wonderful arrangements of other works, and that at least one double concerto and the equivalents of three violin concertos are lost. Their restoration from the clavier versions is possible with a very small margin of error.

The C minor Concerto is twin-brother to the well-known D minor Concerto for two violins: indeed, the slow movement of the C minor contains a figure (marked *a* in Ex. 3) which might easily drift into the other slow movement. But there are notable individual features: e.g. the solo echoes in the opening tutti of the first movement.

Ex. 1 *a.*

Ex. 1 b.

After the tutti paragraph with its two ideas, the solo players enter with a cantabile of their own.

Ex. 2.

Although I have conducted this concerto in a performance with two violins, I ought to have been able to infer from this theme alone what Dr. Max Seiffert has demonstrated: that the work is for oboe and violin, and not for two violins. The instrument that has the cantabile never has the accompaniment figure; and vice versa. I had always noticed this as an unaccountable feature in the clavier version. Its reason is self-evident, if the instrument of the cantabile theme is an oboe. The tone of the oboe is exquisite with the cantabile theme, above a violin as the vehicle of the accompanying figure; but that figure would be detestable on the oboe. Therefore the parts cannot interchange.

The rest of the movement is built up with Bach's usual architecture of solo paragraphs culminating in entries of the tutti in the various related keys until the harmonic ground has been surveyed on all sides. The movement is terse, and the solos remain in close touch with the tuttis throughout.

The adagio (like the well-known largo of the D minor Double Concerto) begins with a broad melody—

Ex. 3.

stated by the violin and answered in the dominant by the oboe. The accompaniment is in rich pizzicato chords, until late in the movement where a deep poetic touch appears in the entry of solemn holding-notes while the solo players develop a wistful new theme.

Ex. 4.

The staccato marks and slurs are Bach's own.

Unlike its famous twin brother, this movement does not complete itself, but leads to the dominant of C minor so as to break into the finale. Of this we need quote only the spirited main theme.

Ex. 5.

In the slow movement a glance at the bass of the extant clavier version will convince any reasonable person that it is a positive duty to restore this work from a condition in which it can be played only on instruments incapable of representing it without makeshifts; while the brilliant passages of the finale, though quite easy to play on keyed instruments, have no particular meaning thereon, but are in the finest style of the violin and oboe in beautiful contrast with each other. If we ask why Bach arranged these works for less effective instruments, the answer is indicated by the survival of the arrangements: he could get them more often played (and probably better played) on the harpsichord.

LXXV. BRANDENBURG CONCERTO IN G MAJOR, NO. 3, FOR NINE-PART STRING ORCHESTRA

1 Allegro. 2 Solo Interlude, leading to 3 Vivace.

This work is a concerto grosso, a term that does not always imply the same thing, but does here very fitly describe a concerto in which there is no actual solo, but nevertheless a clear contrast between the style of a tutti ritornello and the style of solo passages. This is effected by the grouping of the instruments. In the present instance the tutti ritornello, a long single sentence (the melody of which I here give in full), is scored in three-part harmony, which soon coalesces into two parts and finally into octaves, thus attaining a climax of resonance.

Ex. 1.

The orchestra then breaks up into nine parts, plus the bass and continuo (or unwritten harmonic filling-out by a keyed instrument).
These nine parts, three violins, three violas, and three violoncellos,
discuss the figures of the ritornello (I have lettered these figures in
my quotation) and allow themselves at increasingly long intervals
to coalesce again into tutti outbreaks of this or that clause, thereby
marking climaxes in various related keys. There is plenty of
clearly-marked variety in their possible groupings, more indeed
than in any polyphonic concerto with a single solo, or even such a
quartet of solos as the Second Brandenburg Concerto with its flute,
oboe, violin, and sopranino trumpet. For you may have the violins
coalesced into tutti while the violas and 'cellos are divided; and in
one very impressive, Leviathan-like passage the 'cellos are disport-
ing themselves in a vigorous solo style, though, for the sake of
clearness, they are playing in unison. The work was probably
intended for one instrument to each part, on which condition the
contrasts assert themselves automatically. In performances by
larger bands the nine-part passages should certainly be played as
solos. The work then appears in its full vividness as Bach meant it.

To judge by what passes for orthodoxy on the subject of Bach's
scoring you would believe that he never considered how to make
things clear, but only how to keep his contrapuntal schemes complete and methodical. This is not so: often it is only the theorists
who think that a passage is unintelligible unless they can hear 'the
subject', whereas all that really matters is the mass of harmony
and the balance of the musical sentence as a rhythmic whole; and
hardly less often Bach's method of scoring is as carefully balanced
as Mozart's or Wagner's. But you must not be guided by modern
editorial marks of expression, which take no account of the axioms
of Bach's art-forms (e.g. this distinction between solo and tutti), or
the instruments for which he wrote, or the acoustics of the places
where the music was to be played.

From the many episodes which diversify this very large first
movement I quote the surprising fresh start which is made, about
in the middle, by the first theme treated in a new combination
suggestive of the opening of a triple fugue.

Surprises are still in store up to what seems the final ritornello, which is expanded in its last phrase by the interruption of just one more dispersal of the strings into their thrice-threefold division.

Some time after Bach had produced the Brandenburg Concertos, he used this movement as the introduction to a church cantata (*Ich liebe den Höchsten*), and turned the nine parts into fourteen, by adding two horns, two oboes, and a taille or alto oboe. He also greatly lightened and cleared the bass, and gave very complete figuring for the guidance of the continuo player. This figuring should be used without reservation; and, speaking generally, performances of Bach's concerted music without a filled-out continuo are a mistake excusable only on the ground that most of the published fillings-out are worse than nothing at all. The improvements in the bass should also be adopted, but with careful rejection of those particular alterations that result only from the additional wind-parts. It is unfortunately impossible to use these magnificent wind-parts in performances of the concerto as such, for Bach did not arrange the finale for them.

After the first movement there are two queer-looking adagio chords forming a half-close on the dominant of E minor. Handel has familiarized everybody with the effect of a half-close in such a key by way of prelude to a quick movement in the relative major: but the chords as they stand here seem to mean nothing, and are therefore generally omitted. It is as certain as any human inference can be that Bach here extemporized a slow movement or instrumental recitative on the harpsichord, and that these two chords represent its close, as joined in by the orchestra. By great good fortune Bach happens to have written a derelict slow movement in his maturest style which exactly fits this place, except that its last chords are on the dominant of G, a trivial discrepancy which can be easily remedied by altering the orchestral chords to suit it. The last of his six great sonatas for cembalo and violin went through extraordinary vicissitudes in three successive versions, borrowing an aria from a church cantata and a gavotte and courante from a clavier partita. During these changes it shed a beautiful little adagio which had never had any other home and which is undoubtedly wanted here.

Ex. 3.

&c.

It has just the ruminating character which an idealized extemporization should have, though it conceals a close-knit form something like a three-part round that should change its key at each entry, or like a ground bass that every now and then goes to a new key and sometimes rises to the surface. I give its three principal themes in the combination to which they attain in the course of their exposition. Other counter-subjects arise later.

The finale is a kind of gigue in binary form with a second part just three times as long as the first. For the sake of clearness, in all its wheeling dance the basses are never divided; but the upper strings, without sharply marking the line between tutti and solo, bring out every variety of combination, division, and unison.

Bach certainly intended the work to be played by eleven players, the nine concertantists, a double-bass, and the harpsichord. With this combination the distinction between nine-part solo and three-part tutti is very clear. With large string-bands it becomes a mere orchestra *divisi*; and I am sure of the vital importance of my plan of entrusting the nine-part passages to solo players and confining the full string-band to the three-part tuttis.

LXXVI. BRANDENBURG CONCERTO IN G MAJOR, NO. 4, FOR VIOLIN

1 *Allegro.* 2 *Andante, leading to* 3 *Presto.*

Bach evidently aimed at making the six concertos dedicated to the Markgraf of Brandenburg as different as possible in their combinations of instruments, while maintaining throughout the most cheerful of spirits. Lyric sentiment is allowed to luxuriate in the slow movements, but the first movements and finales are among Bach's most brilliant and joyous creations. Each of the six concertos represents not only a different group of instruments, but also a different view of their relation to each other and to the orchestra. The third and sixth are specimens of the concerto grosso, in which there are no solo instruments, but the contrast between solo and tutti is represented by that between the whole mass and smaller groups. The first is also largely a concerto grosso; but a shrill kit-violin gradually emerges from the ensemble, and joins with a solo oboe in the slow movement, while the finale is a minuet for the full orchestra with three trios for three contrasted groups. The second concerto is a quadruple concerto for flute, oboe, violin, and trumpet; and the fifth is a triple concerto for clavier, violin, and flute.

The fourth concerto is often described as a triple concerto for violin and two flutes, but this is not quite correct. It is essentially a violin concerto, and the prominence of the flutes results from the singular fact that the themes of the tutti are delivered by them together with the solo violin in an opening paragraph, throughout which the orchestra is confined to a staccato emphasis on the main points. In other words, the solo violin and the flutes dominate the opening ritornello, which is nevertheless still conceived as a tutti. The gulf between tutti and solo is thus bridged, but the distinction remains perfectly clear, just as in the Italian Concerto, where Bach, writing for harpsichord alone, preserves every possible feature of concerto form and style. And there, as here, the opening tutti is exceptionally long. Bars of 3/8 allegro are indeed short, but 83 of them is a large order. When the whole ritornello recurs at the end of the first movement, it has more the effect of the da capo of the whole first part of an aria than that of a mere final symphony. But the middle episodes show clearly that we are listening to a violin concerto, and not to a triple concerto. The material of the flutes remains that of the ritornello, and if in some passages they are heard with solo matter apart from the violin, this is only because there is no reason to lose the opportunity of so hearing them. They should be *flûtes-à-bec*—something between the flageolet and the recorder.

The following quotations give the themes of the great ritornello:—

and here is the entry of the first genuine solo passage—

Ex. 4.

The six-bar rhythm of Ex. 1 is unusual with Bach, and the listener is likely to apprehend it as 4+2 rather than as the twice three that the eye at once perceives in the groups of notes. And the listener is probably right: for the sequel proceeds in pairs of bars, and, in any case, when Ex. 1 returns, it will take more than one pair to assert its own rhythm. Theorists are apt to vex themselves with vain efforts to remove uncertainty just where it has a high aesthetic value.

The slow movement is unique in Bach's later works for a Handelian massiveness and an abstinence not only from ornamentation but even from anything that might give the violinist opportunity for adding ornament. Indeed, the violin is for the most part a simple bass to the flutes. In the later version of this work as a clavier concerto in F the slow movement has been entirely re-scored, but without any change of its severity. It leads, with a Handelian half-close, to the finale. The following two bars give almost the whole substance of the slow movement.

Ex. 5.

The finale is, if we use terms reasonably broadly, a fugue on the following majestic subject—

Ex. 6.

The exposition of this makes a grand opening ritornello, and the free episodes, while giving scope to the solo violin, do not neglect the fugue-subject for long. Indeed, in the very first solo the flutes accompany the violin with the subject in stretto at two bars. When the ritornello recurs, as it does at the usual intervals and in the usual variety of keys, it is treated with some freedom, and at the end a new climax is provided, thus—

Ex. 7.

LXXVII. CONCERTO IN A MAJOR FOR OBOE D'AMORE
WITH STRINGS AND CONTINUO

1 *Allegro.* 2 *Larghetto.* 3 *Allegro ma non tanto.*

The A major cembalo concerto leaves no doubt in my mind that it was originally intended for the oboe d'amore, an instrument midway between the oboe and the English horn: being in fact an oboe in A with an English-horn bulb-shaped bell. The opening of the concerto in the clavier version, which is all that has reached us, shows, in the clavier arpeggios of its first two bars, that Bach is trying to give the harpsichord player something characteristic to do.

But he abandons the effort except where this part of the theme appears: and it is perfectly obvious that throughout the work he has no other harpsichord style in his mind except in scattered details for the left hand. At first the scholar is puzzled by an equally conspicuous lack of anything like the violin style which is so conspicuous in the other cembalo arrangements; but as soon as we recall Bach's usual treatment of the oboe d'amore the whole thing becomes intensely characteristic, from the sonorous first solo entry—

to the last note.

In the autograph the slow movement is a veritable palimpsest as to the solo part: and the skill of Wilhelm Rust, the editor of vol. xvii of the Bach-Gesellschaft edition, has enabled us to see Bach's mind at work transforming the original solo, with its irreducible minimum of breathing-places, to the more ornate and uninterrupted

flow of rhetoric which fingers can command on keyed instruments.
From the version thus extracted and given by Rust in an appendix
we can get very close to the original oboe d'amore part.

Ex. 3.

Larghetto.
Orchestra.

Oboe d'amore.

&c.

A second theme in a major key, with the ostinato figure of the
strings inverted—

Ex. 4.

&c.

is recapitulated some time afterwards in a lower key, and here it is
interesting to observe that Bach, in copying it out, already fills up
its breathing-spaces, so that the latter part of the movement is not
a palimpsest like the rest. Clearly then, in restoring the work for
oboe d'amore, we must follow the first statement of the theme.

Bach never wrote a more radiant melody than the opening tutti
of the finale—

Ex. 5.

nor a more typically angelic one than the entry of the solo.

Ex. 6.

Every point in this concerto demands a wind instrument, and that the oboe d'amore, to express it convincingly. No other instrument of Bach's time had the exact compass and the exact style. Nowadays a clarinet could do it very pleasantly, and could effectively use the clavier arpeggios of Ex. 1. But it would be dull and cold just where the oboe d'amore is deep and thrilling in Ex. 2.

LXXVIII. CONCERTO IN A MINOR FOR CLAVIER, FLUTE, AND VIOLIN

1 *Allegro.* 2 *Adagio ma non tanto, e dolce; leading to* 3 *Alla breve.*

This is one of Bach's greatest and richest instrumental works: nor has he ever achieved a scoring fuller and more minutely thought out in every bar. Yet it is from first to last an arrangement of older works that were never intended to be in concerto form at all. The astounding result is an arrangement only in an historical sense, for, had the originals been lost, no sensible person would have wished to restore them or would even have suspected their existence.

The loss of the originals of Bach's other cembalo concertos is disastrous, and their restoration a duty, because they were not keyboard music at all, but violin or wind music. But the first movement and finale of this concerto were originally a big prelude and fugue for cembalo alone; every bar of which has been either retained, improved, or expanded in the concerto. The perpetual flow of the original pieces, which, though energetic, verged on monotony, is gloriously diversified by the noble orchestral ritornellos which Bach builds into opening paragraphs, and which recur at the important cadences, expanding the original movements to half as long again. The solo violin and solo flute are additional parts which it is almost impossible to imagine omitted; thus they are freshly invented and are in no sense 'arranged' from anything else, though they are *derived* from the main themes.

Of the first movement I quote, not the whole ritornello, but the transformations of its first figure.

Ex. 1.

The slow movement, in C major, is arranged from that of the organ sonata (or cembalo trio) in D minor. It is transposed from F, and, while the cembalo left hand plays the original pedal part, the right hand plays that of the upper manual, and the flute that of the lower. To this trio the violin adds a new fourth part in pizzicato arpeggios. But the original movement was in two portions with repeats. Now the repeats are written in full, for the upper parts are turned round, the violin taking the clavier melody an octave lower, the clavier taking the flute part *in situ*, and the flute taking the pizzicato arpeggios an octave higher. Ex. 2 *a* and *b* give the two positions.

A couple of extra bars lead into the finale. Here the orchestra makes a ritornello out of a marvellously ingenious transformation of the original fugue theme which the cembalo gives unaltered. Ex. 3 shows the relation between the two versions.

The ritornello version here relieves the tarantella-like perpetual motion of the original composition, but introduces a very much grander idea. A fine cadenza is inserted before the end, and there is a Mozart-like richness and symphonic quality in the accompaniments throughout. And so this work, historically an arrangement, first and finally achieves originality in its present form.

HANDEL

LXXIX. ORGAN CONCERTO, NO. 7 (OP. 7, NO. 1)

Andante (C), *leading to* 2 *Andante* (3/4), *leading to* 3 LARGO, *e piano*
(*D minor*). 4 BOURRÉE: *Allegro*.

Of Handel's fifteen organ concertos this is one which is a little
more completely written down than most. It has only one blank
space marked *ad lib.*, and it actually indicates where the pedals of
the organ are to be used. If we were to attempt to produce Handel's
op. 7, Ex. 3, in accordance with the intentions of the composer, the
margin of conjectural restoration would be so great that we should
be hardly justified in holding Handel responsible for the result.
The direction *Organo ad libitum Adagio e Fuga* leaves a margin for
discretion, or indiscretion, equal to nearly half the work. Handel is
himself to blame if a large portion of what purports to be his organ
music is really the composition of the late W. T. Best. In any case,
if the composer does not condescend to write his music down, some-
body else has to complete the record. The finest performances of
Handel's concertos have been those by musicians capable of extemporizing in the composer's style. From childhood I used to hear
Handel from Sir Walter Parratt, and had no idea that anybody
could play this music with any less Handelian elements. But until
Max Seiffert applied methods of scholarship to the editing of
Handel's concertos, no published edition made any advance
towards the de-Bestification of the text.

The present work is unique, like all Handel's works. If uniformity of procedure were a proof of authenticity, a Higher
Criticism could prove each of Handel's concertos spurious on
the evidence of all the others.

After four bars of grandiose dialogue between the organ and the
orchestra (strings and oboes), Handel drifts into a ground bass;
the dialogue partly anticipates that bass, so that you do not notice
that the composition has settled down thereto until its obstinacy
attracts your notice. Here is the bass—

Ex. 1.

All sorts of things happen on it, and it sometimes changes its key.
Once, when it is in G minor, Handel quotes the *Passacaille* of his
eighth clavier suite, reversing the accents.

Ex. 2.

The fifth variation after this quotation is to be supplied extempore, presumably with a cadenza. The gap can be filled with authentic Handel from the G minor Suite. Then the introductory dialogue is resumed, leading back to B flat and to a pause. We are to begin a new movement.

The new movement, in triple time, turns out to be on the same ground bass! Among its many fancies is the following Hornpipe, such being the rhythm which Handel, in his half-dozen examples, associates with that dance.

Ex. 3.

The third movement, largo e piano, is a solemn elegy in D minor, with a bass which, though not rigid, has still much of the effect of a ground bass.

Ex. 4.

The finale is a bourrée with a tune such as only Purcell achieved before Handel, and nobody has even attempted to achieve since.

Ex. 5.

The original root of Handel's popularity lies here: such tunes devastated the town like any modern music-hall success, though possibly with a little more spiritual nourishment for their victims. The gavotte in *Ottone* was played on all the musical salt-boxes in the three kingdoms. Sir Hugh Allen once suggested that barrel-organs might be employed to spread a taste for good music wherever they grind. Let us equip the first of these noble pioneers with this bourrée and the gavotte in *Ottone*.

JULIUS RÖNTGEN.

LXXX. TRIPLE CONCERTO, IN B FLAT, FOR VIOLIN, VIOLA, AND VIÖLONCELLO, WITH STRING ORCHESTRA

1 *Allegro.* 2 *Lento.* 3 *Allegro.*

The modern composer who writes in the forms of Bach and Handel may do so for various reasons, and with various results. The good reasons are grounded in the nature of music and have nothing to do with fashions, old or new. Nor are they, on the other hand, primarily concerned with points of scholarship, though it is probable that a composer who has mastered the nature of an old art-form is a fine scholar in historical detail.

But it is no part of Röntgen's intention in his Triple Concerto to produce a work that could possibly have been written in the eighteenth century. I have every reason to believe that if he could have been persuaded to forge some posthumous Handel, or (I will even say) posthumous Bach, he could have achieved results which would defy detection. This, however, is not the point of the present spontaneous work of art. It uses eighteenth-century forms because these not only give scope for many aspects of the composer's humour, but are peculiarly convenient for the development of a group of players (instead of a single player) in concerto style. It goes immediately and constantly beyond the scope of the eighteenth century in two important ways: first, it requires no background of continuo to be filled out extempore on a harpsichord: every note is sufficient in its place, and the harmony of the strings is always complete; and, secondly, its old-world themes move into romantic depths of harmony and key-relationship, which, just because they belong to a later musical language, show us the past as seen in a glow of poetic imagination by one whose view of it was neither patronizing nor antiquarian. It is a happy tale of long ago, told without 'tushery', without pedantry, and without affectation.

The short opening ritornello sums up almost the whole first movement in its three clauses.

Ex. 1.

Any impression of mere 'antique style' that might be given by the
first clause is already removed by the unexpected continuation in
the minor key in clauses ii and iii. The three solos then enter with
a new formula.

Ex. 2.   &c.

They build up a clear and broad movement by taking up the second
and third clauses of Ex. 1 in 'augmentation'; i.e. twice as slow, and
by rich modulations on other new themes, such as—

Ex. 3.

Most of the entries of the ritornello (Ex. 1) are connected with
some surprise; e.g. an entry in the bass on the beat, answered
half a beat later by the upper strings.

The slow movement is in a very distant key (C sharp minor,
alias D flat minor). The accompaniment announced in the first
bar persists throughout, while the simple theme given by the violin
is built up into a design that modulates widely and deeply.

Ex. 4.   *Lento.*

In the course of the movement another theme, somewhat resembling an inversion of Ex. 3, contributes a plaintive element; and
the later stages are marked by the appearance, in the major mode,
of an inversion of the main theme. A mechanical inversion would
be as follows—

Ex. 5.

which I, having incautiously quoted from memory, leave in this
form in order that the listener may appreciate the art with which
Röntgen (like Bach) chooses a more expressive position. The
slow movement is followed without break by the finale, of which
the introductory figure—

Ex. 6.

drastically effects the necessary change back to B flat via A minor. The main theme—

Ex. 7.

works up into a kind of free rondo, of which some episodes combine this theme with that of the slow movement, while the central episode begins with a sonorous new tune.

Ex. 8.

At later stages the main theme (Ex. 7) and its accessories go into 9/8 time as follows—

Ex. 9.

and further developments hurry into 6/8 time. The work ends with an allusion to Ex. 1 of the first movement.

One of the finest features in this masterpiece of style and balance is the formal nature of its themes, none of which is allowed to carry an individual character on the surface, though they are all sharply contrasted. The individual character appears in the whole work; and no other themes would have developed anything like it. As a classical example in a different mood we may recall the first movement of the so-called 'Harp Quartet' of Beethoven (op. 74), where any critic who lays down as his *sine qua non* the presence of obviously impressive and original themes will find it impossible to discover that the work exists at all. The same is true of most of Mozart's works for wind instruments. When the composer is producing his purest and loveliest colour-schemes, with masses of delicate, slow-moving harmony, he does not want themes that will distract attention or compel the harmony to change too often for his purpose.

VAUGHAN WILLIAMS

LXXXI. CONCERTO ACCADEMICO, IN D MINOR, FOR VIOLIN AND STRING ORCHESTRA

1 *Allegro pesante.* **2** *Adagio.* **3** *Presto.*

Why *Accademico*? This work is certainly written in no ancient style. Perhaps it is 'academic' in the sense that it is strictly consistent in its own rules; and perhaps the composer wishes to indicate that in his opinion these rules are by this time so well established that they ought to be taught in schools. If such an opinion is correct, I fear that the University of Edinburgh will remain behind the times as long as I am there. It is one thing, and a thing both feasible and necessary, to bring students to understand and enjoy music that would be completely unintelligible to any composer of sixty years ago; it is quite another matter to set about devising exercises in its grammar to students who find the elements of the classical grammar difficult.

If to be academic is to be of crystalline clearness and symmetry, this work is as academic as Mozart or Bach or any classical master, whether he was, like Mozart, abreast of his time, or, like Bach, ninety years behind it and ahead of any assignable future time. Another quality that may be put down to the credit of academic art is consistency of style. Everybody knows that Vaughan Williams is intensely English, that he is an enthusiastic and expert collector of English folk-songs, and that he has learnt much from modern French music in general and from Ravel in particular. But though it may amuse a certain kind of expert to trace these origins in his music, it is quite unnecessary for the intelligent enjoyment of it. He has made a style of his own out of whatever interests him, and no composer is less liable to fall into reminiscences of other music.

So let us listen to this concerto without further prejudice as to what is or is not academic (such as Consecutive Fifths, the Ottava Battuta, the False Relation of the Tritone, and other progressions condemned as licentious by the Great Masters of the Golden Rockstro), and let us also not inquire further into such private affairs as the origins of the composer's ideas. Whatever the origin, the results are true to them, for the results are original. This is no pun, but a statement of fact. The original artist is, as Swift pointed out in *The Battle of the Books*, not the spider whose unpleasant and glutinous web is merely his own unpleasant inside turned outwards, but the bee whose honey is skilfully wrought from its source in the flowers.

The *Concerto Accademico* begins with a spirited ritornello theme—

Ex. 1.

in which the solo violin plays with the orchestra, emerging in a high fifth here and there. Soon the solo makes its official entry with a new theme derived by diminution from the fourth bar (*a*) of the main theme.

Ex. 2.

After a short cadenza Ex. 1 is resumed. With sudden change of key a new theme enters, also derived from (*a*)—

Ex. 3.

and lending itself to decoration by the figure of Ex. 1. An incident in cross-rhythm adds a note of romantic mystery to the Bach-like, imperturbable amble of the whole.

Ex. 4.

Then the figures of Ex. 1 and 2 are developed *seriatim* and combined in new sequences, over which a new theme emerges as a counterpoint in one part after another.

Ex. 5.

This development leads to a recapitulation of the previous themes in the tonic, followed by a coda in which Ex. 4 plays its part.

The slow movement is another Bach-like scheme, in which a

solo violoncello joins with the solo violin. The main theme, in a
Dorian G minor—

Ex. 6.

alternates with a 'soft Lydian air' (Ionian or Aeolian, as you may
prefer)—

Ex. 7.

which eventually modulates widely in combination with Ex. 5, and
finally settles in the original Dorian mode.

The finale is a jig, of which the main theme borrows features
from a theme in the opera *Hugh the Drover*.

Ex. 8.

Another tune in triple time combines with this duple jig-measure.

Ex. 9.

In a kind of Aeolian-Mixolydian dominant key a new jig-theme
forms the second element in a terse binary scheme.

Ex. 10.

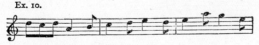

Above it a counterpoint is added.

Ex. 11.

The exposition is repeated from the beginning.
The development section adds a new counterpoint—

Ex. 12.

which is afterwards used to weld the recapitulation to the coda, in which three themes are combined (Exs. 9, 11, 12); the Dorian mode giving place to D major, in which key the concerto comes to the quietest and most poetically fantastic and convincing end imaginable.

GUSTAV HOLST

LXXXII. A FUGAL CONCERTO (OP. 40, NO. 2)

1 *Moderato.* 2 *Adagio.* 3 *Allegro.*

The art-forms of Bach and Handel are gaining influence at the present day in proportion as the later sonata forms of Mozart and Beethoven are ceasing to interest the modern composer. Max Reger's *Conzert im alten Stil* is a somewhat vague imitation of an eighteenth-century concerto grosso, but it does not achieve much more of an 'ancient style' than an impression of remoteness, and it makes no attempt to use the real forms of the old concertos. The happy and inventive Triple Concerto by Julius Röntgen is a real example of the polyphonic concerto form and style; and Holst's Fugal Concerto, for the unusual combination of flute and oboe, turns the genuine old forms to new purposes of wit and fancy.

In the first movement the string orchestra states a fugue-subject in octaves, doing duty (in four bars) for the opening tutti that is to give the gist of the whole movement in one pregnant paragraph.

Ex. 1.

The oboe and flute enter by way of answering this subject in turn. They then introduce a new figure, which has a way of drifting into the scale at the end of the main theme.

Ex. 2.

But its further purpose is to combine, all at sixes and sevens, with the main theme inverted in the bass, coalescing with it at the third bar.

Ex. 3.

(This inversion is all the happier for not being pedantically exact.) On these materials the little movement works itself and vanishes in a merry pianissimo.

The slow movement sheds strange lights on the key of D major and its environs. It is quite diatonic, and D major is the key. And the colour is not modal; there is nothing Doric or Phrygian about it. But our minds are diverted from the tonic throughout, and when other keys are visited we never get in touch with their tonics.

The time is a slow 3/4, but a mysterious bass moves across it twice as slow, while the flute announces a subject for a canon or fugue.

Ex. 4.

A plaintive middle episode takes a new theme into remoter harmonies.

Ex. 5.

While some very beautiful modulations are dying away, the violas drift into the main theme (Ex. 4), in what will be G if Ex. 4 is in D. The movement is thus brought round to a close which clearly is in D. The tonic being thus asserted at last, the music glides in the direction of the dominant. Whereat the finale bursts in with the following quizzical fugue-subject:

Ex. 6.

Tutti.

After various adventures, including lackadaisical cadenzas, apropos of its last notes, on the oboe and flute, followed by attempts at inversion and a ferocious transformation in square time (2/4), this subject fulfils its destiny. For it is obvious to the meanest capacity that it was destined to be a counterpoint to the Old English Dance Tune, 'If all the world were paper'. Even the double-bass knows that, though he has a severe cold in his head—technically known as a sordine.

Ex. 7.

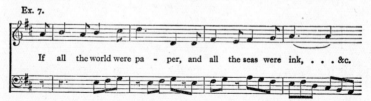

If all the world were pa - per, and all the seas were ink, . . . &c.

After this revelation has been expounded, the little concerto trots peacefully away until, suddenly rearing and scratching itself, it disappears in a trill for the two wind-instruments and a rising pizzicato scale in the absurd rhythm of Ex. 6.

LXXXIII. FUGAL OVERTURE FOR ORCHESTRA

Musical terms are nowadays used in such Pickwickian senses that persons may probably be found who, hearing the following opening of Holst's Fugal Overture—

Ex. 1.

will aver that it is the subject of the fugue. That, together with the supposition that the critic's attention wandered never to return after the first four bars, is the only possibly explanation of the statement, by an otherwise laudatory London musical reviewer, that this overture sounds 'oddly unfugal'. No orchestral writing could well be more fugal, though few things are more whimsical, than the conduct of this overture from the first moment when its main theme starts in the basses, in the Lydian mode.

Ex. 2.

Within the memory of very old persons still living it used to be thought that eight was twice four. The first movement of Ravel's pianoforte trio, however, showed us that eight quavers might fall so persistently into the rhythm of 3+2+3 that no ear could feel the common-time rhythm of four crotchets at all. Holst, in a quicker tempo, here gives us a persistent rhythm of $3+3+2$ (or a $\frac{9}{8}$ minus 1). Being a practical man, he has it conducted by the ordinary four-in-a-bar, and leaves the result to the ear.

A counter-subject in gurgling semiquavers wriggles its way down the wind-band at sixes and sevens.

Ex. 3.

Soon a new subject is announced by the brass. Its rhythmic groups are quite different, and equally removed from those of common time. I draw no bar-stroke, and if, as is probable, I have got the latter part of the theme wrongly grouped, I err in the company of some interlocutors who express divers opinions in its episodic discussion.

Ex. 4.

&c.

A dramatic break-off is followed by the 'augmentation' of the first theme. The rhythm $3+3+2$ (unlike plain common time, and like Beethoven's triple-time fugue-subjects) assumes quite a different ictus by being taken twice as slow.

Ex. 5.

Extremes meet in the combination of the two original subjects on piccolo and contra-fagotto.

Ex. 6.

Piccolo.
Contra-fagotto.

With these resources, together with close stretti (or overlappings
of the subject with its answer), this brilliant masterpiece runs its
classic course in the finest musical language of the present day. It
is used, at the composer's suggestion, as an overture to *The Perfect
Fool* when that one-act opera is given without any other piece.

SET IN GREAT BRITAIN AT THE UNIVERSITY PRESS, OXFORD,
BY JOHN JOHNSON, PRINTER TO THE UNIVERSITY.
PRINTED BY MERRITT AND HATCHER, LTD., LONDON.